高等学校英语专业系列教材
Textbook Series for Tertiary English Majors

高等学校英语专业系列教材 求知 STEM
Textbook Series for Tertiary English Majors

**总 主 编** 石 坚

**副总主编** 黄国文 陈建平 张绍杰 蒋洪新

**编委单位**（排名不分先后）

| | |
|---|---|
| 广东外语外贸大学 | 华南农业大学 |
| 广西大学 | 陕西师范大学 |
| 云南大学 | 武汉大学 |
| 中山大学 | 贵州大学 |
| 中南大学 | 贵州师范大学 |
| 四川大学 | 重庆大学 |
| 东北师范大学 | 重庆邮电大学 |
| 西安外国语大学 | 湖南师范大学 |
| 西安交通大学 | …… |
| 华中师范大学 | |

**策 划** 张鸽盛 饶邦华 周小群

高等学校英语专业系列教材
Textbook Series for Tertiary English Majors

STEM 求知

总主编：石 坚
副总主编：黄国文 陈建平 张绍杰 蒋洪新

# 跨文化交际

（第4版）

# B

# Bridge Between Minds:
## Intercultural Communication

主 编 王 蓉 张爱琳
副主编 彭晓蓉 王 怡
编 者 （以姓氏拼音为序）
代晓莉 彭晓蓉 王 晶 王 蓉
王 怡 吴丽聪 徐 豪 张爱琳

重庆大学出版社

# 内容提要

本书共 8 章,主题涉及文化和交际的内涵、跨文化交际的定义、文化的隐藏核心、语言交际、非语言交际、人际关系、社交习俗、跨文化交际能力提升。本书附录部分为学习者提供了相关阅读书目,供学习者进一步拓展学习。全书以篇章结构为纲,以"案例"解读为引导,兼顾理论系统、实际需要与学习的生动有趣,在培养学习者的跨文化交际能力的同时,提升学习者独立思考和批判性思维的能力。

**图书在版编目(CIP)数据**

跨文化交际:英文/王蓉,张爱琳主编.--4 版.
--重庆:重庆大学出版社,2018.5(2024.7 重印)
求知高等学校英语专业系列教材
ISBN 978-7-5689-0890-0

Ⅰ.①跨…  Ⅱ.①王…②张…  Ⅲ.①文化交流—英
语—高等学校—教材  Ⅳ.①G115

中国版本图书馆 CIP 数据核字(2017)第 270724 号

## Bridge Between Minds:Intercultural Communication
## 跨文化交际
### (第 4 版)

王 蓉 张爱琳 主 编

责任编辑:杨 琪 版式设计:杨 琪
责任校对:邬小梅 责任印制:赵 晟

\*

重庆大学出版社出版发行
出版人:陈晓阳
社址:重庆市沙坪坝区大学城西路 21 号
邮编:401331
电话:(023) 88617190 88617185(中小学)
传真:(023) 88617186 88617166
网址:http://www.cqup.com.cn
邮箱:fxk@ cqup.com.cn (营销中心)
全国新华书店经销
重庆市正前方彩色印刷有限公司印刷

\*

开本:787mm×1092mm 1/16 印张:15.25 字数:430千
2018 年 5 月第 4 版 2024 年 7 月第 17 次印刷
ISBN 978-7-5689-0890-0 定价:45.00 元

# 总　序

进入 21 世纪,高等教育呈现快速扩展的趋势。我国高等教育从外延式发展过渡到内涵式发展后,"质量"已成为教育改革与发展的关键词。由国务院颁布的《国家中长期教育改革和发展规划纲要(2010—2020)》(以下简称《纲要》)明确要求狠抓本科教育人才培养存在的主要问题,厘清高等教育人才培养目标、理念、社会需求,制订本科教学培养模式、教学内容和方法、质量保障与评估机制,切实提高人才培养的质量。我国英语专业在过去的数十年中经过几代人的努力,取得了显著的成绩和长足的发展。特别是近年来随着经济社会的快速发展和对外交流活动的增多,"一带一路"倡议的提出和"讲好中国故事"的需要,英语专业的学科地位也随之大大提升,其规模目前发展得十分庞大。英语专业虽然经历了一个"跨越式""超常规"的发展历程,但规模化发展带来的培养质量下滑、专业建设和人才需求出现矛盾、毕业生就业面临巨大挑战等严峻的现实表明,英语专业的教育、教学与育人又到了一个不得不改的关键时刻。

《纲要》在强调狠抓培养质量的同时,也提出了培养"具有国际视野、通晓国际规则、能参与国际事务和国际竞争"人才的战略方针。基于这样的战略需求,外语专业教学指导委员会明确提出了人才"多元培养,分类卓越"的理念。基于这样的理念,即将颁布的《英语专业本科教学质量国家标准》(以下简称《国标》)对英语专业本科的现有课程设置提出新的改革思路:英语专业课程体系包括公共课程、专业核心课程、专业方向课程、实践环节和毕业论文(设计)五个部分;逐步压缩英语技能课程,用"内容依托式"课程替代传统的英语技能课程,系统建设语言学、文学、文化、国别研究等方面的专业课程。

自 2001 年开始,在重庆大学出版社的大力支持下,我们成立了由华中、华南、西南和西北以及东北地区的知名专家、学者和教学一线教师组成的《求知高等学校英语专业系列教材》编写组,以《高等学校英语专业英语教学大纲》为依据,将社会的需求与培养外语人才的全面发展紧密结合,注重英语作为一个专业的学科系统性和科学性,注重英语教学和习得的方法与规律,培养学生能力和育人并举,突出特色和系列教材的内在逻辑关系,反映了当时教学改革的新理念并具有前瞻性,建立了与英语专业课程配套的新教材体系。《求知高等学校英语专业系列教材》经历了 10 余年教学实践的锤炼,通过不断的修订来契合教学的发展变化,在教材的整体性和开放性、学生基本技能和实际应用能力的培养、学生的人文素质和跨文化意识的培养这三方面上有所突破。通过这套系列教材的开发建设工作,我们一直在探讨新的教学理念、模式,探索英语专业人才培养的新路子。今天,我们以《国标》为依据,回顾我们过去十多年在教学改革上所做的努力,我们欣慰地看到我们的方向是契合英语专业学科定位和发展的。随着《国标》指导思想的明确,为了适应英语专业学科课程设置的进一步调整,我们对《求知高等学校英语专业系列教材》进行了最新一轮的建设工作。

全新的系列教材力求在以下方面有所创新：

第一，围绕听、说、读、写、译五种能力的培养来构建教材体系。在教材内容的总体设置上，颠覆以往"以课程定教材"的观念，不再让教材受制于刻板的课程设置体系，而是引入Program理念，根据《国标》中对学生的能力要求，针对某方面的具体能力编写对应的系列教材。读写和听说系列不再按照难度区分混合编排题材，而是依据文体或专业性质的自然划分，分门别类地专册呈现，便于教师在教学中根据实际需要搭配组合使用。例如，阅读教材分为小说类、散文类、新闻类等；口语教材分为基本表述、演讲、辩论等专题成册。

第二，将五种能力的提升融入人文素养的综合提升之中。坚持英语专业教育的人文本位，强调文化熏陶。在跨学科新专业不断涌现的背景下，盲目追求为每种新专业都专门编写一套教材，费时费力。最佳的做法是坚持英语专业核心教材的人文性，培养学生优秀的语言文化素养，并在此基础上依照专业要求填补相关知识上的空缺，形成新的教材配比模式和体系。

第三，以"3E"作为衡量教材质量的标准。教材的编写上，体现Engaging, Enabling, Enlightening的"3E"功能，强调教材的人文性与语言文化综合能力的培养，淡化技能解说。

第四，加入"微课""翻转课堂"等元素，便于课堂互动的开展。创新板块、活动的设计，相对减少灌输式的lecture，增加学生参与的seminar。

我们希望通过对这套系列教材的全新修订和建设，落实《国标》精神，继续推动高等学校英语专业教学改革，为提高英语专业人才的培养质量探索新的实践方法，为英语专业的学生拓展求知的新空间。

《求知高等学校英语专业系列教材》编委会
2017年6月

# 前　言

　　《跨文化交际》于 2011 年的第 3 版由重庆大学出版社修订再版发行以来,承蒙各地使用者的厚爱,已告售罄。在 2017 年出版社征求再版意见时,我们即认为应对其进行修改,主要基于以下三个方面的考虑:其一,几位作者通过自己以及同行的充分教学实践和学习研究,获得了新的体验和启示,同时也得到一些使用该教材的兄弟院校的积极反馈,故希望对该书进一步充实完善;其二,跨文化交际学科近几年的研究又有长足的进展,其研究成果理应在该教材中及时得到反应和体现;其三,随着全球化的推进,人们的跨文化交际实践不断丰富,无论是商务交往,企业的跨文化管理还是技术传播,都增添了不少新鲜生动的事例。如将之应用于教材,肯定有助于增强教材的趣味性、实用性和时代感。唯其如此,方能更好地适应社会和科学的发展,更好地满足使用者的需要。

　　本书旨在帮助 21 世纪的英语学习者在国际交往日益频繁的今天,进一步增强文化意识和跨文化意识,发展跨文化交际能力,以便在已成为"地球村落"的世界上,在与他人的交往中能如鱼得水、应付自如。修订仍在原书的基本框架内进行,学习方式仍以任务型的案例分析法为主,注重学生的学习主动性、参与性,师生和生生之间的互动性,以及教材与使用者之间的友好性。修订的重点涉及:1.对内容做了较大幅度的增添、拓展和深化,特别补充了一些新的理论研究发现,以使本书更加充实完整,让使用者有更大的选择自由。无论是课程设计还是课堂安排,教师均可针对不同能力的语言学习者灵活地组织教学。2.将原来整体置于章末的参考答案解说部分,分别调整到每个 Activity 之后以方便对照查阅,节省来回翻看的时间,减少麻烦。3.每一章后编写了两类练习。第一类为问答题,通过思考和回答问题帮助学习者复习巩固本章所学内容。此次修订对部分问题进行了删减和修改,拓展了问题的思维深度和知识宽度,从而使学生的学习维度从课堂延伸到课外,充分挖掘了教材的内容,为学生进一步的案例分析讨论奠定了基础。第二类为案例分析题,通过对具体生动真实的事例进行分析和讨论,加深对文化的认识,增强跨文化敏感性和实际交际能力,同时激活思维,培养发现、分析和解决问题的能力,提高英语语言表达能力。此次修订,在案例中增添了许多目前在跨文化交往中比较频繁出现的交际案例,案例所涉及的背景更具有国际化的特点,其时代性和实用性特点鲜明。案例的分析和讨论不仅提升了学生的跨文化交际能力,而且提高了学生的思辨能力。4.附录中推荐阅读书目有少量增加,以方便教师和有兴趣的同学拓展阅读。

　　本书的编写参阅了大量的文献资料，详见参考文献部分。在此谨对各位作者致以衷心的感谢。此次修订工作得到了很多人士的关心、支持和帮助。本书的主编张爱琳教授对本书的再次修订提出了非常中肯的意见。重庆大学出版社外语分社对本书的修订、出版付出了辛勤的劳动。重庆邮电大学外国语学院的部分教师也对本书的修订提出了建设性的意见和建议。借此机会一并对他们表示最诚挚的谢意。

　　此次修订是对原书的改进和提高，但由于编者学识和水平有限，书中定有疏漏和错误，热切希望使用者提出批评建议，以便不断改进。

编　者

2017 年 12 月

# Introduction

Many consultants, distinguished authors and textbooks talk about the need to understand other cultures because of the fact that we live in a global village. From last century's challenge of Jules Verne's *Around the World in 80 Days*, astronauts can now make the trip in under 80 minutes, while the Internet user takes a mere 8 seconds. The media has given us a taste for other countries, and the cost of modern air travel is within the budget of many Western people so we are travelling overseas more regularly than ever before. Holiday travel, business trips, family reunions and overseas conferences to other parts of the world are now commonplace events for professionals and ordinary people alike, with the big trip overseas, a rite de passage for many young people. The closeness of South-East Asia means that Indonesia, Thailand, Hong Kong of China, Singapore, Vietnam and Malaysia are favourite destinations for many westerners. Trades between countries are more frequent and in much larger quantities. Through all kinds of social media and advanced communication tools, such as the mobile devices and palm devices, we are increasingly linked across the globe and this has enabled us to connect with people on the other side of the world as quickly as it takes us to contact and converse with those who inhabit our neighborhood physical space. We can no longer remain detached and isolated from global issues, tensions and conflicts. The 2014 World Cup in Brazil stimulated fans all over the world. The fluctuation of the oil price is felt everywhere. The 2016 Olympic Games in Rio de Janeiro attracted sports lovers in countries all over the world. The military conflicts in the Middle East concern all peace-loving people everywhere on the earth. The list is endless. What naturally follows is that contact between nations has become more frequent, more numerous and more significant than ever before. We need to understand each others' cultures because we are increasingly visiting other cultures and interacting with them.

How do we manage this change process? How do we deal with the ever increasing intercultural contact? A good knowledge of a foreign language, mainly English—the most widely used language in the world today—is of course indispensable. But language alone does not ensure successful communication, especially communication. Let's look at some of the communication cases between people from Chinese and English cultures:

1. One cold winter day in a Chinese city, Wang Lin on his way to the library met an American professor who knew very little about China. After greeting him, Wang said: "It's rather cold. You'd better put on more clothes." but the professor didn't appear happy on hearing this. Why?

2. You are the only Chinese among some Americans. One of them is telling joke. You feel good because you understand every word. All of a sudden, everyone is laughing. Everyone except you. Why?

3. There has been a very famous brand of battery in China: White Elephant. Suppose this product is to be exported to the UK or the USA, it's very likely to fail without changing its brand name. Why?

In each of the above situations there is something "wrong." But this "something" has nothing to do with the language, which is acceptable. The problem lies in the culture in which the language is used. In the first case, for instance, Americans (and many Westerner too) don't like to be told what to do as they tend to be independent; while Chinese are in the habit of showing and accepting concerns. The second case tells us that sometimes connotations (the implied meanings) of words are keys to our understanding. In the third case, a white elephant, which arouses beautiful associations in the minds of Chinese, stands for something big, probably expensive but useless in the English culture. From the above simple cases, it's not difficult to see what an important role culture plays in communication and why language alone doesn't guarantee successful intercultural communication.

Why do these problems arise? There are many factors of course. One very important factor may be that people are not usually aware of culture due to their familiarity with it. It sounds paradoxical but it is true. This is just like what air is to people who never give it a thought until it is taken away.

That is why we need to develop our cultural awareness, and improve our intercultural communication competence, so that we can better meet the challenges which are inevitable in this globalizing world. This is what this book aims to achieve, the increase in global intercultural awareness and competence. Together we will enhance our awareness of culture, and explore diverse cultural aspects such as beliefs, values, world view, discourse patterns, body language, time and space views, human relationships, and behaviors. We know that it is impossible to expound all the details of any culture in one book alone, as culture covers almost every aspect of a person's life as well as that of a group. Armed with this contribution of cultural and intercultural awareness and basic knowledge and skills, we can design our own strategies for dealing with difficulties when they arise in specific intercultural communication situations.

During the learning process we will access the visible aspects of culture (like culturally conditioned behaviors of distinctive people) and the invisible aspects (such as beliefs, values, worldviews and relationships). Moreover, we will appraise the diversity of cultures, appreciate the similarities, respect the differences, anticipate potential problems in intercultural communication and develop an ability to deal with them. Through comparing and contrasting, we will have a better understanding of our own native culture as well as other cultures. This will make us more qualified citizens of China and of the world.

The above aim will be achieved through this thought-provoking, task-based interactive learning experience. We are about to discover a lot about culture both as readers and participants.

# CONTENTS

# Chapter *1*

# Communication and Culture

*The life which is unexamined is not worth living.* (Socrates)

*Every tale can be told in a different way.* (Greek proverb)

*The greatest distance between people is not space but culture.* (Jamake Highwater)

# I Warm-up: Look and Say

Study the picture on the left showing a "mature couple" on a tandem bike. Try to give a brief account of what you have seen from the picture to your partner, and then think about whether this picture can tell you something about the relationship between communication and culture.

Both the two wheels of a tandem bike and a mature couple in life have something in common: they work together with each other to get the best result. This may shed some light on how culture and communication are related. They "work in tandem" and they are so closely linked that it is often difficult to decide which is the voice and which is the echo.

We humans cannot live in a culture-free situation, nor can we survive without communication. In today's "shrinking" world, our communication behavior is extended from that within our own community to that among and between others. As a result, intercultural communication competence becomes necessary. In this chapter, we begin with communication, the basis of all human contact. Then we will look at aspects of culture, and the relationship between culture and communication.

# II Basics of Communication

## A Communication: Broad Types and Essential Elements

The American anthropologist Edward T. Hall says communication is culture, and culture is communication. It means that communication and culture are directly linked. Since they are two different concepts, we'd better deal with them one at a time. Let us begin with communication. Communication is the term we are too familiar with to give it a second thought. Familiarity, however, does not mean good understanding. We need to understand communication to be better communicators.

## 【Activity 1】

*Study the following communication situations. Work in groups to identify as many types of communication as you can. Then try to figure out the criteria on which you base your classification.*

1. A car dealer delivers a speech to a large audience in the auto exhibition.

2. You complain to online sales about the late delivery through Wechat(微信).

3. Two blind people exchange ideas in Braille.

4. A jockey gives instructions to his horse in the horsemanship performance.

5. A programmer issues commands to a computer.

6. Tom talks to himself while brandishing his toy gun.

7. An archaeologist is deciphering a mysterious sign on the recently unearthed pot.

8. An Arabic traveler talks to you in Arabic that is Greek to you.

9. A hen clucks to her chicks.

10. My wireless earphones receive commands from the cellphone.

## Discussion

You may use human beings as the criteria for classification; then you have two categories: human and non-human communication. If we extend our horizon a little, then we can have roughly six types:

1. Human communication

2. Animal communication

3. Human-animal communication

4. Human-machine communication

5. Machine-to-machine communication

6. Human-machine-Human communication

From the above situations, we see that communication occurs when:

1. there are at least two or more communicators, human or non-human;

2. there must be some contact between communicators;

3. there must be a language shared by communicators;

4. an exchange of information has taken place, however much it is.

For Rules 1, 2 and 4, it is self-evident; otherwise, no communication happens. For Rule 3, languages used by communicators vary.

We now move to the communication process between humans, since it is our primary focus. When we mention the term "communication" in the remainder of the book, we mean human communication.

## B Communication: Definition and Components

What is communication? What does it have to do with us? In fact, communication occurs in any place where there are human beings. When a baby is just born, it usually cries. Does the crying communicate anything? When you graduate, your friends usually say "Congratulations!" to you. When a driver sees the red light, he/she will stop. All these are cases of communication. Our experiences tell us that communication is closely connected with our everyday life; without it we can hardly survive. Communication, the basis of all human contact, is as old as humankind. Today it has become even more important. Some people believe that information (the content of what is communicated) means power and money. Whoever has information has power, and hence has control over those less informed. Whether you agree or not, it indicates that we have to take communication very seriously.

Although it constantly occurs around us, human communication is not at all a simple matter. That is why so far no single definition of human communication has been agreed upon.

## 【Activity 2】

Study the pictures below. Work in small groups and identify the many ways in which people usually get ideas and information across. Then try to 1) define communication in your own words, 2) work out as many components or steps involved in communication as you can, and 3) list the Chinese characters that are usually employed to translate communication.

## Discussion

Human beings are social creatures who need to connect and interact with other humans for survival. However, it is not easy to find a single definition due to its complexity. Up to now there are as many as over 100 definitions of communication. The pictures above give us some clues in defining communication.

We see that communication involves a message exchanged between a sender and a receiver, a channel (face to face or through the telephone) for the message to be conveyed, a setting in which the communication event occurs, a feedback from the receiver and possibly a noise and/or gesture accompanying the process of message sharing.

From these components of communication, we can draw some definitions. In its most general sense, communication refers to the sharing or exchange of information, ideas, feelings and so on. Put simply, it means getting across our ideas, views, feelings, emotions, etc. Since it involves an exchange process between humans, communication is never static. Instead, it is a dynamic, systematic process in which meanings are created and reflected in human interaction with symbols. But this definition doesn't mention whether communication behavior is intentional and/or unintentional. There are two schools of thought on this. The first believes that in a communication event one intentionally attempts to induce or illicit a particular response from another person. The second holds that the concept of intentionality is too limiting because there are instances where messages are conveyed unintentionally. In nonverbal communication cases, more messages are likely to be conveyed without the sender's awareness. This is what we have to be especially alert to in intercultural communications.

Owing to its complexity, the term communication does not have a single equivalent in Chinese. Many terms have been used to translate communication. They are 交际, 交流, 传播, 沟通, 通信, 传通. In mainland China, each of these terms is preferred by a certain discipline: 交流 in the field of psychology, 沟通 in management, 传通 in journalism, 通信 in communication. The first one, 交际, is mostly adopted by people with a linguistic background.

## Ⓒ Communication: Characteristics

It is a great challenge trying to search for a universal definition of communication. Communication is a term that has been used in many ways, for diverse purposes. In addition to the definition and the components of communication, the study of its characteristics helps us to have a better understanding of how communication actually works.

## 【Activity 3】

*Study the definition of communication and see what characteristics you can derive from it. Group discussion is recommended.*

Definition: Communication is a dynamic, systematic process in which meanings are created and reflected in human interaction with symbols.

### Discussion

From the above definition we know that communication is a process with several distinctive characteristics. Here are some important ones.

Communication is *dynamic*. It's more like a motion picture than a single snapshot. When we communicate, we interact with each other. When we don't like one idea, we replace it with another. We sometimes even shift topics in the middle of a sentence.

Communication is *irreversible*. Once a person has said and another has received and decoded the message, the original sender cannot take it back. Once a communication event takes place, it is done. Even if you can experience a similar event, it cannot be an identical one.

Communication is *unavoidable*. It is impossible not to communicate, since we communicate unintentionally all the time, even without the use of words. Our body language, the way we dress, the importance we give to arriving on time, our behavior and the physical environment in which we work, all convey certain messages to others.

Communication is *a two-way exchange of information*. Communication is sharing of information between two or more persons, with continuous feedback.

Communication is *a process*. Each message is part of a process and does not occur in isolation. This means that the meaning attached to a message depends on what has happened before and on the present context. It involves a sender and a receiver of information.

Communication is *systematic*. It is part of a large system. We send and receive messages not in isolation, but in a specific setting or context. The nature of communication depends to a large extent on this context. Settings and environments help determine the words and actions we generate and the meanings we give to the words and actions of other people. The elements of this system include a) the place or location: school buildings, theaters, public squares, homes etc.; b) the occasion: wedding, funeral, academic conference, class, graduation ceremony, etc.; c) the time when the communication takes place; and d) the number of participants: two people, a group, or a large audience. Perhaps now you may see how the people in the pictures of Activity 2 communicate and why they communicate the way they do.

Communication is *meaning loaded*. Humans are meaning-seeking creatures. Throughout our lifetime we have accumulated various meanings as the outside world has sent us trillions of messages. These meanings are stored somewhere in our brains for us to retrieve and employ. In each communication event participants attribute meaning to a behavior. Then meaning exchange is more obvious.

Communication is *symbolic*. Humans are symbol-making creatures. We are able to generate, receive, store, and control symbols. Human symbolic communication is the difference of man and the difference it makes. In other words, it is man's alone.

Today we have at hand very different types of symbols to conduct communication with: sound, light, a mark, a statue, Braille, or a painting etc. that represents something else. When we look at the road signs or no-smoking sign, we learn something. Our words and actions are other sets of symbols (very important ones) through which we convey our messages, ideas and feelings to other people.

Communication is *self-reflective*. Just as we use symbols to reflect what is going on outside of us, we also use them to reflect ourselves. This unique ability enables us to be participants and observers simultaneously: we can watch, evaluate, and alter our performances as communicators in communication events.

Communication has a *consequence*. That is to say, when we receive a message, something happens to us. For instance, when someone asks you how to go to the Dean's office, your natural response is to say, "It's over there." And you might even point to that direction. Moreover, you sure feel happy on hearing "You look great!" So regardless of the content of the message, it should be clear that the act of communication produces changes in people.

# III Understanding Culture

In this part we move from communication to culture. Like communication, culture is a term that still challenges scholars owing to its extreme complexity. Culture is not at all strange to us. We hear, read and even talk of it, such as Chinese culture, English culture, tea culture, campus culture, and so on. But when it comes to the meaning of culture, it may not be easy to give a conclusive definition. For example, you would find it difficult to define the Chinese culture even though you have grown up in it. The problem may lie in the fact that you are too familiar with it. Now let us approach culture from different aspects.

##  Culture: Too Familiar to Be Noticed

### 【Activity 4】

*How important is air to us human beings? How often are you aware of its existence around you? When do you think you will be aware of it? Why? Discuss these questions with your neighbors.*

### Discussion

The fact is that we rarely think about the existence of air, because it is always there and so we have taken it for granted. We are usually not aware of it until there is a lack of it. In this sense we are similar to the fish that seems to notice everything around it except the water in which it is swimming. Then a somewhat strange phenomenon appears before us: we have distinct explanations for what is abstruse or complicated; however, when it comes to what is essential for our survival and familiar to us, we are often at a loss as to give it a definitive description. Familiarity does not necessarily mean good understanding. This is true of culture. We live in culture; we meet culture; we behave under the guidance of culture; we transmit culture; we enrich culture. In other words, we human beings are basically cultured animals. But when we stop to think about the meaning of culture, we find we are puzzled. This is perhaps why we should spend some time on its study.

## B Culture: Definition

## 【Activity 5】

*Study the pictures and identify which of them shows a meaning of culture. Discuss this issue in small groups and try to define culture. Reference to an English and/or Chinese dictionary would be helpful.*

### Discussion

The answer is that each picture shows a meaning of culture, as each of them reflects the creation of man. Now look at how culture can be defined.

## ■ Definitions of Culture

Semantically, the word "culture" stems from the Latin term "colere," translatable as "to build on, to cultivate, and to foster." This term, referring to something constructed willingly by men, composes the opposite of "nature" that is given in itself.

As has been mentioned above, culture is a very large, complicated and elusive concept. Up to now no agreement has been reached on its definition. "As early as 1952, Kroeber and Kluckhohn listed 164 definitions of culture that they have found in the anthropology literature. And, of course, many new definitions have appeared since then."

The following are just a few of them that may help us gain some general ideas about culture.

Culture may be defined as what a society does and thinks. ——Sapir

Culture is that which binds men together. ——Ruth Benedict

By "culture," anthropology means the total life way of a people, the social legacy the individual acquires from his group. Or culture can be regarded as that part of the environment that is the creation of man. ——Kluckhohn

Culture is a system of shared beliefs, values, customs, behaviors, and artifacts that the members of a society use to cope with their world and with one another, and that are transmitted from generation to generation through learning. ——Bates and Plog

We define culture as the deposit of knowledge, experience, beliefs, values, actions, attitudes, meanings, hierarchies, religion, notions of time, roles, spatial relations, concepts of the universe, and artifacts acquired by a group of people in the course of generations through individual and group striving. ——Samovar et al

From the above few definitions, we see that culture is complex, covering almost every aspect of our life. A simpler definition can be derived: culture is the total way of life that a (usually very large) group of people share.

## ■ Importance of Culture

From the above we know that culture is what we cannot do without in our life process. The importance of culture can also be understood from other perspectives. Here we are going to talk about it in terms of satisfying basic human needs and overcoming the innate human deficiencies.

Culture is a particular way to satisfy human needs. Human beings are basically the same, with similar needs to be met. Abraham Maslow(1908-1970, American psychologist) has proposed the theory of a five-type hierarchy of human needs. One of the basic axioms of his theory is that once the lower needs are satisfied, higher needs materialize to take their places.

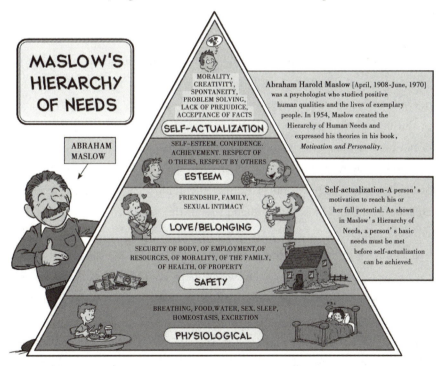

At the very bottom are the basic needs such as air, water, food, sleep, sex, etc. When these are not satisfied we may feel sickness, irritation, pain, discomfort, etc. At the second level, we see the needs for safety—the needs to do with establishing stability and consistency in a chaotic world. These needs are mostly psychological in nature, such as the security of a home and family.

Then next on the ladder come the needs for love and belongingness. Humans have a desire to belong to groups: clubs, work groups, religious groups, family, gangs, etc. We need to feel loved (non-physical) by others and accepted by others. What then follows are the needs for esteem. There are two types of esteem needs. First, it is the self-esteem which results from competence or mastery of a task. Second, there is the attention and recognition that comes from others. This is similar to the belongingness level; however, wanting admiration has sometimes to do with the need for power. Finally, at the top of the hierarchy there are the needs for self-actualization— "the desire to become more and more what one is, to become everything that one is capable of becoming." People who have everything can maximize their potential. They can seek knowledge, peace, esthetic experiences, self-fulfillment, etc.

Though we have basically the same needs, ours are satisfied in different ways. For example, all people need food. This is universal. But how to eat food is modified by culture. Some use chopsticks, others knives and forks, still others their fingers. In all human history, there are love stories. But how love is expressed differs from culture to culture. A point in case is the difference between the Chinese story of *Liang Shanbo and Zhu Yingtai* and the English one of *Romeo and Juliet*. Therefore, culture provides us with a way to satisfy our needs.

Culture is man's second nature, an effective way to overcome the essential vulnerability (unspecialization or deficiency) of human beings. Culture is what distinguishes humans from animals. According to some scholars, man differs biologically from animals in that they are not as specialized as animals. In other words, they do not have built-in instincts for survival that are biologically predetermined. Birds learn to fly by instinct. Cows are predetermined to eat grass. But man has no wings to fly, no teeth for grass, no claws to get food. Man is thus biologically weak. But it is just this inborn weakness that makes man exceed animals in earning himself a better life. Nature does not predetermine what man should do, or what they should not do. This leaves room for humans to find a way to compensate for their very weakness. The human activities that try to make up for the weakness compose human culture. It is human culture that allows man to adapt to almost all situations, and thus be superior to animals. In this sense, culture serves as the "artificial, secondary environment."

Clyde Kluckhohn[1] sums up the importance of culture when she stated that culture regulates our lives at every turn, and from the moment we are born until we die, and there is—whether we are conscious of it or not—constant pressure upon us to follow certain types of behavior that other men have created for us.

Geert H. Hofstede[2] compares culture to the software of the mind. This software takes time to acquire. That is the process of socialization, the process of learning culture. Therefore, man is the producer of culture and also the product of culture. It means that man makes culture, and is also

---

① Clyde Kluckhohn (1905—1960): a cultural anthropologist with a deep interest in culture and personality.

② Greert H. Hofstede (1928—present): a Dutch scholar who has contributed a lot to intercultural communication.

shaped by culture once culture is produced.

When we talk about culture, we had better distinguish it from society as they often appear in the same context. It seems that we cannot talk about culture without mentioning society. According to some researchers, a culture is the way of life of a nation, while a society is a community organized in accordance with a certain way of life. In other words, a society is composed of people with a distinct identity, a territorial area, and a distinctive way of life. Put simply, a society is a people with a common culture, and a culture is the transmissible way of life within a society. Cultures can exist apart from their societies: the Roman Empire disappeared, for example, but much of its culture was preserved and handed down through manuscripts and works of art.

 ## Culture: Elements

As we know, culture is an umbrella term that refers to everything concerning our life. In order to have a better and fuller understanding of culture, we will see how scholars classify culture.

In very general terms, culture can be roughly divided into three categories: material or artifact (物质文化), including such items as dresses, buildings, food, etc.; institutional (制度文化), including family, education, law, etc.; values/beliefs (观念文化), including ideas like freedom, democracy, equality, etc.

From the point of view of visibility, culture can be seen as composed of two parts: the visible (material/artifact and institutional) and the invisible (values/beliefs).

From the perspective of levels, culture is classified into two categories. One concerns intellectual and artistic activity, and the works produced by it, including things like education, history, geography, institutions, literature, art, music, and so on. The other refers to the way of life of a given people who share values, beliefs, customs, norms, etc. Some scholars name the first one "Big C" (Culture with a big C) and "small c" (culture with a small c). Another version of "Big C" and "small c" is "high culture" and "anthropological culture." High culture focuses on intellectual and artistic achievements. One might speak of a city as having a great deal of culture because there were many art exhibits, concert performances, and public lectures. Or we might say so of a particular period in history, such as the Tang Dynasty (618-907 AD) in Chinese history.

According to the sphere of influence, culture is divided into dominant culture and sub-culture. No matter how diverse a culture can be, within each society there is always one part of the culture that is shared by most people and exerts greater influence. It is to this part—the dominant culture, or umbrella culture, or mainstream culture—that we refer to when we are applying the term culture. At the same time, we should not neglect the fact that numerous sub-cultures that co-exist within each culture in addition to the dominant one. Sub-cultures refer to the groups or social communities exhibiting communication characteristics, perceptions, values, beliefs, and practices that are significantly different enough to be distinguished from the other groups, communities, and the dominant culture. This distinction can be made based on race, ethnic background, gender, sex, sexual preference, locality, and so forth. In the United States, for example, there are such sub-cultures as those of African Americans, native Americans, women, youth, gays and lesbians, and so on. Please think about the sub-cultures in China.

## 【Activity 6】

*It is the "small c" discussed above that plays an essential part in intercultural communication. It defines people's thinking, action, etc. For example, culture decides:*

—how people get married (their customs);
—what people teach their children about right and wrong (their values);
—what people think is beautiful (their beliefs);
—how people look at each other when they are talking (their nonverbal communication);
—what people study in school (their institutions)...

Now work with your neighbor and continue the above list. Please find out more aspects of human life that are affected by culture. This activity helps us see how culture affects our life.

## 【Activity 7】

*Read the following stories and decide what caused the difficulties in communication.*

A. It was my first visit to Chongqing, southwest China. I felt uneasy when I asked the way to some place. In my hometown in the North, directions are given in terms of East, West, North and South. We may easily find the way when local people there tell you whether the place is in the direction of North or South; while in Chongqing the local people tell you the way in terms of direction on the right, or on the left, to which we Northerners are quite unfamiliar. And I guess people from Chongqing may meet the same problem as I had when they were in the North.

B. 古时候有个不学无术的人,好不容易用钱买了个县官,却不会说"官话",上任之后,照例要去拜访顶头上司——知府,在闲聊中知府问:
"贵县风土怎么样?"
"并没有大风,更少尘土。"
"百姓怎样?"
"白杏只有两棵,红杏不少。"
"我问的是黎庶!"
"梨树很多,结的果实很小。"
知府动气了:"我不是问什么梨树,我是问你的小民!"
县官见知府生气,急忙站起来回答到:"卑职的小名叫狗儿。"

## Discussion

It is very likely that problems arose in the above communication events because the communicators came from different co-existing cultures, and they did not share enough to carry a smooth communication. In the first case, there is the difference between regional cultures. In the second, a gap is obvious between the levels of education.

The fact that many sub-cultures co-exist within a dominant culture tells us that there are usually many cultural differences within a single race or nationality. When we use culture in this book, we refer or relate to the dominant culture as it is the culture that most people within a nation share. However, we have to always remember that when we say Chinese are modest, we do not mean that every Chinese possesses the same degree of modesty. It only means that most Chinese display a relatively large degree of modesty in many occasions. There are always differences!

##  Culture: Characteristics

## 【Activity 8】

*Read the following story and rank the five characters according to whom you approve of most and whom you approve of least, and write a sentence or two explaining your first and last choice. Next, think about what made you rank them as you did, and try to identify where you learned the values that underpinned your reasoning and choice for the particular ranking. Do you think the values that guided your decision were personal or cultural or both? Share your opinions in pairs or in small groups.*

*Rosemary* is a woman of about 21. For several months she has been engaged to a young man named *Geoffrey*. The problem she faces is that between her and her fiancé there lies a river. No ordinary river, but a deep, wide river filled with hungry alligators.

Rosemary wonders how she can cross the river. She remembers *Sinbad*, who has the only boat in the area. She then approaches Sinbad,

asking him to take her across. He replies, "Yes, I'll take you across if you'll spend the night with me." Shocked at this offer, she turns to another acquaintance, *Frederick*, and tells him her story. Frederick responds by saying, "Yes, Rosemary, I understand your problem—but it's your problem, not mine." Rosemary decides to return to Sinbad, spends the night with him, and in the morning he takes her across the river.

Her meeting with Geoffrey is warm. But on the evening before they are to be married, Rosemary feels she must tell Geoffrey how she succeeded in getting across the river. Geoffrey responds by saying, "I wouldn't marry you if you were the last woman on earth."

Finally, Rosemary turns to her friend *Dennis*. Dennis listens to her story and says, "Well, I don't love you... but I will marry you." And that's all we know of the story.

### Discussion

This story provides us with some clues that help us understand the characteristics of culture. Let us see how this story can be possibly interpreted. (1) People do not always have similar interpretations of the world around them. They perceive and interpret behavior in different ways; (2) as a result of different values, people's beliefs, behavior and reactions are not always similar; (3) no two people, even from the same culture, have exactly the same perceptions and interpretations of what they see around them; (4) many interpretations, however, are learned from within a person's culture. Therefore, those who share a common culture will probably perceive the world more similarly than those who have different cultural backgrounds. The conclusion we can draw is that individuals are unique with different views, but individuals who share a common culture have more similarities with each other than with those from different cultures.

From this story we learn some characteristics of cultures. Can you find some more from the passage below?

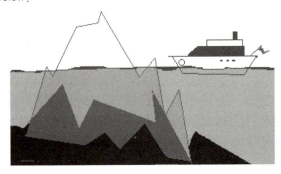

Here are five metaphors of culture. First, the popular iceberg metaphor illustrates "hidden culture": the world of assumptions, habits, beliefs that may not be consciously articulated or taught. Culture in one sense is like an iceberg. Only a small part is visible. What we can see of culture is the tangible part like food, dress, paintings, architecture, statues, etc. However, the majority of culture is like the iceberg hidden under the water, and we don't see with our eyes the intangible aspects of culture such as views, ideas, attitudes, love, hatred, customs, habits, and so on. It means that most of culture is out of our immediate conscious awareness and thus the study of culture is no easy job.

Second, culture is like the water a fish swims in. A fish notices everything around it except water in which it is swimming. The fish just takes the water for granted as it is always there around it. The same is true for us. We are usually not aware of culture, because it is so much a part of us as our environment.

Third, culture is our software. Our physical selves can be seen as the hardware. Hardware does not work without software. Culture is what provides us with the needed software. However, as with any good software, we are only vaguely aware of it when we use it.

Fourth, culture is Jelly Beans. All jelly beans in the organizational jar are "diverse" not just the red ones or purples ones.

Fifth, Culture is like melting pots and salad bowls. Popular metaphors for the relationship of immigrant cultures within a larger nation or dominant culture have shifted from the melting pot to the salad bowl. In the latter, immigrant cultures maintain their original integrity in the new national salad. More cynical observers may note that whether it is stew or salad, it all gets eaten and assimilated in the end.

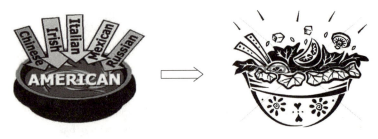

Culture is extremely complicated; some of its characteristics can be seen in the passage and the story above, and the definitions in Activity 5. The following is a list of some more important ones that may help you understand culture better.

a) Culture is *learned*, not hereditary. Because culture is a shared symbolic system within a relatively large group of people, the only way for group members to integrate into, reinforce, and co-create this shared symbolic system is through a learning process of socialization or enculturation. Interaction with family members and friends is the most common way for us to learn about our culture. Other sources for learning our culture are schools, media, folk tales, and art.

The needs that we are born with are basic needs such as food, clothing and shelter. Humans need food, but what to eat, when, where and how to eat is learned. That's why we Chinese use chopsticks while Westerns prefer knives and forks; and we like rice while Americans prefer bread. Sneezing is physiological, but after the other person sneezes, a Guangdong person says "吉星," while an English native says "God bless you." When we cough in public places, we Chinese tend to ignore it, but an American usually says "Excuse me" immediately after he/she does so.

We learn our culture in many ways and from a variety of sources, either consciously or unconsciously. One way is by means of proverbs that offer in a vivid way an important set of instructions for members to follow. For example, the English proverb "*The squeaky wheel gets the grease*" encourages people to "speak up" and make sure their views are heard. What are the other sources for people to learn culture? You should be able to list some now.

b) Culture is *transmitted* from generation to generation. Without the advantage of knowledge from those who lived before us, we would not have culture. A culture is but one link in the whole chain of generations, some of which have become history and some of which are in transition.

c) Culture is *dynamic*. Cultures are constantly changing over time. Some cultures are more open and accepting of change, others tend to resist it. Cultures change in the process of transmission from generation to generation, group to group, and place to place. The Chinese culture has experienced great changes in its long history, especially since the May 4th Movement in 1919. For example, handshaking that was not practiced before is popular now, yet in some remote rural areas, elderly farmers still don't shake hands. Today changes in China are even more obvious and prominent, as contact with other countries is getting more frequent than ever before. Contact, by its very nature, brings change. Cultures also change through several mechanisms: innovation, diffusion, and acculturation being the most common.

One point needs emphasizing. Although many aspects of culture are subject to change, the deep structure of a culture resists major alterations. That is, changes in dress, food, transportation, housing and the like are likely to occur very quickly. However, values associated with such things as ethics and morals, work and leisure, definitions of freedom, the importance of the past, religious practices, the pace of life, and attitudes toward gender and age are so deeply embedded in a culture that they persist generation after generation.

d) Most of culture is *hidden*, like the part of the iceberg under water. It's difficult to study culture because most of what we call culture is of an intangible nature and cannot be seen. That is to say, most of culture exists in the subconscious mind of people, who therefore aren't aware of the fact that their actions are governed by their own culture, or cultural rules.

e) Values are the *core* of culture. Cultures are mainly differentiated from others by way of different values people hold. Many of these differences can be seen from what people do. For example, Western people celebrate Christmas; people in East Asia celebrate the Spring Festival. Some people speak Spanish, but others speak English. Some people talk to God, but others have God talk to them. And still others say there is no God. Some people paint and decorate their entire bodies, but others spend millions of dollars painting and decorating only their faces. People like to hear compliments and praise, but people from different cultures respond differently to the same compliments and praises.

f) Cultural elements are *integrated*. They are closely linked as if in a complex chain like system. You touch a culture in one place and everything else is affected. A good example of this is the Opening and Reforming in China, which has brought huge changes not only in the areas of the economy, but also in many other sectors including politics, education and so on.

g) Culture is *ethnocentric*. Practices that differ from one's own are usually considered strange, even abnormal or barbarous. This is the manifestation of ethnocentrism. Ethnocentrism, the belief that one's culture is primary to all explanations of reality, is usually learned at the unconscious level. It often leads to a negative evaluation of another culture's ways of doing things, because a logic extension of ethnocentrism is that *our way is the right way*.

# **IV** Communication and Culture

## **A** Communication: Culture Bound

Communication permeates our life, and our life is guided by our culture. Communication itself is the basic human need, but the way an individual communicates emanates from his or her culture. In other words, communication is a product of culture. This can be seen in the fact that when communicating some cultures prefer debate, while others value silence more. Therefore, "communication is culture, and culture is communication" (Hall). The following part will tell us how the human communication style is modified by specific cultures.

## **B** Communication: High-context and Low-context

From the study of communication characteristics, we see that communication is systematic. We send and receive messages not in isolation, but in a specific setting or context. Before we discuss high and low context, let us first engage in two activities (9, 10) and think about how people get meanings from the context and what elements are included in the context.

## 【Activity 9】

*Read the dialogue below and see what the conflict is between the two speakers. Discuss in groups the questions following the dialogue.*

In Hong Kong, a Chinese policeman (A) goes to his British superior (B) and asks for leave to take his mother to hospital.

A: Sir?

B: Yes, what is it?

A: My mother is not very well, sir.

B: So?

A: She has to go into hospital, sir.

B: Well, get on with it. What do you want?

A: On Thursday, sir.

B: Bloody hell, man. What do you want?

A: Nothing, sir.

## Questions

1. What do you think the Chinese policeman wants?
2. How do you know his meaning?
3. What do you think of the British officer's response?

## Discussion

A Chinese professor has made a survey among both Chinese (including foreign citizens of Chinese origin) and the native speakers of English. The respective responses may surprise you. The Chinese respondents said that the British officer had no human feelings whatsoever! However, the native English speakers' reaction was that the Chinese policeman was a terrible guy; he was not clear or specific at all!

The possible cause of the conflict is that the Chinese policeman makes the request by stating the reason only. In the Chinese culture, this is a clear contextual clue with which the hearer can indirectly get the message. The officer, as a superior, should have shown his concern and understanding for the policeman and taken the initiative to grant him a leave of absence. However, in the English culture, "Your mother's illness is your personal and private business, what you should make clear to your superior is what you want from him". What the Chinese policeman said cannot give the British officer any clue for asking for leave, because the latter is not accustomed to the culture where a lot of meaning comes from the context instead of explicit verbal message.

# 【Activity 10】

*Now you will find another kind of difference. Study the paragraph and discuss the questions below.*

If you are one of the residents of the global village who actually get on airplanes and fly from country to country, you will notice an interesting phenomenon at the arrival gates of international airports. Usually there is a group of family members or a host waiting to meet the Chinese, Japanese, and other Asians who are getting off the airplane. Often there is no one waiting to meet the Westerners who are arriving. They just collect their luggage and then take a taxi or a bus to their destination.

## Questions

1. How do you account for this difference?
2. If you were to arrive at New York for the first time, would you like to have some friends or relatives meet you at the airport? Why or why not?

## Discussion

We tend to believe that you would prefer to have some people to meet you at the airport the first time you arrived at certain place in a foreign country. We are Chinese. Our social norms tell us that no one arriving at an unfamiliar place should be left to find their way on their own, if that could be avoided. That is why whenever foreign teachers come to our campuses, they are always met at the airport. Moreover, a Chinese, usually a person who speaks their language, is often assigned to be their contact who is supposed to help them with any difficulties they might encounter in the new culture. Westerners, however, are more likely to get enough explicit information in the form of a guidebook, a brochure, a manual, etc. before they arrive. Then they tend to assume that certain predictable services will be available and that they can find these and use them without any assistance.

## ■ Context

From the previous two activities, we see that meanings do not come from the verbal language alone. They are also implied from the context in which communication takes place. For example, the real intention of the Chinese policeman is not expressed through words, but is to be inferred from the relationship of the communicators. And being present at the airport to meet guests is also meaningful. In other words, setting and environment help determine the words and actions we generate and the meanings we give to the words and actions of other people. Therefore, the meanings that people exchange in ways other than language are usually referred to as context. According to Hall, context is the information that surrounds an event, and bound up with the meaning of the event.

## ■ High-context and Low-context

Anthropologist Edward Hall categorizes cultures as being either high or low context, depending on the degree to which meaning comes from the settings or from the words being exchanged. This helps us to see more clearly the relationship between culture and communication, and provides an effective means of examining cultural similarities and differences in communication.

A high-context (HC) communication or message is one in which most of the information is either in the physical context or internalized in the person, while very little is in the coded, explicit, transmitted part of the message. A low-context (LC) communication is just the opposite, i.e., the mass of information is vested in the explicit code.

Any transaction can be characterized as high, low or middle context. HC transactions feature programmed information that is in the receiver and in the setting, with only minimal information in the transmitted message. LC transactions are the reverse. Most of the information must be in the transmitted message in order to make up for what is missing in the context.

**High-context cultures**

|

Japanese

|

Chinese

|

Korean

|

African American

|

Native American

|

Arab

|

Greek

|

Latin

|

Italian

|

English

|

French

|

American

|

Scandinavian

|

German

|

German-Swiss

|

**Low-context cultures**

According to Hall, Native Americans, Latin Americans, Japanese, Chinese, and Koreans belong to high-context cultures, where people are very homogeneous and so they tend to share more common experiences. In these kinds of cultures, information is provided through gestures, the use of space, and even silence. Meaning is also conveyed through status ( age, sex, education, family background, title, and affiliation ) and through an individual's informal friends and associates. At the other end of the spectrum lie the low-context cultures such as German, Swiss, and American. The population there is less homogenous. It leads to the lack of a large pool of common experiences, and so each time they communicate they need detailed background information. This largely explains why in low-context cultures, people input meanings in explicit verbal codes. A study shows that the American adults in Hawaii talk on average 6 hours and 43 minutes every day, while Japanese adults talk only 3 hours 31 minutes a day on average. The scale on the left indicates how much people in diverse cultures depend on context in communication.

This continuous scale tells us that no culture exists at either end and the difference lies only in degree. What we have to remember is that this categorization, based on national cultures, is general and in each culture there are both high-context and low-context situations. For example, communication between close friends and family members that is high-context situation exists in any culture. Moreover, banquets, the typical example of high-context situation, and contracts, the typical low-context documents, are not restricted in a certain culture. American culture, for example, is generally low-context, but there are also many high-context communication transactions. A case in point is the mother-son talk when each knows the other too well to use many words. Again, cultures vary only in degree in this regard.

## ■ Characteristics of High/Low-context Communication

Each style manifests its own characteristics. First, as we have noticed before, high-context communication tends to be more personal while low-context communication seems more impersonal. In general, people in high-context cultures prefer to get information from other people—neighbors, friends, colleagues, and acquaintances, while those in low-context cultures tend to look for trust and use impersonal sources such as newspapers, textbooks, guidebooks, lectures, roadmaps, announcements and instruction sheets.

Second, high-context communication is often economical, fast, and efficient, because participants share many common experiences and so they do not have to rely on speaking out as much as low-context culture communicators do. However, this way of communicating takes a long time to learn. When we turn to low-context communication, we find that it is an effective way of transmitting information among people who do not share the same experiences.

Now we know why the British officer did not recognize the implied meaning. The problem is that he comes from a low-context culture. Low-context communicators tend to pay little attention to messages sent non-verbally. They think communication is the exchange of verbal messages that are meaningful apart from the context in which they are said. They are aware of some non-verbal behavior such as facial expressions and tone of voice, but to them these behaviors only emphasize and modify what people say rather than how they are behaving and why. They pay little attention to the situation, the roles of participants and other factors that make up the context of the words. This means that they often fail to note things such as the status of the people they are communicating with, what the other person is not saying, and any social expectations that are not expressed in words. Usually high-context communicators have no difficulty understanding the meaning of these contextual messages. Because of these differences, problems or misunderstandings may arise when people from high and low-context backgrounds are communicating.

| 高情景文化 | 低情景文化 |
| --- | --- |
| 多表达含蓄的信息，使用比喻，有很多言外之音 | 信息表达比较简单、直接 |
| 很多非语言交际 | 语言交际多余身体语言 |
| 价值观倾向于团队意识 | 价值观倾向于个人主义 |
| 倾向于花时间培养和建立长期的个人关系 | 倾向于发展短期的个人关系 |
| 强调螺旋式逻辑 | 强调线性逻辑 |
| 重视非言语的互动，更容易读懂非言语表达方式 | 重视直接的言语互动，很难读懂非言语的表达方式 |
| 倾向于在表达中加入更多"情感" | 倾向于在表达中加入更多"逻辑" |
| 倾向于传递简单、含蓄、模棱两可的信息 | 倾向于传达有组织的信息，基于足够的细节、强调重点词语和技术标识 |

# REVISION TASKS

1. *Review this chapter with the help of the following questions.*

(1) What is communication? What are the characteristics of communication? Can you give some examples of these characteristics?

(2) What role does communication play in your life? Do you know your communication style? Can you design a communication model of your own?

（3）How much do you know about high-context and low-context communication? Can you give some examples of the differences between high-context and low-context communication?

（4）What is culture? What is its nature? Is culture important to you? why or why not?

（5）Is culture unique to humankind? Why or why not?

（6）Do you agree that culture is man's second nature? Please give your reasons.

（7）Do you think there are differences between cultures? If yes, please give examples.

（8）What do you think is the relationship between culture and communication?

（9）Have you ever experienced cultural puzzles and/or conflicts?

（10）How do you look at sub-cultures? How do sub-cultures affect communication?


## 2. *Complete the tasks below.*

（1）Read the story told by Litz, a Finnish, who married a Chinese doctor. Misunderstanding between the mother-in-law and the daughter-in-law is obvious in the story. Try to explain why. You may use the framework we have learned in this chapter.

My husband and I had long wished to bring his mother to stay with us for a while. Last summer, after we re-decorated our house, we invited her over. You can well imagine how happy my husband was! And I was just as happy. I know being filial to parents is a great value Chinese people cherish. As a wife of a Chinese man I try to be as filial as my husband.

Two days after my mother-in-law's arrival, I talked to my husband while his mother was sitting in the garden enjoying the sunshine.

Litz: Dick, how long is your mum going to stay?

Dick: I don't know. I haven't asked her.

Litz: Why not ask her?

Dick: What do you mean by asking her?

Litz: I mean what I said. Just ask her how long she's going to stay.

My mother-in-law overheard our conversation, and decided to leave for China the very afternoon. I had never expected that her visit should be so short. I tried very hard to persuade her to change her mind, but in vain.

（2）In the following story, David's strategy worked well in Australia and New Zealand, but failed in China. Read it and try to diagnose what was wrong with David's strategy in China by using the high / low context frame.

Glorious Paints, a Singapore manufacturer, is a fast-growing company headed by three young Western-educated directors.

In early 1990s, the firm decided to sell a large quality of paint to Australia and New Zealand. Director Tan achieved this success by 1) sending information to potential candidate firms, 2) negotiating a distribution agreement with the company he decided was best qualified to handle that market area. This process took about 4 months and sales volume is already exceeding expectations.

Then the company decided to do business in China, which was a very promising market with high demand and little local competition. So David was instructed to set up distribution there using the same approach that succeeded in Australia and New Zealand.

After necessary research, David sent off brochures and product information to the prospective candidate firms, enclosing a cover letter requesting an appointment to discuss possible representation. He expected perhaps 5~6 of them to reply.

Six weeks went by without a single response. Then David sent off the second mailing, this time in Chinese. Still no answer.

Mr. Tan was upset. He expected David to come up with a solution. David was at a loss. "What have I done wrong?"

(3) Read the following story about Walmart's failure in Germany, and then think about what it tells us about doing business in foreign countries.

Walmart (a famous US super-market) that entered Germany in 1997 and took over 95 stores quit the country in July 2006. What was wrong with Walmart's operation in Germany? The main factor by many analysts is the cultural philosophy. Walmart tried to relocate the American model: service with a smile from the bag-packer at the end of the band, employees chanting W-A-L-M-A-R-T to raise morale and an ethics code which included banning sexual relations between employees. The latter was overturned about a year ago by the German courts, which supported the German custom by which man and wife can often be found across the hall from each other in the same firm after romance blossomed in the workplace. And clerks ordered by supervisors to smile at customers are reported as invitations to unwanted social interaction. It is because in Germany smiles are exchanged between friends, but not between strangers. And raising morale? Well, in Germany that is the job of the workers' council, a group of employees quite akin to a union, which ensures employee concerns are represented during management meetings on the one hand, and organizes employee activities such as the company soccer competition or discounted access to mind and body classes on the other.

(4) Study the unhappy experience of an Australian student who learned Chinese in a University in Beijing and try to explain why she felt unhappy.

She taught some non-English majors of the second year. She found that the Chinese students were not good at speaking in discussion. Every time she asked questions in Chinese, the students laughed. Then she picked up a basketball at hand, and said that anyone who got the ball had to answer, which is often used in Australian high schools. She explained the rules and then threw it to a male student. The whole class burst into laughter. She was so confused that she shouted: "Nothing funny. Answer!" Again another fit of laughter.

(5) Read the story about Mr. Geddy Teok who was in trouble and give him advice on how to deal with the problem.

Mr. Geddy Teok, an American-Chinese (second generation) employee of a large New Jersey pharmaceutical firm, was based in Tokyo, Japan. His main aim was to get a major joint venture going with one of the largest Japanese pharmaceutical manufacturers. After four years of negotiating, the supreme moment had come for signing contracts. Obviously the lawyers from HQ in New Jersey were well prepared and sent the contract to Geddy one week before the "ceremony."

Geddy was shocked when he received the document from the USA. "I could not even count the number of pages. I would guess the Japanese would leave the room when they saw the thick pile."

Geddy called HQ. The legal department said that the relationship was so complex that the contract needed to cover many possible instances. Moreover, a consultancy firm that advised them regularly said that Asians in general and Japanese in particular had a reputation of being quite loose in defining what was developed by them and what came from the USA: "We'd better have some pain now and be clear in the terms of our relationship, than to run into problems later because of miscommunication. If they sign it at least they show they are serious."

The meeting was scheduled for tomorrow. Geddy was in despair. His dilemma was: "Whatever I would do, it would hurt my career, if I insist on the Japanese signing it they will see it as proof of how little trust that has been developed over the years of negotiation. This might mean a postponement of the discussions and in the worst case the end of the deal. If I reduce the contract to a couple of pages and present it as a "letter of intent," HQ in general and even worse the whole legal department will jump on me, jeopardizing my career."

If you were Geddy, what would you do?

# Chapter 2

# Intercultural Communication

*Wisdom begins when you realize that there are other points of view. ( Author Unknown )*

*All life is an experiment. The more experiments you made the better. ( Ralph Waldo Emerson )*

*Diversity... will be the engine that drives... the corporation of the 21st century. ( Stephen H. Rhinesmith )*

# I Warm-up: Read and Say

*Study the following scenario and discuss with your group members why the Japanese and the Americans behaved differently.*

Early during the Suzuki family's stay in the United States, Mr. Suzuki went out after work with several American businessmen. They went to a small restaurant and ordered a pitcher of beer. As is the custom in Japan, Mr. Suzuki filled the glass of everyone at the table but himself. He left his own glass empty. The American men at the table looked at Mr. Suzuki in surprise. One asked if Mr. Suzuki didn't want a drink. Mr. Suzuki smiled and nodded. The men waited for him to fill his own glass. When he did not, they dismissed it

and began to talk. Throughout the night, the Americans continued to fill their own glasses or have them filled by Mr. Suzuki. They assumed that Mr. Suzuki did not drink and left his glass empty.

Why did Mr. Suzuki leave his own glass empty? What would a Chinese man do in similar situations?

# II Intercultural Communication

In Chapter One, we dealt with communication and culture, and their relationships. We now have to move on to intercultural communication. First, we will begin from what it is about and how many levels it involves. Then we will see why it is necessary for us to devote time to it and what difficulties are involved. Finally, we are going to address the practice aspect and the discipline aspect of intercultural communication.

## A Intercultural Communication: Definition and Levels

Both cross-cultural communication and intercultural communication have been translated as 跨文化交际 in Chinese. Some scholars maintain that these two terms are interchangeable, being basically the same in meaning. Other scholars argue that they are different in that cross-cultural communication implies static comparison between cultures while intercultural communication focuses on the process and interactions. In this course we prefer the latter, emphasizing interactions.

Intercultural communication may be understood as a practice, called in Chinese 跨文化交际. It can also be understood as a discipline 跨文化交际学. Some people do not make such a

distinction. They just use 跨文化交际 for both.

As the term suggests, intercultural communication occurs when a member of one culture produces a message for consumption by a member of another culture. To put it simply, intercultural communication means the communication between people from different cultural backgrounds. It consists of several levels of communication.

# 【Activity 1】

*Study the following communication events and discuss each question.*

1. If a Japanese Prime Minister communicates with an American President, what kind of communication is it?

2. If an Afro-American interacts with a White American, what kind of communication is it?

3. If in China a Tibetan Chinese communicates with a Han Chinese, what kind of communication is it?

4. If in China a northerner interacts with a southerner, what kind of communication is it?

## Discussion

In the first event, it is an international communication because it occurs between two countries. The second case involves interracial communication, because Afro-Americans and White Americans are of two different races. The communication between a Tibetan Chinese and a Han Chinese is inter-ethnic in essence, because they are from different ethnic groups. The last one belongs to the category of inter-regional communication, because the speakers come from different regions within one country. This categorization helps us to have a clearer idea of intercultural communication.

However, some scholars such as the Scollons deny that there is intercultural communication. They argue that cultures do not talk; individuals do.

## B  Intercultural Communication: Importance and Difficulties

Culture and communication act on each other. As the carrier of culture, communication influences the structure of a culture, and culture is necessarily manifested in our communication patterns by teaching us how we should talk and behave. We know from our experiences that today's world is becoming smaller because time and space are "shrinking", the result of the rapid advancement in the areas of telecommunication and transportation. Other factors contribute too, such as international economic relationships, economic cooperation through regional organizations, the movement of people, people's higher standard of living, and

environmental issues that include over-fishing, global warming, deforestation, endangered species, waste disposal, and air and water pollution. All these indicate that we have come into more frequent, abundant and significant contacts with people from other countries. We are facing the reality of intercultural communication in a global environment. The following activities will alert you to the importance and difficulties involved.

# 【Activity 2】

*Contacts with people from different cultural backgrounds inevitably involve miscommunication, misunderstanding, and even serious conflicts. Read the following cases and decide what different behaviors, norms and values are reflected.*

A. Shanghai: A Washington State agriculture official who was touring China a few years ago handed out bright green baseball caps at every stop without noticing that none of the men would put them on or that all women were giggling.

B. A leading U.S. golf ball manufacturer targeted Japan as an important new market for its product, but even after heavy advertising, the sales of the company's golf products were well below average. As it turned out, the firm had offered its product in white packaging, and in groups of four.

## Discussion

Both cases involve cultural differences. In Case A the response of the Chinese is affected by the Chinese expression "绿帽子", the symbol of a cuckold. In Case B, the U.S. manufacturer failed to learn that in Japan white is a color often associated with mourning and that the number four signifies death there.

From the cases above, we see that failures can often result from a lack of knowledge about other cultures. The case in the Warm-up Activity also implies that it is important to know something about intercultural communication before we actually participate in the practice. Mutuality is the underpinning of Japanese drinking culture. It comes across in the general tolerance for the excesses it spawns, but more directly in the practice of pouring your drinking partner's drinks for him or her. Most drinking is done from small glasses decanted from bottles or cans. Never pour your own!

In that scenario, Mr. Suzuki acted as his culture required of him. Everyone at some stage has, by the end of the evening, poured everyone else a drink. It is probably the only ceremony that really deeply matters in Japan, and one that is heralded and acknowledged by all involved with bowing of heads, grunts, groans, brilliant smiles or gales of laughter. In Japanese society, one defers to the needs or wants of others. Thus, in Japan, one does not serve himself/herself; to do so would put oneself above others. Mr. Suzuki, a polite Japanese man, showed his respect for the others in the group. He always filled the others' glasses but never filled his own glass. He waited patiently, assuming that the other men, operating under the same custom, would fill his glass. In the United States, however, one person may pour another's drink but would not ignore himself/herself in the process. The Americans probably assumed Mr. Suzuki did not drink and, rather than embarrass him, did not make an issue of his empty glass. Both the Americans and Mr. Suzuki probably left the restaurant confused and wondering. Mr. Suzuki probably thought the Americans were rude or selfish. The Americans probably thought Mr. Suzuki was strange.

# 【Activity 3】

*Read the story and think about why so many problems may arise in the practice of intercultural communication. The questions below each case may help you form some ideas on this issue.*

A. Once upon a time a marmoset ( monkey) decided to leave the forest and explore the great, wide world. He traveled to the city and saw many strange and wonderful things but finally he decided to return home. Back in the forest his friends gathered around. "Well," they cried, "what did you see?" "I saw many buildings made of concrete and glass. Buildings were so high that they touched the sky," said the marmoset. And all his friends imagined branches scratching the sky. "The buildings were full of people walking on two legs and carrying briefcases," said the marmoset. All his friends could almost see people running along the branches with their tails wrapped firmly around their briefcases.

## Questions

1. Why did they imagine people with tails?
2. What made them misrepresent the image of people?

B. In the TV series *Genghis Khan* (《成吉思汗》) produced by the CCTV studio, Genghis Khan①, on one occasion after heavy drinking, lay down on his "bed" and said to his subordinates, "How delighted I am today! You have never known that the bed of middle China is supported on four legs. You can never imagine how comfortable it is lying on it." The subordinates racked their brains to understand. What they had in mind, however, was but a horse, or a cow, or a camel that had four legs.

## Questions

1. Why could they not be able to construct in their mind the image of a bed as it is?
2. What does this story tell us about understanding between cultures?

## Discussion

People are very much limited by their own environment. When they first come in contact with cultures other than their own, they often behave like the marmosets or the subordinates of Genghis Khan. They can only interpret what they see or hear of the unfamiliar culture in terms of what they are familiar with.

---

① Genghis Khan (1162—1227): the Mongol conqueror who united the Mongol tribes and in 1206 took the name Genghis Khan ("supreme conqueror"). He annexed northern China, central Asia, Iran, and southern Russia.

This is probably why misunderstanding in interpretation results.

One more thing we can infer here is that it is very difficult for people to understand each other if they do not share the same experiences. It is true that as human beings we share commonalities, but there are many differences that distinguish us from one another. It is just these differences that make the world diverse. However, this is where miscommunication, misunderstanding and even conflict may occur. It is natural enough that is that we need to know something of other cultures as well as our own if we hope to achieve development and harmony in the world.

To sum up, our culture shapes the way we think; it tells us what "makes sense." It holds us together by providing us with a shared set of customs, values, ideas, beliefs, rituals, practices as well as a common language. We live enmeshed in this cultural web: it influences the way we relate to others, the way we think, our tastes, our habits; it enters our aspirations and desires. But as culture binds us together it also selectively blinds us.

# 【Activity 4】

Jane, an American, had a very good Japanese friend Suki living in Japan. Suki was a talented designer working for a famous company. Suki decide to get married and invited Jane to her wedding. Thus, Jane flew to Japan to meet Suki. Suki wanted to introduce her fiance to Jane, so they all had dinner together. During dinner, they began a pleasant conversation, and Suki's fiance was nice and polite to Jane. Then Suki told Jane that she would quit her job and be a housewife after marriage. Jane was surprised. She told Suki that she should not waste her talent and that she still should continue to work even after marriage. Suki said that as a housewife she would be very busy and that there would be no time for work. Besides, they had decided to have a baby, and this would increase the workload for Suki. Jane suggested that Suki could share the housework with her husband so she could have time to develop her career. Suki seemed embarrassed, while her fiance remained silent for the rest of the evening. Jane felt that his attitude toward her become cold.

## Questions

1. What do you think the differences in the values of marriage and family between the American and the Japanese?
2. Why was there a change in the attitude of Suki's finance toward Jane?

## Discussion

Marriage rituals vary based upon family expectations. This really isn't much different from the United States. I will instead focus on the reality of marriage in Japan: the trends and ideas behind it.

Like many societies, marriage in Japan was arranged for much of its history. The purpose of marriage was the continuation the family line. Women were raised to be the "good wife, wise mother" and sacrifice herself for the good of family and country (Bardsley, 2004). The traditional gender roles still persist: married women in Japan feel the household tasks are unfair. Japanese men often do not share in housework. Because of this view, women who work are often not seen as contributing to the household. (Kaufman & Taniguchi, 2009).

In this case as a traditional Japanese husband, Suki's fiance naturally wanted her wife to be a good mother and a dedicated housewife to this family. Thus, he was quite cold when he heard Jane's advice. Jane, as a well-educated and physically independent, white-collar worker , insisted that woman should still have the rights of work and career after getting married. Being a wife, a mother is equally important as a self-sufficient whit-collar worker. In America, most of the modern women believe that work could offer their chances to establish themselves and hold certain social status. That's why Jane insisted on persuading Suki to go for a job.

# 【Activity 5】

*Study the poem① and see what messages you can draw from it that are relevant to intercultural communication study.*

横看成岭侧成峰，远近高低各不同。<br>
不识庐山真面目，只缘身在此山中。

## Discussion

One of the messages we can derive from this poem is that "outsiders" often see things we do not usually see because they are contrasting our ways with their different ways. That is, the "otherness" (other cultures) provides an alternative frame of reference for us to know ourselves. This involves comparison that has always been an effective way of cognition.

Knowing only one culture is just like having only one torch in a dark room. Your sight is so limited that you might ignore the rest of the visible and invisible world. Imagine that there is more than one torch available and you will see more of the world from another perspective. This other perspective can be provided by the knowledge of another culture. This also illustrates the importance of intercultural communication and the benefit of engaging in it.

In order to live in harmony with other world "villagers," we need to know that all peoples in the world are both similar and different. The similarities that unite us should be appreciated and the differences that divide us should be respected, so that harmony and development will be enhanced in the world community. In the process of communication, we should develop cultural awareness, being alert to the fact that in spite of our commonalities, we behave in diverse ways. We need to know each other well. Thus, we could obtain a useful frame of reference against which we can know ourselves better. This is reciprocal.

The following principles may help us in our study of intercultural communication:

---

① 《题西林壁》by 苏轼 (1037-1101).

- Remember that communication is a process and that the process varies among cultures.
- Learn to understand different communication styles—you could even benefit through expanding your repertoire.
- Communicating across cultures requires extra efforts. Good communication requires commitment and concentration.
- When communications cause conflict, be aware that problems might have more to do with style or process than with content or motives.
- Although culture affects differences in communication patterns, there are many exceptions within each group depending on social class, age, education, experience, and personality.
- Look at what might be getting in the way of understanding. Constantly ask "What's going on here?" and check your assumptions.
- Use language that fosters trust and alliance.
- Respect differences; don't judge people because of the way they speak.
- Target language alone does not guarantee effective intercultural communication.

# III Overview

Intercultural communication can be understood as both a practice and a discipline. As a practice, it dates back to thousands of years ago. It has been around with us for so long that it often escapes our consciousness. Wandering nomads, religious missionaries, and conquering warriors have encountered people different from themselves since the beginning of time. A typical example is the famous "Silk Road"① in Chinese history through which peoples of Asia, Africa and Europe interacted with each other. Today, we do not have to go abroad to interact with members of other cultures. Even at home, we watch overseas movies, read novels by overseas writers, meet overseas tourists, employ overseas teachers, and interact with others over the Internet. It has become a practice that we perform everyday. In this sense, intercultural communication is universal.

Intercultural communication (ICC) as a discipline has but a short history. It was started in the United States, a country of immigrants. Edward T. Hall is accepted as the founder of intercultural communication, and his book *The Silent Language* (1959) marked the beginning of this field of study.

What follows is an outline of the development of this field of study.

Culture and communication were studied separately until the early 1970s when scholars started to relate culture to communication. In 1970, intercultural communication was recognized by the International Communication Association (ICA). Since then, many changes occurred. One of them is that intercultural communication was offered as a course of study at American universities.

---

① Silk Road: an ancient caravan route linking Xi'an in central China with the eastern Mediterranean. It was established during the Han Dynasty (206 B.C.-220 A.D.) and took its name from the silk materials which were brought by the early traders to Western Europe from China.

Since the early 1970s, cross-cultural training started. Trainees were Peace Corps members who were sent to countries in Asia and Africa. Most of them were university graduates and volunteered to go overseas. But when they were actually there, many experienced what Ruth Benedict called "culture shock." This kind of training was thus started.

In 1975, Society for Intercultural Education, Training and Research (SIETAR) was set up. It probably is the biggest international organization engaged in intercultural communication.

In 1977, an academic journal, *International Journal of Intercultural Relations*, was published.

Today this discipline is widely acknowledged and extensively researched all over the world.

Intercultural communication in China has a shorter history. It was not until the early 1980s when ICC was introduced into China. Since then more and more researchers and teachers of English have become interested. Well-known scholars in this field in China include Professors Hu Wenzhong, Le Daiyun, Guan Shijie, Jia Yuxin, Lin Dajin, Gao Yihong, etc. who have contributed a lot to the study.

In 1995, the China Association for Intercultural Communication was founded. It holds an international symposium on intercultural communication biannually. Scholars attending these symposiums are mainly teachers of foreign languages, teachers of Chinese as a foreign language, linguists, as well as psychologists. Their research aspects cover verbal communication, nonverbal communication, comparative study of customs, values, and behavior patterns in China and other countries, and so on.

ICC is of a multidisciplinary nature. It concerns anthropology, philosophy, psychology, physiology, sociology, history, religion, tradition, geography and so on. Of all the studies, anthropology contributes most substantially to the study of culture and that of intercultural communication. For example, Sapir, Whorf, Benedict, Kluckhohn, and Mead did a lot of work in the field of cultural studies.

# REVISION TASKS

*1. Review this chapter with the help of the following questions.*

(1) What does intercultural communication mean to you?

(2) What principles may help us in our study of the of intercultural communication?

(3) What do you think are the affecting factors contributing to misunderstanding in intercultural communication?

(4) What accounts for the difficulties in conducting communication across cultures?

(5) What benefits can you gain from learning intercultural communication?

(6) How do you understand "cultures are both similar and different"?

(7) How should we look at the cultures of some small nations?

(8) How does "Silk Road" promote intercultural communication?

(9) In what sense do we say that ICC is of a multidisciplinary nature?

(10) What knowledge and competence do you think is needed for conducting intercultural communication?

## 2. Complete the tasks below.

(1) Study the following statements and see whether you agree with them and why.
- Communication is a risky business.
- Target language alone does not guarantee effective intercultural communication.
- You will not know your own culture well until you communicate with another.

(2) The Golden Rule for treating others is "Do unto others what you would have them do unto you." Which Chinese saying is similar to this? Do you think this is a good rule to guide interaction between people of different cultures? If yes, why? If not, give your advice.

(3) Comment on the English maxim "If you want to know about water, don't ask a fish." Does it indicate the importance of intercultural communication in some way?

(4) Some suggest that foreign language learners should not only learn about culture, but also "do culture." The latter term underscores the idea that communicating across cultures is a process of making meanings, and of people understanding one another so they can get to know one another, build relationships, and solve problems together. What do you think this imply? Share your ideas with your classmates.

(5) Find out the main message conveyed by the remark (below) of Carlos Fuentes, and then deliberate on it in small groups.

"People and their cultures perish in isolation, but they are born or reborn in contact with other men and women, with men and women of another culture, another creed, and another race. If we do not recognize our humanity in others, we will not recognize it in ourselves."

Chapter 3

# The Hidden Core of Culture

*Culture hides more than it reveals, and strangely enough what it hides, it hides most effectively from its own participants.* (Edward Hall)

*One man's meat is another man's poison.* (English proverb)

*Mind is actually internalized culture.* (Edward T. Hall)

# I Warm-up: Read and Say

A. A Chinese man married an American woman who was twenty years younger. They bought a house in the suburb of the U.S. city where they lived. Since it was a two-story house, there were enough rooms for the couple to use. The husband suggested renting the basement so that they could have some extra money to pay for the mortgage. However, the wife would never agree. Unhappiness resulted.

*Work in pairs.*

One takes the side of the husband and lists the possible reasons for renting the part of their house. One takes the side of the wife and lists the possible reasons for not doing so. Then discuss what accounts for their differences.

B. If a lady was harassed in the office at work, what would you disapprove of? Is it that the conduct rule was violated or the lady was left with terrible experiences?

Your opinions on the above issues have a lot to do with values, which are what we will address in this chapter.

# II Understanding the Core of Culture

When we study something, we want to know not only what it is, but also why and how it is so. This is very true of culture, which as we noted in Chapter 1 is what we live in and thus what we can never pay too much attention to. In this chapter, we will identify some whys in the study of intercultural communication. We know that there are many differences between distinct cultures. But why is this so since we are basically the same human beings with basically the same needs, the needs for food, dressing, shelter, security, love, esteem, etc.? Why do some cultures frantically cling to youth, whereas others welcome old age? Why do some cultures worship the Earth, whereas others molest it? Why in some cultures independence is emphasized while in others interdependence is preferred? There is no end to such questions. It is the deep structure or the core of a culture where we have to turn to find possible answers.

## 【Activity 1】

*Where is the deep structure or the core of a culture? What does it include? How can we find it? Please look at the pictures of an iceberg below. Discuss these questions in small groups.*

### Discussion

What is visible is only the tip of the iceberg. It means that, as we noted in Chapter 1, most of culture is hidden, out of sight as if under water. However, this is the most important part (the deep structure or the core of culture) as it makes up the massive foundation of culture. This invisibility suggests that most of culture exists in the subconscious mind of people, who therefore are not usually aware of the fact that their actions are governed by their own culture, or cultural rules.

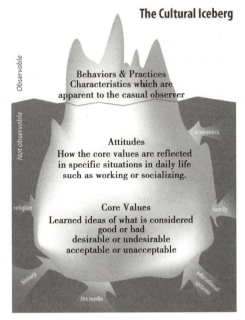

The core part of culture includes things like perceptions, views, beliefs, values, attitudes, tradition, history, and so on. Some scholars maintain that the essential core consists of traditional (i.e. historically derived and selected) ideas and especially their attached values. All these are abstract, and thus invisible. What we can do is to observe people's behaviors and actions which reflect their values, beliefs, etc.

## III Recognizing Key Elements in the Core of Culture

The culture iceberg indicates that the core of culture is composed of different views which we have to address when we study culture. They are often termed in various ways, such as meanings, perceptions, views, beliefs, values, attitudes, tradition, history, cultural patterns, value orientations, value dimensions, and so on. It is true that there are differences between these terms which can be independently examined. It is still true that these terms, more often than not, intertwine and overlap.

In this part, our main purpose is to foster cultural and intercultural awareness, and develop a general picture of culture so as to better conduct communication across cultures, facilitate mutual understanding, and achieve peaceful coexistence of different peoples. Therefore, we will just focus on history, worldviews and values. History is the soil where a culture's myriad of ideas grows. The worldview usually underlies the values shared by members of a culture, which are closely related to history, tradition, attitudes, beliefs, practices and institutions.

# Ⓐ The Axial Age and the Different Cultural Spirits

It is common sense that cultures do not come all of a sudden from nowhere. Each culture is like a stream which flows from its source. This source plays an essential part in determining the specific spirit of a culture. So the sources should never be neglected in our study of cultures. There are many ways to trace their histories. The theory of Axial Age proposed by Karl Jaspers (1883–1969), the famous German philosopher, in his book *The Origin and Goal of History* may provide an interesting frame of reference for us to have some ideas about the founding of ancient philosophies and religions. Knowledge of ancient philosophies and religions is indispensable in the understanding of cultures.

Jaspers defined the Axial Age as the period from 800 B.C. to 200 B.C. during which the same intensity of thought appeared in three different regions: China, India and the Occident which include, very roughly, Ancient Greece and the Middle East. This era is a watershed point in ancient civilizations of the East and the West. Great thinkers in those civilizations independently turned to the similar basic questions concerning man such as the meaning and purpose of life( Who am I? Where am I going? Where do I come from? ), the meaning of suffering, how to distinguish good from evil—were of universal interest and their answers were meant for people everywhere, not just for their own clan or even just for their own time. Man for the first time in history began to be conscious of themselves and started using reason to search for the ultimate reality of universe and human destiny.

The central Axial Age thinkers in ancient China are numerous. Here we mention only three of them. Confucius (551–479 B.C.), whose philosophy was legitimatised by the later dynasties to become the ruling ideology of the Chinese culture; Lao Tze (approximately 580–500 B.C.) whose idea of Tao contributed to the development of philosophical and religious Taoism; Mo Tze (approximately 468–376 B.C.) who preached the concept of  universal love in contrast to the Confucian hierarchy of social rites and filial piety.

The Axial Age in India is the time of the beginning of Buddhism. Buddhism is one of the great world religions founded by Siddhartha Gautama① who is usually revered as the Buddha (i.e. the enlightened one).

---

① Siddhartha Gautama (563–483 B.C.): Indian founder of Buddhism. He began preaching after achieving supreme enlightenment at the age of 35.

In ancient Greece, at the time of the Axial Age there are great minds, such as Homer[①], author of *Iliad* and *Odyssey*; Parmenides[②] who founded the philosophy of being that emphasized being as the unchangeable reality of the essence of all existence, Heraclitus[③] who believed in change and held the philosophy of becoming; Socrates[④], together with Plato[⑤] and Aristotle[⑥], became the founder of Western philosophy; and Archimedes[⑦], legendary for his Eureka and his Archimedean point: *Give me a place to stand on and I will move the Earth*, was the founder of Western mathematics and physics.

The central Axial Age figures in Palestine are the 8th century B.C. Hebrew prophets. Their prophetic message of ethical monotheism set the Hebrew religion sharply in contrast to the polytheistic religions of the Ancient Near East and permanently shifted the course of development of Judaism. Zoroaster[⑧] represents the Axial Age breakthrough in Persia (Iran). His teaching is basically monotheism with a dualist cosmology. He preached that the Wise Lord is the highest god of the world who is opposed by the evil deity. The Wise will achieve final victory over the evil and thus gives joy and hope to all followers.

There are similarities and differences among the Axial Age thinkers. One of the striking similarities is their common sociological background. They are all born into a time of social upheaval and political turmoil. One of the major dissimilarities among them is their different philosophical and religious outlook, i.e. the direction and way of thinking. The Socratic and Platonic way of thought can be described as speculative. The Greeks tend to use their reason as a spectacle in which to see the world. Hence thinking is the means to understand the world. While the Greeks think in order to understand, the Hindus think in order to think, i.e. to take thinking

---

① Homer (about the 9th century B.C.): Greek epic poet. Two of the greatest works in Western literature, the *Iliad* and the *Odyssey*, are attributed to him.

② Parmenides (approximately 510–450 B.C.): Greek philosopher and poet. Parmenides was a student of Ameinias and founder of the School of Elea.

③ Heraclitus (540–480 B.C.): Greek philosopher who is called founder of metaphysics; be lieved that constant change from being to not-being is fundamental principle of universe, and that all things are part of one primary substance, fire.

④ Socrates (469–399 B.C.): Greek philosopher who initiated a question-and-answer method of teaching as a means of achieving self-knowledge. His theories of virtue and justice have survived through the writings of Plato, his most important pupil. Socrates was tried for corrupting the minds of Athenian youth and subsequently put to death.

⑤ Plato (428–348 B.C.): Greek philosopher. A follower of Socrates, he founded the Academy (386 B.C.), where he taught and wrote for much of the rest of his life.

⑥ Aristotle (384–322 B.C.): Greek philosopher. A pupil of Plato and the author of works on logic, metaphysics, ethics, natural sciences, politics, and poetics, he profoundly influenced Western thought. In his philosophical system theory follows empirical observation and logic, based on the syllogism, is the essential method of rational inquiry.

⑦ Archimedes (287–212 B.C.): Greek mathematician, engineer, and physicist.

⑧ Zoroaster (628–551 B.C.): Persian prophet who founded Zoroastrianism(索罗亚斯德教/祆教).

not as a means but an end. The Hindu meditation is the most abstract of all because it is the thinking of thinking. Thinking becomes the subject of its own investigation. The Chinese way of thinking is contemplative because it takes the person as the subject. It is to think oneself as a person and thus contemplation becomes a form of self-cultivation. The end of thinking is not to understand the world from without but the person from within. Thus a very rough generalization is that thinking for the Greeks is to look outward, for the Hindus is to look upward, for the Confucians is to look inward. Although this may be too simple a generalization, it helps us to understand the difference.

Many scholars believe that the Axial Age has significance for the development ever since, because the influence of this period's philosophy and thinking on later generations till now is too great to be neglected even a little. The idea that we should treat others as we would like them to treat us, known as the Golden Rule, is an ethic that emerged almost universally during the Axial Age. For example, Confucius said: "What I do not wish others to do to me, that also I wish not to do to them" (Analects, 5.11) while Zoroaster (628–551 B.C.E.) said, "That which is good for all and any one, for whomsoever—that is good for me... what I hold good for self, I should for all. Only Law Universal is true Law" (Gathas, 43.1). The book of Leviticus says, "You shall love your neighbor as yourself" (Lev. 19:18). And also, the Confucian tradition is not just philosophical ideas for the elite or for the scholars. It's also what we call "habits of the heart" for the people. Many people do not know anything about the Analects, or about the major thinkers of the Confucian tradition, but they act in a way that is not only compatible with but in a way influenced deeply by the Confucian ideas. They understand the self not as an isolated individual but as the center of relationships. They are very concerned about long-lasting friendship based on trust, about the society which is harmonious rather than simply conflicting. And there is a very great commitment to the well-being of the family as one of the most important units in society. One expects the government to act in a just way for the community as a whole. The leaders ought to be responsible for the well-being of the people. So many things that function very pervasively in Chinese society are connected with Confucian values. In the West, the profound influence of ancient thinkers on later generations has been self-evident. To sum up, the ideas of ancient thinkers that help form the traditions of different peoples can never be neglected when we study culture.

## B Worldviews

People are not always fully aware of the historical origins of their roots or culture. It is a subject that seems academic and irrelevant to daily living. Without such knowledge we can feel a sense of detachment from our roots and loose the true value of our cultural identities which can result in feelings of disconnection and identity confusion.

Sometimes when we are not fully educated as to the reasoning behind cultural norms, relationships can become unbalanced and conflict and misunderstandings can quickly follow.

Each group of people has, from the very beginning of civilization, seen the need to evolve a worldview. A culture's worldview, as stated before, belongs to the core part of culture, for it influences all aspects of our perception and consequently affects our belief and value systems as well as how we think and act. In short, it produces great effects on the social, economic, and political life of a nation. But what does it really mean? Let us begin from the following activity.

## 【Activity 2】

You know that today there have been many environmental problems around us: killer smog, water pollution, global warming, and the ozone hole, lack of resources, deforestation and so on. For example, the dramatic loss of ozone in the lower stratosphere over Antarctica was first observed and noted in the 1970s by a research group from the British Antarctic Survey.

*Discuss with your neighbors why environmental problems have become so serious, and try to find some causes that are more fundamental.*

### Discussion

We know that our actions are governed by our ideas and views. The above problems are caused directly by humans' over-exploitation of the Earth's resources. Why have we done so? What is behind such actions of ours? One interpretation is that we think we are the masters of the Earth and the outside world is at our disposal. We can do whatever we like to it so long as we can improve our life on the Earth. Where does this idea come from? The root cause is probably that we distinguish the objective (the world) and the subjective (human mentality). The objective is what we can take advantage of. Since the Earth is the objective world outside of us, it is natural for us to exploit it. Here we come to the dualistic worldview of objectivity and subjectivity. But all peoples in the world do not hold the same worldview.

It is no easy matter to define a worldview. Up to now numerous authors have offered a variety of definitions. Generally speaking, because worldviews deal with the topics that penetrate all phases of human existence, they start with questions about what we commonly call the meaning of life. Therefore, worldview is a culture's orientation towards God, humanity, nature, questions of existence, the universe and cosmos, life, death, sickness, and other philosophical issues that influence how its members perceive their world. To put it simply, our worldview is a unified, shared outlook on the world that guides us in our actions on the Earth. Our worldview is so much a part of our lives that we see and hear them daily, whether we are aware of them or not. For example, we are now trying to make our society more harmonious. The worldview behind may be that "Nature and Man are blended into one harmonious identity" (天人合一).

Deep questions addressing the nature of man, life and death, the creation of the world, the origin of the society, the relationship between man and nature, and the relationship between individuals and groups, etc. are the concerns of both religion and philosophy. So Samovar et al say that what one person might call religion or worldview, another might call philosophy. If we understand a culture's worldview and cosmology, reasonable accuracy can be attained in predicting behaviors and motivations in other dimensions. This knowledge helps us in our communicating with people from that culture.

In the world there are many different worldviews. It is impossible for us to touch all of them. Here we will focus on just two.

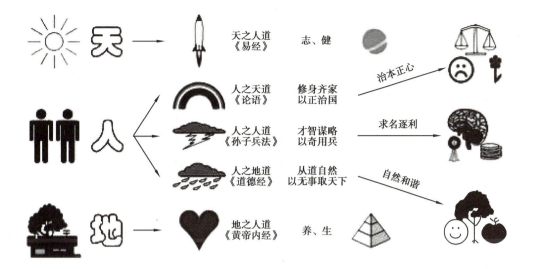

| | | | |
|---|---|---|---|
| 天 | 天之人道《易经》 | 志、健 | |
| 人 | 人之天道《论语》 | 修身齐家 以正治国 | 治本正心 |
| | 人之人道《孙子兵法》 | 才智谋略 以奇用兵 | 求名逐利 |
| | 人之地道《道德经》 | 从道自然 以无事取天下 | 自然和谐 |
| 地 | 地之人道《黄帝内经》 | 养、生 | |

## C Holistic vs. Dualistic Worldviews

As has been stated, culture is a product of history passed down from generation to generation. To study its core part, we have to go into the past. In the following activity we are going to have a glimpse of two distinct worldviews that have exerted great impact on the Eastern and Western cultures.

## 【Activity 3】

Now let's compare the propositions advanced by some ancient Greek and Chinese philosophers, as they contributed a lot to the foundations of Western and Eastern civilizations. The pre-Socratic philosophers like Thales①, Pythagoras②, Heraclitus and Democritus③ tried to find what the world was made up of: water, fire, numbers or atoms. This implies a view of division which was explicitly stated by Plato. "He (Plato) conceived of reality as consisting of two parts. The lower part included material things. The higher part consisted of the ideas on which material things were always patterned. These were the eternal Forms... (which) lay behind material things and gave shape to ordinary life. The Forms were known by reason, which was the divine element in humans. From this set of concepts came the Greek definition of man as a rational soul in an animal body." Aristotle continued this view, though he was much more concerned with the natural world. In other words, they advocated dividing the world into two opposing parts in spite of the different concepts they put forward: "element" and "form," "reality" and

---

① Thales (624–545 B.C.): ancient Greek philosopher, mathematician, and astronomer who proposed that water was the primary substance from which all things were derived.

② Pythagoras (580–500 B.C.): Greek philosopher and mathematician.

③ Democritus (460–370 B.C.): Greek philosopher who developed an atomist theory of the universe.

"reason," and "matter" and "form". Later European philosophers like Descartes① and Hegel② consolidated the theoretical basis through different notions such as "matter" and "mind," and "real object" and "absolute spirit."

The ancient Chinese proposition "Tao consists of Yin and Yang" in the *Book of Changes* (about 600 B.C.) initiated the notion of Tao. Lao Tzu, who lived about 500 years before Christ, further developed this concept of Tao in Chapter 42 of his *Tao Te Ching*: "Tao gave birth to the One, the One gave birth successively to two things, three things, up to ten thousand. These ten thousand creatures cannot turn their backs to the shade (*Yin*) without having the sun (*Yang*) on their bellies, and it is on this blending of the breaths (both *Yin* and *Yang*) that their harmony depends".

*Discuss in small groups whether ancient Western and Chinese philosophers looked at the world in a similar or different way. If similar, how were they similar; if different, how were they different?*

## Discussion

From the propositions of both ancient Greece and China mentioned in Activity 3, we see that they looked at the world in different ways. The ancient Greek philosophers, whose ideas exerted great influence over the whole Europe, tended to believe that the Universe is divided into two opposites and there is a clear-cut demarcation (划界) between the two: man and nature, subject and object, mind and matter, the divine and the secular. Even Christianity prevalent in the West helps explain this. Christianity holds that God creates Man and Man sins against God. Throughout the *Bible* the theme of the redemption of humanity is developed. There exists a clear division between God and Man. The "dividing" worldview is the starting point of Western culture's initiative in exploring and transforming Nature. This accounts for—at least partly—the rapid development of science and technology in the West. The intent to transform the world is manifest in what Archimedes said "Give me a place to stand on and I will move the Earth" and in proverbs like "Nature is conquered by obeying her."

Let's briefly summarize the core beliefs of western world-view. Western world-view (Europe, and those countries influenced by European culture such as America, Canada, Australia, New Zealand) are rooted in ancient Greece under philosophers like Plato, Socrates and Aristotle who's philosophies shaped the Western world and its belief system to this day.

- The central belief is based on the principle that man is an individual at the centre of his universe.
- The world is dualistic meaning that body, mind and spirit are seen as being separate from each other.
- The world is stable and unchanging so therefore the pursuit and curiosity of knowledge was pursued in order to explain the universe.
- This is achieved through valuing linear thinking, reasoning with the categorization of things and events. In this way rules reasoning and formal logic are applied to explain events. Scientific

---

① Descartes (1596−1650): French philosopher, mathematician, and man of science.
② Hegel (1770−1831): German philosopher.

scrutiny is required as the basis of accepting new evidence into formal structures.

In contrast, the ancient Chinese philosophers emphasized the "One," the "blending" and the "harmony." Chang Tzu (369−286 B.C.) developed the concept of Tao by saying that the "One reality is all men, gods and things: complete all-embracing and the whole; it is an all-embracing unity from which nothing can be separated." When it comes to the relationship between Man and Nature, he proposed the concept that Man is part of Nature. In addition, Confucianism, the dominant ideology in China seeks to teach the proper way for all people to behave in society, with the purpose of promoting harmony. Zen (a Chinese Buddhism school) maintains that the world and its components are not many things, but one reality. Since then this notion of stressing oneness or wholeness began to take root in the minds of the Chinese people. A number of Chinese idioms mirror this idea of identifying Man with Nature rather than separating the two:

- Nature and Man are blended into one harmonious identity. (天人合一)
- Nature affects human affairs and human behavior finds response in Nature. (天人感应)
- Nature accords with human wishes. (天从人愿)

From the above we see that both Western and Chinese cultures recognize opposing elements in the universe, and the difference is that Western culture emphasizes their co-existence and opposition while Chinese culture stresses their interdependence and integration as is indicated by the diagram of *Taigi* (太极). Remember, this comparison is done in very general and broad terms and we can never say that all the people in either culture demonstrate that particular view all the time, in any situations and in any or all of their actions.

Let's briefly summarize the core beliefs of eastern world-view. The Eastern world-view (China, Japan, Korea, and countries influenced by Chinese philosophy) are rooted in China under philosophies of Confucius, Buddhism and Daoism.

- The core value is based on the principle of collectivism which places man as a member of a multiple collective rather than an individual.
- Maintaining relationships is key to ensuring a harmonious society. Control of oneself is required in order to maintain harmonious relationships. Hierarchy within relationships are observed and respected.
- Filial Piety which is a reverence for ancestry and family are valued.
- The world is seen as holistic and changing. Events are explained in terms of context.
- The midway or compromise is favoured to resolve contradictions.

**Differences Between East & West: Spirituality**

| West | East |
|---|---|
| Christianity, Judaism, Islam | Buddhism, Daoism, Confucianism |
| God is separate to mankind: Dualism—there are two worlds—the Natural and the Supernatural. | God is Within. |
| God is on the outside. | God is on the inside. |
| We only live once but our souls are immortal. | We live many lives and born again through reincarnation. |
| We are judged for our deeds when we die. | Karma is part of our life and we get what we deserve on the Earth depending how we lived our lives in previous incarnations or lives. |
| Human beings are sinful and need to control their impulses in order to stay good. | Human beings are ignorant but can become enlightened or wise. |
| Spiritual practice is based on developing a personal relationship with God. | Spiritual practice is based on quietening the mind through meditation. |
| Jesus and Mohammed are intermediaries between mankind and God. | No Intermediaries—only one reality. We access divine through inner reflection. |

# 【Activity 4】

*We know from the previous part that Westerners tend to distinguish mind from body, people from nature, and God from humankind, while Chinese are used to looking at the world as a whole unit. Now compare the Western Medicine and the Traditional Chinese Medicine (TCM). Are there any differences? If yes, what? Do the differences reflect different worldviews to some extent? If yes, try to name these two world views.*

 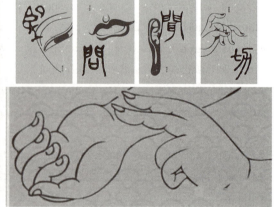

## Discussion

Western Medicine lays emphasis on the parts that make up a man. The human body is taken as an object that can be studied and controlled. In contrast, TCM stresses the whole human body that is composed of different parts. Being part of nature, the human body, if it isn't functioning well, needs to be brought back into balance. So medicine has to stimulate the body's own resources which work to restore normality. This difference lies, it is believed, at least in part in the distinct worldviews of the East and the West.

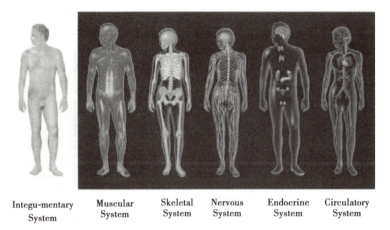

| Integu-mentary System | Muscular System | Skeletal System | Nervous System | Endocrine System | Circulatory System |

Let's briefly summarize the differences between East and West toward health and wellness.

**Differences Between East and West: Health & Wellness**

| Eastern | Western |
|---|---|
| Eastern treatments include herbal remedies, food therapy, acupuncture, reflexology. | Western medical techniques include laboratory testing, pharmaceutical medicine and surgical methods with diagnostic tools. |
| Holistic & Integrative: look to find the root of illness before treating. | Exercise is focused to treat the muscles of the body as mind, body and spirit are seen as separate. |

The dividing worldview is called the *dualistic view* (distinguishing mind from body, people from nature, and God from humankind), also referred to as a mechanistic view. It goes by many different names—reason versus intuition, objectivity versus subjectivity, or science versus religion. This view characterizes many Western cultures. It shows in a number of ways. For example, it makes a sharp distinction between religion and science as alternative ways of discovering truth. It separates mind and body. Westerners also hold that reasoning is humankind's highest faculty and achievement. There is also a strong reliance on "facts" as opposed to "opinions." For them, Americans in particular, facts are more reliable and dependable than subjective evaluations based on "feelings" and "intuition."

Because of this basic worldview, Westerners tend to perceive the world as being composed of separate pieces to be manipulated and examined. We'll take the American view as an example. As American culture is deeply rooted in Western culture, their view represents to a great degree that of the West. According to Hoebel & Frost, "American thought patterns are rational rather than mystic; the operative conception of the universe is mechanic. The bedrock proposition upon which the whole world view stands is the belief that the universe is a physical system operating in a determinate manner according to discoverable scientific law... Because they view the universe as a mechanism, Americans implicitly believe that individuals can manipulate it. Human beings need not accept it as it is; they may work on it, and as they gain in knowledge and improve their techniques, they even redesign it so that it will be more to their liking."

The American mode of living is characterized by confrontation with and exploitation of the external world and by humanity being armed against it. The conquest of natural conditions is the dominant assumption in the United States. The Americans' relationship with nature may be called a "master-slave" relationship. Linell Davis makes this clear when she says:

> I think there are two basic reasons why Americans climb mountains. The most important reason is to get to the top. This is a matter of meeting the challenge of the mountain. Can I do it? Do I have the physical fitness, strength and endurance to meet the challenge? Can I conquer nature by conquering the mountain? How fast can I do it? The second reason is to see the view from the top.

However, the Eastern view of the world is profoundly holistic. It is believed to have emerged in many Asian countries. It sees the world as a whole unit, not as separate pieces. With this view in mind, the Eastern peoples tend to look at humanity and nature in total harmony and in eternal inseparability. They then stress adapting to nature instead of conquering it. For example, when they climb mountains, they expect to enjoy the experience and to feel their connection with nature rather than their power over it. When it comes to finding truth, this worldview stresses intuitive wisdom which cannot be verified by the senses or the scientific instruments that Western people use to extend the range of perception. People with this worldview believe that man should always be in harmony with nature rather than manipulate it, and then they must act carefully so as not to upset the balance.

Here are some very insightful perspectives on East and West thinking suggested by Richard Nisbett (professor of social psychology and co-director of the Culture and Cognition program at the University of Michigan at Ann Arbor).

| Western Worldviews | Eastern Worldviews |
| --- | --- |
| Greece origins. | China origins. |
| Individualistic. | Collectivist. |
| Personal agency—self centred. | Member in multiple collective. |
| Linear focus—focus on details. | Interrelated and changing. The whole is more than the sum of its parts. |
| Developed knowledge and rules to master the world. | Developed relationships. Hierarchical family orientation. |
| How questions. | Why questions. |
| Control environment. | Control oneself to maintain social harmony. |
| Either/Or. | Middle way to maintain harmony. |
| Backward reasoning. Looking for principles that justify events. | Causal analysis. Events are described in terms of context. |
| Nouns: eg. more tea? | Verbs: eg. Drink tea. |

The above analysis, however, doesn't mean that the distinction between the holistic and dualistic views is absolute or that they are polar opposites. In fact, both the peoples recognize that in the world there is the wholeness and there are many parts that make up the whole. The only difference is that different people lay emphasis on different perspectives of views.

# 【Activity 5】

It is said that the way to a person's heart is through the tummy. The sharing of meals always plays a central part in keeping family and community together. Through food we are able to bond with family, friends and community. We get to know about our way of life, our values how we identify ourselves.

*Now try to discuss the differences between the Western meals and the Traditional Chinese meals, and what makes us similar and different to others when celebrating special occasions around meals. Do the differences reflect different worldviews to some extent? If yes, try to name these two worldviews.*

## Discussion

Western values of Individuality, detail and science are strongly featured in the way Westerns eat. Meals are served in individual portions and eaten with a knife and fork. This reflects an individualist culture. In the West meat and fish are main dishes whilst vegetables are side dishes.

The value of science and detail is expressed in the focus of the nutritional value of food.

Eastern values of Collectivism, group or communal minded are expressed in the sharing of meals which helps to promote family relationships. Meals are placed at the centre of the table so everyone can share. Meals are eaten with chopsticks— Confucius believed that knives and forks might promote violence. In the East vegetables are the main dish served with grain usually white rice or noodles and meat is used in small portions.

Spiritual, aesthetic (the way something looks) and holistic values are expressed in that the taste and look of food is more important with balance being achieved by combining both Yin and Yang food in a meal.

Being part of a multicultural community or family has the advantage of being exposed to different types of cuisines and cooking styles. Meals revolve around individual preferences and a combination of food rather than a preference for one type of cuisine. For instance some meals may be Asian in origin such as Sushi, Chinese stir fry whilst other meals might reflect a western preference for instance spaghetti bolognaise, Pizza, Hamburger, or perhaps a fusion dish or style might be selected on other days.

## Differences Between East & West: Cuisine

| West | East |
|------|------|
| Knife & Fork Isolated setting. Cutlery provides more distance between food and preparation area and the individual. | Chopsticks communal seating (bringing people together around a dish). Unity of family and community. Less distance between food and place of preparation. |
| Condiments that cater for your individuality. | shared condiments. |
| Measured, technical. More solitary experience. Buying frozen food to shorten the food preparation time. | Intuition and rule of thumb. Social experience involving others. Buying partly frozen food. Eating at street market. |
| Protein or meat is the main portion with vegetables as side portions. Food portions are bigger and cut with knife and fork. Rice is not usually served with the main meal. | Vegetables are main portions, grains then protein or meat which is usually a side portion. Food is bite size and eaten with chopsticks. Rice usually white rice is served with main meals. |
| Tend to nutritional value of food. Cold Drinks. | Tend to value the flavour of the food. Warm Drinks. |
| To Promote social relationships. | To promote intimacy and strengthen family ties. |

# 【Activity 6】

The term "aesthetics" concerns our senses and our responses to an object. If something is aesthetically pleasing to you, it is "pleasurable" and you like it. If it is aesthetically displeasing to you, it is "displeasurable" and you don't like it. Aesthetics involves all of your senses—vision, hearing, touch, taste, and smell—and your emotions.

*Now try to discuss the differences between the Western and the Traditional Chinese views toward aesthetics. What makes these differences and do the differences reflect different worldviews to some extent? If yes, try to name these two worldviews.*

## Discussion

The Western view of beauty is rooted in ancient Greece—as Western cultural values are. For something to be considered beautiful it needs to have three elements:

- Harmony
- Balance
- Symmetry

Western art is also concerned with detail, geometric lines and point of view of the artist. This reflects the Western value of logic, linear perspective, detail, external perception, individuality.

Western aesthetics is reflected in Leonardo da Vinci's painting capturing the proportions of man reflects Western values on lines, geometry, detail of externals, harmony symmetry and balance.

The Eastern view tries to capture the spirit of the artist or the work of art. Rather than detail, emptiness and space are used to reflect the

Eastern view of holism. Everything being inter-connected. Nature is often used as the subject matter reflecting the Eastern value of being close to nature. The artist aims to look through the eyes rather than with his eyes in order to create a spiritual sensibility and a heartfelt experience.

Eastern Zen aesthetic values try to capture the stillness of the universe which is puzzling because it is empty but full at the same. The essence of empty space and mystery through the artist vision of sincerity, mysterious profundity, pathos, sublime beauty, emotional beauty, melancholy, loneliness are among the most valued aesthetic ideals.

Eastern aesthetics reflect values of holism with the artist attempting to capture the spirit of a subject matter. Nature scenes are especially valued.

### Similarities Between Eastern and Western: Worldviews

| West | East |
| --- | --- |
| Rooted in ancient Greece. | Rooted in China, Japan. |
| External focus. | Internal focus. |
| Harmony, balance, symmetry. | Zen's seven principals: sincerity, mysterious profundity, pathos, sublime beauty and emotional beauty, melancholy, loneliness. |

Much has been written about the differences between Eastern and Western worldviews but little has been said about similarities and parallels between the two seemingly opposite worldviews.

- East and West like all humans search for meaning and purpose to life.
- Historically both philosophies seek the truth—the one through science and the other through spirituality.
- Treating people the way you would like to be treated was taught by both Confucius and Jesus Christ.
- Both see the universe as consisting of elements—water, air, earth, metal and fire.
- Both East and West agree that all is energy and that there are other dimensions to our greater universe even although it might not be visible to the naked eye.
- Both have a predictive zodiac system. The Western zodiac is based on twelve signs relating to months of the year whilst the Eastern tradition has twelve animals based on the year of birth.
- Both used parables to relate concepts.
- Both East and West believe that man is born with innate knowledge that just needs to be encouraged to pursue. We love our children and want to see them prosper.
- Both East and West pursue the meaning of good and evil.
- Both Easterners and Westerners have a hierarchy of needs as described in Maslow's theory of needs. Starting from Physiological, security, belongingness, self-esteem and self-actualization.

In general the needs are the same but the method of finding answers and solutions are somewhat different—with the West flavouring a scientific approach with focus on specific elements whilst the East focus, being more holistic and general.

## ■ Intersections Between East and West

Both Taoism and complementarism as defined in quantum physics agree that the universe consists of polar opposites that need each other to maintain a harmonious whole. Each opposite cannot occupy the same space at the same time but together they form a complementary whole.

For instance, night and day, male and female, good and evil, left brain and right brain. Likewise the East and West are viewed as complementary opposites.

It follows that East and West agree on the same things but their methods are often at polar opposites when it comes to finding solutions and outcomes. For instance, the West is generally more external focused whilst the East is internal. The West values individualism whilst the East Collectivism. The West is associated with left brain thinking whilst the East is associated with right brain thinking.

The intersection of complementarism with the growing awareness that the world is interconnected and interdependent creates the need for co-operation between the East and West in order to produce outcomes that are complementary and holistic.

Eastern and Western values shaped their cultural expressions. Today's post modernism era reflects the blending of time, space and culture, where the blending of Eastern and Western ideals increasingly shape our reality. To understand these values and how they are expressed in our personal lives and society provides an enriching and empowering experience for personal growth and enlightenment.

## D Values: Definition

Values fundamentally influence our behavior in society. They do not describe how we act in a culture but dictate what we ought or ought not to do. Values tend to be the basis of all the decisions we make and provide standards for us to evaluate our own and others' actions. We all hold certain values though we may not be conscious of them. Values develop standards and guidelines that establish appropriate and inappropriate behaviors in a society. People usually exhibit and expect behaviors according to their value systems. Without any knowledge of each other's values, participants in intercultural communication may encounter misunderstanding, confusion or failure. So values deserve much of our attention.

According to the *Concise Oxford Dictionary*, values are: one's principles or standards; one's judgment of what is valuable or important in life. Values are generally normative. They can be taken as a learned organization of rules for making choices and for resolving conflicts. These "rules" and guideposts tell us what is good and bad, what is right and wrong, what is true and false, what is positive and negative, what to strive for, how to live our life, and even what to die for. For example, in our culture love of one's country is an important value, and so is filial piety. If somebody treats his parents badly, we tend to be very critical of him.

Values are broad, abstract concepts which provide the foundation that underlies a people's entire way of life. Then where can we find them? They are reflected in many aspects, such as people's remarks and actions and behaviors. From what historic heroes said and did, we get our values. The media around us such as literature, arts, films and TVs are also channels that send value messages to us.

## E Values: Types

According to the scope to which values apply, there can be three types. Universal values come first. They are values common to all human beings. For instance, the desire to live a happy life is a universal value, as everybody wants to have a happy life.

Culture-specific values follow. They are values that apply only to one particular group of people. In other words, they are specific to a particular culture. Take individualism. It is a culture-specific value, upheld by some cultures, while many others in the world are collectivist in nature.

Finally, we come to peculiar expressions of individuals within cultures. People in the same culture possess somewhat different values depending on age, gender, generation, etc. Though individuals have some deviations, there are values that tend to permeate a culture.

## F Values: Characteristics

## 【Activity 7】

*Values are learned through diverse ways. Proverbs, short, pithy sayings in frequent and widespread use, reflect values of the users. Now study the following proverbs and decide what value(s) they represent, which of them are still strong in Western culture and Chinese culture respectively, and which don't apply any longer.*

### Proverbs

1. Blood is thicker than water.
2. Too many cooks spoil the broth.
3. God helps those who help themselves.
4. Time is money.
5. A man's home is his castle.
6. Think three times before you take action.
7. Nothing done with intelligence is done without speech.
8. A single arrow is easily broken, but not a bunch.
9. He who stirs another's porridge often burns his own.

10. However crowded the way is, the hen will reach her eggs.

11. A stitch in time saves nine.

12. Don't cry over the spilt milk.

13. Don't count your chickens before they are hatched.

14. Take care of today, and tomorrow will take care of itself.

## Discussion

Proverbs'value explanation:

| | | |
|---|---|---|
| 1. Value: family; loyalty | Origin: Scotland |
| 2. Value: the individual | Origin: England |
| 3. Value: self-help | Origin: Greece |
| 4. Value: efficiency | Origin: USA |
| 5. Value: privacy, male orientation | Origin: England |
| 6. Value: caution | Origin: China |
| 7. Value: talk | Origin: Greece |
| 8. Value: group over individual | Origin: Asia |
| 9. Value: privacy | Origin: Sweden |
| 10. Value: mother's love for children | Origin: Africa |
| 11. Value: time and action | Origin: North American |
| 12. Value: practicality | Origin: North American |
| 13. Value: practicality | Origin: North American |
| 14. Value: future orientation | Origin: North American |

Many proverbs, examples of folk wisdom, remind people of the values that are important in their culture, such as the above listed. Many are very old. So some of the values they teach may not be as important in the culture as they once were. For example, Americans today do not pay much attention to the proverb *Haste makes waste* because patience is not important to them now. But if you know about past values, it helps you to understand the present. And many of the older values are still strong today. Benjamin Franklin, a famous American diplomat, writer, and scientist, died in 1790. But his remark "Time is money" is taken more seriously by Americans of today than ever before.

A study of proverbs from around the world shows that some values are shared by many cultures. In many cases, though, the same idea is expressed differently. Two examples are: *The squeaky wheel gets the oil* and *He who does not cry does not get fed*. Both teach that it is important to make people know what you want, which is the value of assertiveness. Another example is the value of caution, which is communicated in different ways by the following proverbs: *Turn the tongue seven times, then speak* (French); *Have an umbrella before getting wet* (Japanese); *Before you drink the soup, blow on it* (Arabic); *First weigh [ the consequences ], then dare* (German); *If you don't know the ford, don't cross the stream* (Russian); *Be careful bending your head—you may break it* (Italian); *Look before you leap* (English). You must know how this idea is expressed in Chinese.

## 【Activity 8】

Christianity teaches kindness and morality. However, it is well known that the trade in drugs, which ultimately resulted in the fact that Hong Kong was under the British rule for so long, was carried out by people who professed the most Christian of beliefs. In the U.S., people believe that all people are created equal, yet there is pervasive prejudice and racism. Equality of opportunity is an ideal value, but it is not always put into practice. In reality, some people (those who are born into rich families, inherit money, etc.) have a better chance for success than others (those who are born into poorer families). Americans believe that they are a moral people, yet there is a lot of violence in their society. In China, it is a virtue to help each other. But there is also a saying that goes. *Sweep the snow in front of his door, and not bother about the frost on his neighbor's roof.*

*Work in small groups and see what characteristics of values are reflected in these examples. Then try to list other characteristics that you can think of.*

## Discussion

The above examples tell us that in many instances *contradictory values are found in a particular culture*. There is often a gulf between the values that are articulated (idealism) and the values that are acted out (reality). Another example is the third President of the United States Thomas Jefferson (1743—1826), who upheld equality but at the same time owned about 200 slaves.

Some other characteristics of values are listed as follows. *Values are learned* from people around: family, school, peer groups, mass media, and so on. Once learned, they tend to be stable. And they govern people's beliefs, attitudes, ideas and actions.

*Values are hidden.* We do not see them as they exist in our sub-consciousness. We are not always aware of them, but we make judgments according to them. Values can be compared on a continuum rather than one of only two possible choices. As mentioned above, people everywhere possess the same values to different degrees. Every culture teaches their young to be civil, yet the importance of that common value, and how it gets acted out, is a matter of degree.

*Values are interrelated.* They don't work alone. For example, the value toward family usually leads to those toward age, status, etc.

*Values of a culture change with time just as cultures do.* They change, of course, much more slowly than do the way people dress, the artifacts people make, and other parts of a culture that are easily seen. But changes do happen. The Women's Movement of the late 1960s and early 1970s, for example, has greatly altered the value system in the U.S.

# IV Instruments Comparing Cultural Values

From the previous study, we have learned that cultures are both similar and different at the same time, and the differences are where misunderstanding and even conflicts may arise when peoples of different cultural backgrounds meet. So it is necessary to have some knowledge of them. But how do we talk about the similarities and differences? Comparison, a very good way to increase and deepen the understanding of our life and the world, is helpful. To compare we need some instruments. Scholars have proposed different frames of cultural comparison. The four most common models for the study of cultural values orientations were developed by Kluckhohn and Strodbeck (1961), Condon and Yousef (1975), and Hofstede (1980,1983,1984). In this part we will present two classifications developed by Kluchhohn and Hofstede respectively. Hopefully the classifications will help us have a deeper understanding of different cultures and become better intercultural communicators. After that, we will look at some of the differences between the Chinese cultural values and the Western ones. As would-be intercultural communicators, we should know our home culture as well as the target culture.

##  Kluckhohn's Value Orientations

In every culture a limited number of general, universally shared human problems need to be solved. One culture can be distinguished from another by the specific solutions it chooses for those problems. American anthropologists Florence Kluckhohn and Fred Strodtbeck identify five universal problems faced by all human societies and cultural value orientations they represents after studying values in the five communities within fifty miles of each other in southwest USA (first study in 1936, second one in 1951). They argue that all societies are aware of all possible kinds of solutions but prefer them in different orders. In other words, all cultures are similar in the dilemmas or problems they confront, yet different in the solutions they find.

1. What is the character of innate human nature? (the human nature orientation)

2. What is the relationship of people to nature (and supernature)? (the man-nature orientation)

3. What is the temporal focus of human life? (the time orientation)

4. What is the modality of human activity? (the activity orientation)

5. What is the modality of a person's relationship to other persons? (The relational orientation)

| Orientation | Basic Values | | |
| --- | --- | --- | --- |
| Human nature | Basically evil | Mixture of good and evil | Basically good |
| Relationship to nature | Nature controls humans | Harmony with nature | Humans control nature |
| Sense of time | Past | Present | Future |
| Activity | Being—who you are | Growing—becoming | Doing—what you are doing |
| Social relationships | Hierarchy | Group | Individual |

The basic values in the chart above are the source of more specific values we use to guide our decisions. These more specific values are expressed as social attitudes reflected in proverbs, slogans, wise sayings and advice from others, and the principles on which we rely when we exchange advice.

Florence Kluckhohn's original idea was to compare the basic values of various cultures. More often than not, it is only by looking at our own values in contrast with other values that we really understand them.

## ◼ Human-Nature Orientation

Three types of responses to this orientation are identified: 1) evil but perfectible; 2) the mixture of good and evil; and 3) good but corruptible.

The traditional Western belief about human nature is that humans are basically evil. We see this in the Biblical story of Adam and Eve. God throws them out of the Garden of Eden because they ate the fruit from the Tree of Knowledge. Since then, according to Christian teaching, all human beings have been born with original sin. Humans do evil as part of their nature and only be saved from evil by God. People have to try to perfect their nature by keeping doing good things. Some personal remarks can also serve as evidence of this. Robert Sunley quoted a New Englander as saying that all children are born with an evil disposition: "No child has ever been known since the earliest period of the world, destitute of an evil disposition—however sweet it appears." Immanuel Kant observed, "Out of the crooked timber of humanity no straight thing can ever be made." The psychological theories of Sigmund Freud include the idea that infants are controlled by primitive desires (evil) and learn to control them (become good) as their personality develops. This traditional view has also been incorporated into Western institutions in various ways. The distrust of human nature can be seen in American political institutions with their checks and balances. As a result of the rise of humanism in the West, the basic belief has changed to one of seeing humans as a mixture.

In contrast, the Asian people who have accepted Confucianism believe that human beings are basically good. The very typical embodiment of this idea is the *Three Character Classic* [1] that begins with "Man, by nature, is good; people's inborn characters are similar, but learning makes them different." What follows logically is that people have to see that they are not corrupted by the society. There are no lack of stories and teachings on this point, such as the story of Mencius' mother moving three times in order that her son could be in a good neighborhood, and the saying that "Your character will be tinted 'red' (good) if you are in the company of 'redness', but 'black' (bad) if you are in close contact with ink."

---

[1]  *Three Character Classics*: *San Zi Jing* (Southern Song Dynasty, 1127−1279 A.D.).

## ■ Man-Nature Orientation

There are also three general approaches under this category: 1) subjugation to nature; 2) harmony with nature; and 3) mastery over nature.

If you have the first type of orientation, you believe that basically human beings are powerless. Human beings are at the mercy of nature.

We Chinese believe that man should live in harmony with nature. The philosophy holds that a "power" links all things and creatures together. This cooperation view is found in Chinese medicine, architecture, proverbs, etc. Typical Chinese gardens and houses reveal their social attitudes toward the relationship between humans and nature. Pavilions, paved pathways, and other structures are integrated with natural features of water, trees and rock. There is no sharp distinction between being inside a building and being outside in nature. In the West, buildings tend to dominate their surroundings and their interiors and exteriors are distinct spaces. Nature is outside of human society.

The Western experience of human life being separate from nature can be found in the Biblical story of creation. When God created Adam, God gave him dominance over all of God's creation. As masters of nature, humans are encouraged to control and exploit it in any way they choose. This view (man being separated from nature) has contributed to the development of Western science and technology. But today more and more people have come to see that the Western mastery-over-nature philosophy causes problems, even though it has brought benefits for humans. Many people believe that we should protect the environment. The Greenpeace Organization which is gaining in world influence is an example.

## ■ Time Orientation

Cultures vary widely in their conceptions of time. Where they differ is in the value placed on the past, the present, and the future and how each influences interaction. Past-oriented people tend to believe tradition is important. To them, the cultural memory is rich and deep. They like to look back to a period when their culture was at the height of its power and glory and may quote respected philosophers and leaders

from the past as a guide for action in the present. They may feel more secure when something new is defined as similar to something that occurred in the past. Asian cultures including the Chinese are believed to hold this orientation. But some Chinese scholars think that now the Chinese view is changing from the past-oriented to the future-oriented.

Present-oriented cultures maintain that the moment has the most significance. For them, the future is vague, ambiguous, and unknown and what is real exists in the here and now. Samovar et al states that people of the Philippines, Mexico, and Latin America usually have these beliefs.

PAST PRESENT FUTURE

If you tend to look to the future and make plans for the future, you're future-oriented. Cultures with this orientation tend to emphasize the future and expect it to be grander and nicer than the present. This does not mean that people in those cultures do not have negative expectations for the future and their efforts may be directed at preparing for or preventing bad times ahead.

Whether the future is seen as probably good or bad, future-orientated people tend to see time as a straight line that leads from the past and is swiftly moving into the future. In other words, time is a linear concept. In present and past-oriented societies people are more likely to experience time as a cycle, as repeating itself according to some pattern.

## ■ Activity Orientation

This orientation is the way a culture views activity. Three common modes of activity expression are being, being-in-becoming, and doing.

In being-oriented cultures, people are satisfied with what they have, and family background is more important than what they accomplish. Their actions express who they are. For that reason people behave in ways appropriate to their positions (status, social roles, and characters) in life.

Being-in-becoming-orientations often correlate with cultures that value a spiritual life more than a material one. For instance, in both Hinduism and Buddhism, people spend a great portion of their lives in meditation and contemplation in an attempt to purify and more fully advance themselves. For them, this inner or spiritual development represents one of the main purposes of life.

Doing-orientation leads to external accomplishments. The goal is to achieve as much as possible. You want to do things and to achieve success. So you tend to be more active. Because the emphasis is on action in doing culture, the goals toward which action is directed are also emphasized. And there is often a sense of urgency about getting things done. Deadlines are important, as is the schedule. To have a full schedule indicates that you are accomplishing things.

# ■ Relational Orientation

This value orientation is concerned with the ways in which people perceive their relationships with others. From the chart on page 58 we find three types of orientation: hierarchy, group and individual. In fact, any society consists of hierarchies. The difference is whether and how much hierarchy is emphasized or deemphasized. In a hierarchy people have clearly defined privileges and obligations according to their positions. But

hierarchical societies differ from one another depending on the criteria used to assign a person a place in the hierarchy. If the criteria depend upon race, ethnic group, or inheritance from one's parents, then the hierarchy may be rigid and unchanging with certain groups permanently at the bottom and others permanently on the top.

In societies where relationships are based on groups, each person's social identity comes from their group memberships. People feel dependent on the group, safe within it, proud of it, and competitive with other groups. Loyalty is important in group-oriented cultures. In this pattern the group act out of concern for all its members and make decisions by consensus, and members are loyal to the group.

In individualistic societies, social relations are based on the autonomy of each person. There are many hierarchies in individualist cultures such as the USA, but people are uncomfortable with them and try to communicate with one another in a way that denies their existence or reduces their impact. For example, people prefer to use first names; high-ranking people send messages that they are just like everyone else. People tend to be less aware of others' feelings and may talk more than people from group-oriented cultures. Self-reliance and independence are important and it is considered weak to be dependent on others.

# Ⓑ Hofstede's Value Dimensions

Dr. Geert Hofstede, Dutch scholar, conducted perhaps the most comprehensive study of how values in the workplace are influenced by culture. From 1967 to 1973, while working at IBM as a psychologist, he collected and analyzed data from over 100,000 individuals from 40 countries. From those results, and later additions, Hofstede developed a model that identifies four primary dimensions to differentiate cultures: Individualism-Collectivism, Power Distance, Masculinity-Femininity, and Uncertainty Avoidance.

Hofstede's dimension analysis that emphasizes national cultures can assist us in better understanding the intercultural differences found in communicating with people of other cultural backgrounds. However, as with any generalized study, the results may or may not be applicable to specific individuals or events. There are many differences between people within any culture.

## Individualism—Collectivism

This describes the degree to which a culture relies on and has allegiance to the self or the group. A High Individualism ranking indicates that individuality and individual rights are paramount within the society. Individuals in these societies may tend to form a larger number of looser relationships. In such cultures, an "I" consciousness prevails: competition rather than cooperation is encouraged; personal goals take precedence over group goals;

people tend not to be emotionally dependent on organizations and institutions; and every individual has the right to his/her private property, thoughts, and opinions.

Collectivism typifies societies of a more collectivist nature with close ties between individuals. These cultures reinforce extended families and collectives where everyone takes responsibility for fellow members of their group. A "we" consciousness prevails: identity is based on the social system; the individual is emotionally dependent on organizations and institutions; belonging to organizations is emphasized; and group goals rather than personal ones take the precedence.

What Hofstede adds to the understanding of individualism and collectivism is the concept of in-groups and out-groups. In-group includes people who have a closer relationship with you, e. g. your immediate and/or extended family members, relatives, friends. Out-group refers to people who are basically strangers. You take care of your in-groups and keep the out-groups out. All people make this distinction, yet collectivist people lay more emphasis on it.

## Power Distance

This is an attempt to measure cultural attitudes about inequality in social relationships. It concerns how institutional and organizational power should be distributed (equally or unequally) and how the decisions of the power holders should be viewed (challenged or accepted). Power and inequality are extremely fundamental facts of any society, and anybody with some international experience will be aware that all societies are unequal, but some are more so than others.

In low power distance countries, for instance, if a teacher reports to parents that their child has misbehaved, the parents will try to find out if the teacher used his authority over the student in the proper way. To those people, power distance between teachers and students, between parents and children, and between bosses and workers should be reduced and not emphasized.

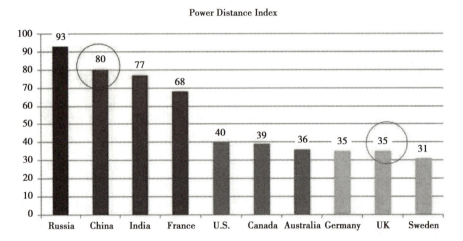

Power Distance Index

## ■ Masculinity—Femininity

These two terms do not refer to men and women, but rather to the degree to which masculine or feminine traits prevail. Masculinity is the extent to which the dominant values in a society are male dominated and is associated with such behaviors as ambition, differentiated sex roles, achievement, the acquisition of money, and signs of manliness. According to Hofstede, Ireland, the Philippines, Greece, South Africa, Austria, Japan, Italy and Mexico are among countries that tend toward a masculine worldview.

Cultures that value femininity as a trait stress caring and nurturing behaviors. A feminine worldview maintains that men need not be assertive and that they can assume nurturing roles; it also promotes sexual equality and holds that people and the environment are important. Scandinavian countries in Hofstede's scale tend toward femininity.

## ■ Uncertainty Avoidance

This dimension focuses on the level of tolerance for uncertainty and ambiguity within the society. A High Uncertainty Avoidance ranking indicates the country has a low tolerance for uncertainty and ambiguity. This creates a rule-oriented society that institutes laws, rules, regulations, and controls in order to reduce the amount of uncertainty. A Low Uncertainty Avoidance ranking indicates the country has less concern about ambiguity and uncertainty and has more tolerance for a variety of opinions. This is reflected in a society that is less rule-oriented, more readily accepts change, and takes more and greater risks.

## ■ Hofstede Scheme and Kluckhohn Scheme

Kluckhohn scheme:
1. Human nature
2. Relationship to nature
3. Sense of time
4. Activity
5. Social relationships

Hofstede scheme:
1. Individualism-Collectivism
2. Power Distance
3. Masculinity-Femininity
4. Uncertainty Avoidance

In the Kluckhohn scheme, there is only one category for social relationships, which she divides into three basic values: hierarchy, group, and individual. In the Hofstede scheme, there are two pairs for social relationships. The first, power distance, is roughly similar to the value Kluckhohn calls hierarchy. The second, individualism versus collectivism, is roughly the same as individual values and groups values.

These two schemes have been widely used in the study of cultures because of their obvious merits. Still, there is criticism against them. Some argue that Kluckhohn's scheme is general rather than specific, so it can only be used to examine general trends in behavior, and not used to predict specific behaviors in any one situation. Moreover, most behavior is multiply determined, so the theory may be termed simplistic in that it attempts to explain one dimension at a time. The criticism against Hofstede's study is that most of his findings are work-related because the people he surveyed were middle managers in large multinational organizations, and that many important countries and cultures were not included such as Arab countries and most African countries.

## V Study of Specific Cultural Values

The above frameworks provide two taxonomies that can be used to analyze key behavioral patterns found in particular cultures. As we are Chinese and expect to conduct intercultural communication, it is helpful for us to have some knowledge of certain specific values prevailing in the mainstream cultures of China and some other countries.

In many countries there are both similar and different cultural assumptions[1]. For example,

---

[1] A cultural assumption, shared by the people of a culture, is a belief about the way the world works, a way to understand reality.

Confucius teaches: Don't do to others what you don't want others do to you, and Christianity has similar teachings. We Chinese value hard work, honesty, kindness, and so do Americans. However, differences are distinct in value assumptions. But these contrasting assumptions should be viewed as differing in degree or in emphasis rather than as strictly dichotomous (二分的) in substance.

## ■ Western Cultural Values

## 【Activity 9】

*Have you ever seen the film Kramer vs. Kramer (1979)? It is about the aftermath of divorce of Ted and Joanna Kramer. Joanna, a dutiful wife and mother, decides to leave Ted, an advertising executive. Ted is a good husband who works very hard and does not have any affairs. Why do you think Joanna makes such a decision? The following passage presents a story somewhat similar to that of the Kramers. Read it and in small groups discuss the questions that follow.*

My best friend called late one night to tell me she was leaving her husband. Her mind was made up—16 long years of marriage, with children—and she was leaving!

My friend and I and both our husbands, like a majority of our friends, are Nigerians. While we've lived in the United States for most of our adulthood and for all intents and purposes live like Americans, we identify closely with our traditional Ibo culture.

"Why? What happened?" I asked.

"Nothing, really," she answered, "nothing I can put my finger on."

"Is he having an affair? Is he involved with someone else?" He didn't strike me as the cheating type, but why else would she be leaving?

"No, nothing like that."

"Did he beat you up?" Women don't end marriages for nothing.

"It's nothing in particular." She spoke haltingly, weighing every word. "All I know is that I've been very unhappy lately."

"Are you having an affair?"

"No! Are you crazy? How can you even ask me that?" She laughed out loud.

She has everything any Ibo woman would want: a professional husband (from a good family back home) with a good income, who allows her to pursue her own career; not one, not two, but three sons and a daughter; a huge house in the suburbs.

"What about the children?" I heard her muffled sobs and sensed her struggle to regain composure. "They'll stay with their father." she said. She has no right to the children. That is the Ibo tradition, American laws or not.

"How can you do this to yourself?" I lost all control, "Have you gone mad?"

"I need to try to find happiness. I really thought that you, of all people, would understand," she said coldly, hanging up before I could reply.

## Questions

1. What do these two women in the story have in common and where are they different?
2. Why did the writer's friend make such a decision?
3. Why was the writer surprised on hearing the news?
4. Would a Chinese woman in the same situation of the writer's friend leave her husband?

Joanna, the heroin of the film *Kramer vs. Kramer*, gives the reasons why she wants a divorce when she says that in the past years she has always belonged to others: first she is her parents' daughter, then her husband's wife after marriage, and then her son's mother. She has been and fulfilled all these roles except being herself. Professor Zhu Yongtao discussed this issue with some Chinese students in the 1980s, and he found that the students didn't understand how Joanna could make such a decision.

*Think about why the students found it hard to understand her. Does it have anything to do with Chinese values?*

## Discussion

In the story above we find some cultural conflicts. According to traditional Ibo culture, a woman is born (educated if she is lucky), marries, has children (a definite must, male children preferably), and dies when her time comes. God rest her soul. Women of the writer's generation, educated and all, are expected to live through their husbands and children as their mothers and grandmothers did before.

An Ibo woman has very little personal identity, even if she lives in the United States and has success in her career. Ibos cling to the old saying that a woman is worth nothing unless she's married and has children.

The writer is different from her friend. Professionally, she is more successful than the majority of Ibo men she's met in the States. At work, she's as assertive as any American-born female. She raises her voice as loud as is necessary to be heard in meetings. At conferences where she presents papers on "Women from the Third World," she makes serious arguments about the need for international intervention in countries where women are deprived of all rights. Yet as easily as she switches from speaking English to Ibo, she is content to slide into the role of the submissive and obedient wife. She never confuses her two selves. When they gather for a party, usually to celebrate a marriage or birth, she joins the women in the kitchen to prepare food and serve the men. She remembers to curtsy before the older men, looking away to avoid meeting their eyes. She glows with pride when other men tease her husband about his "good wife." She often leads the women in the Ibo wedding song: "It is as it should be; give her the keys to her kitchen." At birth ceremonies, she starts the chant: "Without a child, what would a woman be?" It is a song which every Ibo woman knows like her-own name.

The Ibo culture is unforgiving of a stubborn woman. She always gets the maximum punishment—ostracism (放逐,排斥). "She thinks she's smart; let's see if she can marry herself" is how treatment of a non-conforming woman is justified.

Now her best friend, steeped in the Ibo culture as much as she is, says she's leaving her husband—not for any offenses he's committed but because she is unhappy. The writer is, of course, surprised.

Later the writer realized what was going on with her friend. She thinks herself American. She has bought into America's concept of womanhood (*individualism*)— personal satisfaction, no matter the cost. She wants to be happy!

# 【Activity 10】

*Read the short story and discuss with your neighbors the questions following the stories.*

A. During the American Civil War, a very hungry young man fell down in front of a farm gate. The farmer gave him food but in return he asked the young man to move a pile of wood in his yard—in fact it was not at all necessary to move the wood. When the young man left, the farmer moved the wood back to its original place. Seeing all this, the farmer's son was confused.

## Questions

1. Why did the farmer not just give the young man some food for free?
2. What values underlie the behavior of the farmer?

B. An American couple came to Beijing to work as foreign teachers for the first time in their lives. They had a three-year-old son. Since both of them worked, they hired a Chinese housemaid, who was in her late 40s. One of her jobs was to take their son to a kindergarten in the morning and pick him up and bring him home again in the afternoon. She found this the most difficult among all her tasks. Every day when it was time to take the boy to kindergarten there was bound to be a fight with the boy because she insisted on carrying the boy in her arms or at least holding his hand; but the boy never liked it. He preferred to walk by himself. After a few days, she quit the job.

## Questions

1. Why did the Chinese woman quit the job?
2. What made the little boy behave as he did?
3. Would Chinese children in general always fight to be on their own?

## Discussion

For the first story, the farmer explained to his son after the young man left that one could never at any time in any way make other people feel inferior, even unintentionally and out of goodwill. What accounts for the farmer's behavior is that he believed in individualism that leads to other values like independence, self-reliance, self-esteem, and egalitarianism, the major values in the West, especially in the USA.

For the second story, the boy had been nurtured to be independent, to do whatever he could by himself, ever since he was born. He felt uncomfortable about being over-protected. From this we can assume that the American parents hold the value of individualism. The Chinese woman quit the job because she couldn't bear it any more. She was nervous and worried that she could not act out her responsibility of the boy. You can offer your own answers to the last question. Then think about whether Chinese mothers would first and foremost make sure that their children do not get hurt.

# 【Activity 11】

*Read the following story and in small groups work out at least two reasons why Jim insisted on returning the money to Jose, and why Jose refused?*

Jose and Jim worked together in a restaurant. They had become friendly because both of them were also studying. Jim was studying business, and Jose was taking English classes and planned to study engineering.

One day, as they were leaving work, Jim asked Jose, "Jose, I need a favor. I have to go over to school, and I'm out of money. Could you lend me a dollar so I can take the bus over there and then get home? I'll pay you back tomorrow."

"Sure, Jim. No problem. You don't have to pay me back," said Jose, as he handed Jim a dollar.

As soon as he got to work the next day, Jim went over to Jose and handed him a dollar, saying, "Thanks, Jose. I really appreciated this last night. It sure was too cold to walk."

"Forget it." said Jose, as he handed Jim back his dollar.

"Oh, no, I insist. I don't want to take advantage of a friend. What if I needed to borrow money again sometime? If I didn't pay you back now, I would feel wrong asking to borrow money again," said Jim, as he put the dollar into Jose's shirt pocket.

Jose answered, "But that's what friends are for. In Spanish, we have a saying, 'today for you, tomorrow for me.' If you pay me back, I will feel that I won't be able to ask you for money when I need it. I will feel like you are closing the door on me, that there is no trust between us. I thought we were friends. How can I take the money?" Jose handed back the dollar.

"But I won't feel right if you don't take it!" said Jim.

## Discussion

One reason Jose did not want to accept Jim's dollar was that in his culture it is very important to be generous. Generosity and respect for others' generosity are two values that explain many Hispanic and Middle Eastern customs and attitudes. That is why Jim's refusal to accept Jose's generosity made Jose question their friendship. In cultures where generosity is such an important value, most people do not like to think of themselves as stingy or cheap, and these are terrible insults to a Hispanic or an Arab. One reason Latinos do not try to return small amounts of money is that one does not want to suggest that the other person is stingy. To a Latino, Jim's insistence on returning the dollar might mean that Jim thought Jose was stingy and had to have his dollar back.

Americans see it all differently. Jim felt that it would be rude if he did not try to return the dollar as soon as possible. To understand the American point of view, it is necessary to know how important the value of self-reliance is to Americans. Americans do not feel it is right to rely on others for too much. In American culture, owing too many favors suggests being dependent. Americans see this as a weakness. They do not like to think of themselves as "sponges," or "leeches," or "moochers," words used to describe people who take too much from other people. Americans cannot respect themselves if they feel too much "in debt" to other people, financially or otherwise. Instead, they prefer to be "free" of obligations to others. Americans feel strongly about paying their own way. To let someone else pay for them is "to take advantage," which is morally wrong. But if Jim and Jose were close friends, Jim would feel that he was not taking advantage of Jose. He would not need to pay back the dollar.

This trait of American culture is also seen in their custom of "going Dutch" when it comes to paying the bill in a restaurant.

# 【Activity 12】

*Read the quotation from Abraham Lincoln and in small groups work out what value he expressed. If a poor man were to get rich as Lincoln said, what would he do to succeed?*

We do wish to allow the humblest man an equal chance to get rich with everyone else. When one starts poor, as most do in the race of life, free society is such that he knows he can better his condition; he knows that there is no fixed condition of labor for his whole life.

## Discussion

The value President Lincoln expressed is "equality of opportunity," by which Americans mean that each individual should have an equal chance for success, *not that everyone is—or should be—equal.* They see much of life as a race for success. For them, equality means that everyone should have an equal chance to enter the race and win. In other words, equality of opportunity may be thought of as an ethical rule.

If much of life is seen as a race, then a person must run the race in order to succeed; a person must compete with others. That is a price to be paid for the equality of opportunity. If every person has an equal chance to

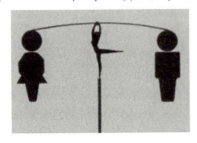

succeed, then it is every person's duty to try. Americans match their energy and intelligence against that of their neighbors in a competitive contest for success. People who like to compete and are more successful than others are honored by being called "winners." The pressures of competition in the life of an American begin in childhood and continue until retirement from work. Learning to compete successfully is part of growing up in the United States. People believe that competition and the desire to win are healthy and desirable. Young people are even advised that if they lose and it does not bother them, there is something wrong with them.

This value can be traced back to ancient times in the West. At the beginning of the first century the Roman philosopher Ovid wrote: *A horse never runs so fast as when he has other horses to catch up and outpace.* The message was clear then and it is clear now—we need to "outpace" all other horses. In contrast, competition was never encouraged in the long history of China.

# 【Activity 13】

We know that in Western countries certain questions are not supposed to be asked. For example, it is considered impolite to inquire about a person's age, marriage status, income, religious belief, choice in voting, property, and others. Of all the aspects, one's income is the most personal or secret. People at the same office don't have the faintest idea of how much each person earns, except the boss.

*With this information in mind, read the following two passages and try to answer the questions below each one.*

A. Simon and Cheng Feng often studied together to prepare for exams. One day, in the middle of a study session, Simon said he wanted to get a coffee. He asked Cheng Feng if he wanted any, but Cheng Feng said, "No." When he came back, he found Cheng Feng reading his notes. He was upset and, although he didn't say anything at the time, he never studied with Cheng Feng again. Cheng Feng noticed the change and wondered what had happened.

## Questions

1. Why did Cheng Feng do this?
2. Why was Simon upset? If you figure out, tell Cheng Feng why.

B. A foreign teacher in China once asked a Chinese student a polite question about his parents. The student's answer revealed serious difficulties the family was experiencing. The teacher felt embarrassed. She regretted that her question had caused the student to reveal such personal information.

## Questions

1. Why did the foreign teacher react the way she did?
2. Would a Chinese teacher have similar feelings? Why or why not?

## Discussion

In case A, Simon's attitude is that "If I write it, it's mine." For him, though the notes that he took were based on the professor's lectures and the textbook, they represented his own interpretation of what he had heard and read. Thus, they were essentially private and should not be looked at by anyone without his permission. In North America, one would be unlikely to pick up anything from someone else's desk or bed to read, even if only a newspaper. Strangely, perhaps, the physical contact of something as a desk or bed imbues the newspaper with the same degree of privacy as the desk or bed.

In contrast, if one is visiting a friend at her/his home, and some magazines are laid out on a coffee table, it is acceptable to pick them up to read. The presumption is that anything displayed on "public" is available to be picked up. But anything on private furniture is definitely private and should not be touched. Bookshelves, however, are a grey area. Sometimes they may be considered private, but other times public. Sometimes the physical location may give a clue: if they are in a public or open area, they can be considered to be available for browsing. If they are behind a person's desk, they should be considered to be private. When in doubt, assume something is private and should not be touched or read unless invited.

We know in China things are different. Among friends, people would pick up magazines, books from a friend's desk or bed and read without even thinking of asking for permission to do so. The difference may lie in the fact that in our tradition, there was no such concept as privacy. Instead, sharing was valued. Today even though some people in China begin to be aware of this idea, still they are not so much as conscious of it as are Westerners.

The foreign teacher in case B was from an individualist culture where a student would have answered her question in a way that protected the privacy of his family. In that culture questions concerning personal information are discouraged because of their strong concept of privacy. Privacy refers to the state or condition of being free from being observed or disturbed by other people, or being free from public attention. It has a lot to do with the value of individualism. In order to understand the Western idea of personal privacy, you should start by thinking of a nation's concept of "territoriality." A nation has borders or boundaries, and everything within those boundaries belongs to that nation and no other. And so is it in the cases concerning personal affairs. Examples are many. Take a private house. If one enters a private house without asking for permission, he is likely to be accused of trespassing or even burglary. And there is, again, individual territory, even in a house: a person's bedroom, for example, is his/her territory. Those who do not live in that bedroom must not enter without asking and must not open the closet or drawer in that room. On top of the desk, there may be letters, business papers or other articles. You must not pick up one of these and read it. If a person is reading something, you must not lean over his shoulder to "share" it with him. It is his private property. The same concept is true in an office. If it is somebody else who wants to enter the office, he usually asks, "May I come in?" and waits for an affirmative answer or response before entering the room.

## ■ Chinese Cultural Values

## 【Activity 14】

We have discussed values of other countries. Now Let's turn to the Chinese values. In the early 1980s, a group of social scientists from around the world conducted a survey of Chinese values. In order to avoid making the research biased by using Western values as their starting point—as has happened frequently in cross-cultural research—they approached a number of Chinese social scientists and asked them to prepare a list of at least ten "fundamental and basic values for Chinese people." Then they summed up the values which are presented in the following composite list. There is no particular order in it.

*Study the values below. Work in small groups and decide five Chinese values that you think are still important today, and five values that you believe have changed. Remember that you don't have to agree with each other, but be prepared to give reasons for your choice.*

1. filial piety                               服从、孝敬、尊崇、赡养父母
2. industry (working hard)             勤劳
3. tolerance of others                  容忍
4. harmony with others                随和
5. humility                                     谦虚(贬己尊人)
6. observance of rites and social rituals    礼仪
7. loyalty to superiors                 忠于上司
8. reciprocation of greetings, favors and gifts    礼尚往来
9. kindness (forgiveness, compassion)    仁爱(恕、人情)
10. knowledge (education)             学识(教育)
11. moderation, following the middle way    中庸之道
12. solidarity with others              团结
13. sense of righteousness            正义感
14. self-cultivation                   修养

15. ordering relationships by status and observing this order    尊卑有序

16. benevolent authority    恩威并重

17. personal steadiness and stability    稳重

18. non-competitiveness    不重竞争

19. resistance to corruption    廉洁

20. patriotism    爱国

21. sincerity    诚恳

22. keeping oneself disinterested and pure    清高

23. thrift    俭

24. patience    耐心

25. persistence（perseverance）    耐力（毅力）

26. sense of cultural superiority    文化优越感

27. repayment of both the good or the evil that another person has caused you

    报恩与报仇

28. adaptability    适应环境

29. prudence（thoughtfulness）    小心（谨慎）

30. trust-worthiness    信用

31. having a sense of shame    知耻

32. courtesy    有礼貌

33. contentedness with one's position in life    安分守己

34. being conservative    保守

35. protecting your "face"    要面子

36. close, intimate friendship    知己之交

37. chastity in women    贞节

38. having few desires    寡欲

39. respect for tradition    尊敬传统

40. wealth    财富

## Discussion

The list above helps us to know that there are many values that guide our behaviors. In the previous part we have touched on some of them, like filial piety. Here we will consider a few more.

One of the characteristics of the Chinese culture is hierarchy which is implied in the list. Every person is supposed to have a set position in family and society in order to achieve harmony between people. One of the famous sayings of Confucius is *Let the emperor be an emperor*, *the subject a subject*, *the father a father*, *and the son a son*, the implication being that within the family as within the nation, persons are not equal; each has to mind his/her own position and role and act accordingly. Personal desires are best subjugated to the will of the patriarch（the male head of a family or a tribe）. Confucius found that there was nothing wrong with inequality because, in his view, the obligations between senior and junior ran in both directions. The senior party had his duties for the junior, and vice versa. These reciprocal obligations were expressed in the Chinese virtue known as *li*, which means "right conduct in maintaining one's place in the hierarchical order."

Large power distance characterizes a hierarchical culture in which people are comfortable with an unequal distribution of power and thus do not try to bring about a more nearly equal distribution. Throughout Chinese history, people have shown respect for age, seniority, rank, maleness, and family background, from which hierarchy is clearly seen. In the language we use everyday there is no lack of terms that imply hierarchy such as 上下一心, 上下级, 禀报, 汇报, 通报. Of course, this way of thinking has noticeably eroded since the 20th century. A lot of changes have taken place. The basic assumptions, however, are still there.

So it's not difficult to see that humility is an important value in China, and the concern for humility is apparent everywhere, though often without our awareness. Humility includes two corresponding sides: self-disparaging or self-denigrating and respecting or glorifying others. Professor Gu Yueguo (顾曰国) sums up this principle as self-denigration and other-elevation (贬己尊人). Examples are many. When the Chinese entertain a guest or guests with a sumptuous dinner with the table overflowing with six or eight beautifully presented, mouth-watering dishes, the comment of the host/hostess is likely to be (in a suitably apologetic tone of voice) "We hope you won't mind joining our simple home meal. We're not very good at cooking, so we've only prepared a few dishes for this evening." Or a very renowned artist usually writes in the corner of their exquisite painting something that means "trying one's hand" or "daubing." Another example is about taking a photo. When a large number of people are preparing themselves for a group photograph, they usually begin by crowding into the back row(s), because they understand that the front row, especially the center-front location, is the place of honor. They recognize that proper humility requires them to be reluctant to place themselves in the front row. Only after some good-natured scuffling and earnest appeals from the junior members and the photographer to the senior ones, the situation resolves itself appropriately with the most important seniors at the center-front, which also reflects the hierarchical concept. The usually polite way of inquiring of another's name is "May I know your respectable family name." The following table helps give us a clearer idea of this concept. Some of the terms are no longer used today, but quite a few are still often employed.

| | 自称（自贬、自谦） | 他称（抬高、尊人） |
|---|---|---|
| 人 | 鄙人、小弟 | 您、您老、先生、阁下、师傅 |
| 姓名 | 鄙姓、贱姓 | 尊姓、贵姓 |
| 妻室 | 内助、老婆、拙荆 | 夫人、太太 |
| 子女 | 小儿、小女 | 令郎、令爱 |
| 亲属 | 舍弟、舍妹 | 令弟、令妹 |
| 工作 | 卑职 | 尊职 |
| 意见 | 愚见、拙见 | 高见、尊意 |
| 作品 | 拙作、拙著 | 大作、佳作、杰作 |
| 家 | 寒舍、舍下、陋室 | 贵府、府上 |
| 处所 | 敝处 | 贵处 |
| 探望 | 拜访、拜见、拜会 | 赏光、赏脸、光临 |
| 单位 | 敝校、敝厂 | 贵校、贵厂 |
| 读书 | 拜读 | 过目 |
| 告别 | 拜别 | |

As harmony is the goal in a hierarchical society, courtesy or good manners have always been stressed by the Chinese tradition when interacting with other people. One important way to achieve this harmony is to accept and respect each person's need to preserve face.

"Face" has been a very important concept in China and other Asian countries. "Face" can be used in many different ways. It can be "thick" or "thin," lost or gained, borrowed or given, augmented or diminished, to name just a few. "Face" carries a range of meanings based upon a core concept of "honor": identity, dignity, integrity, self-esteem, vanity, admiration, etc. Within sociological and sociolinguistic studies it is generally defined as "the negotiated public image, mutually granted each other by participants in a communicative event." It refers roughly to a set of  claims one makes regarding their characteristics and traits. These characteristics and traits are usually what a society thinks are good and desirable. Having some of these characteristics of a certain person called into question would mean that that person was likely to be looked down upon by others. They thus lose face, and are likely to feel embarrassed, upset, and angry. If that happens, there is little likelihood for harmony. Face-saving is employed to achieve harmony, avoid conflicts and protect the integrity of the group. Thus the importance of the "face" concept can hardly be overemphasized.

The "face" concept is not limited to Asians. People in Western countries are also conscious of it. Ideas like dignity, pride and ego refer to what the "face" concept includes. A case in point is mentioned by Fons Trompenaars, a Dutch author:

> On a cold winter night in Amsterdam I sees someone enter a cigar shop. His Burberry coat and horn spectacles reveal him to be well off. He buys a pack of cigarettes and takes a box of matches. He then visits the newspaper stand, purchases a Dutch newspaper and quickly walks to a wind-free corner near the shopping gallery. I approach him and ask if I can smoke a cigarette with him and whether he would mind if I read the second section of his paper. He looks at me unbelievingly and says, "I need this corner to light my paper." He throws me the pack of cigarettes because he does not smoke. When I stand back, I see that he lights the newspaper and holds his hands above the flames. He turns out to be homeless, searching for warmth and too shy to purchase a single box of matches without the cigarettes.

To the mind of Asians, "worry about losing face" accounts for the homeless man's behavior. However, the difference is great. "Face" has much greater social significance for the Chinese and other Asians. An oft-repeated Chinese proverb puts it this way: "A person needs face as a tree needs bark." Moreover, "face" in individualistic and low context cultures concerns mainly the individuals, while in Asia one's face is also the face of one's group, whether that group is thought of as one's family, one's cultural group, or one's corporation.

## ■ Relevance of Face and Negotiation in Different Countries

France is a good example of a Western country in which face matters. For the most part, the French try to avoid negotiation altogether. They have little belief in the values of negotiation and compromise, because, in their view, concessions tend to lead to loss of power and status. "The

French have a strong sense that their own status and prestige is constantly at stake in any negotiation, and it often can be protected best by rejecting discussion or concessions, or taking a conflictual stand on grounds of principle." The importance of maintaining national honor is important, but unlike in high-context societies, failure to reach an agreement does not cause loss of face. Instead, unnecessary concessions are more cause for concern about national face.

In the former Soviet Union, compromising was only for the weak. A strong person, someone with self-esteem, would choose a confrontational strategy and would only agree to compromise if it could be proven that the negotiator had struggled very hard. The Russians seem to fall between the U.S. and France in regard to negotiating styles and importance of face. The Russians still prefer progress to abandoning the process altogether. However, they prefer to do this by getting the other side to make the first concession. They make every one of their own concessions seem like a huge burden, and so increase the appearance of benevolence to the other group and to outsiders.

For Egypt, the use of a third party was a key factor in saving face for the Egyptians and achieving the Camp David Accords in 1978. Shuttle diplomacy, which is a common way of negotiating in the Middle East, enabled Egypt to make concessions to and for the U.S. that Egyptian President Sadat could not have made directly to Israel without suffering severe loss of face.

The key to resolving the stalemate at Camp David had to do with realizing that Egypt's main concern was restoring lost face. Because Egypt had been sorely humiliated after the 1967 war, Egypt's need to regain all of the Sinai was about restoring lost face, whereas Israel's need was for security. The solution was a demilitarized Egyptian Sinai and everybody was relatively happy. This formed the basis of the 1978 Camp David Accords.

The Chinese term "lian" is the source for the concept of face. "It represents the confidence of society in the integrity of moral character." Loss of face occurs when one fails to meet the requirements of one's position in society. The cornerstone for the conflict resolution process in Chinese culture is for both parties to care about the other's face. In many cases, in order to save face, as in Middle Eastern countries, respected third-party mediators are needed to manage the communication between parties in conflict.

According to Harry Irwin, author of *Communicating with Asia*, in order to understand Chinese personal corporate and national identities, one must get a feel for all of the face work that is needed. For the Chinese, proper conduct of face maintenance is equivalent to being a moral member of society; the most important social value is creating and perpetuating group harmony. Gaining face is as important a concept as losing face. A primary goal in many Asian cultures is to increase one's face value or standing in society, while successfully avoiding the loss of face.

## ■ Bamboo, a Symbol of Traditional Chinese Values

China is not only famous for its national treasure, the giant pandas, but also the giant panda's staple food—bamboo. The Chinese love bamboo, and bamboo culture has been rooted in their minds for a long time. To the Chinese people, bamboo is a symbol of virtue. It reflects people's souls and emotions.

# 【Activity 15】

*Work in groups and discuss what traditional Chinese values are reflected from the following pictures according to your knowledge.*

Bamboo is viewed as a symbol of traditional Chinese values. It is an example of the harmony between nature and human beings. Ancient Chinese people designated the plum, orchid, bamboo and chrysanthemum as the "four gentlemen," and pine, bamboo and plum as the "three friends in winter." Ancient Chinese literature held bamboo in profound esteem. This explains why there are so many writings and paintings dedicated to the plant throughout history. Bamboo has the title of "gentleman" among other plants. As a symbol of virtue, bamboo is always closely related to people of positive spirits. Famous Tang Dynasty (618—907) poet Bai Juyi (772—846) summarized the merits of bamboo according to its characteristics: its deep root denotes resoluteness, straight stem represents honorability, its interior modesty and its clean exterior exemplifies chastity. Bamboo culture always plays a positive role in encouraging people to hold on when facing tough situations.

## ■ Implications of Individualism and Collectivism

From Activity 7 to Activity 12, we sense that individualism and collectivism are very important in our study of cultures. According to cross-cultural theorists, individualism and collectivism are basic clusters of values and assumptions. Values like self-reliance, independence, equality, fairness, privacy, and competition derive from individualism, while values such as harmony, "face"-saving, humility, courtesy, group loyalty, and interdependence have a lot to do with collectivism. Therefore, it is appropriate to give them more time and consideration.

# 【Activity 16】

*Work in small groups to find out what individualism means, what it implies, how people who believe in that value will behave, and how it is translated in Chinese? And then consider whether individualism is also an important value in China? After that study the meaning of collectivism.*

## Discussion

According to *Webster's New Collegiate Dictionary* individualism is "a theory maintaining the political and economic independence of the individual and stressing individual initiative, action and interests; also:

conduct or practice guided by such a theory" (主张政治与经济上的独立，强调个人主动性、行为与兴趣的理论，以及由这种理论指导的实践活动). The connotation of individualism is quite positive, contrary to the Chinese term "个人主义." So some scholars suggest that individualism be translated as "个体主义" to avoid the negative implication of "个人主义."

Individualism was first used by the French historian and politician Alexis de Tocqueville[①]. Individualism is then used by anthropologists to designate one of the basic orientations of some cultures. Individualistic cultures have been described as "I" cultures. In those cultures, the basic social unit is the individual who is seen as having intrinsic worth. Individuals tend to define themselves by the extent to which they are different from, rather than similar to others; and they tend to subordinate the goals of collectives (groups like families) to their personal goals. Thus self-examination and self-disclosure are important activities. People learn to express their uniqueness: self-confidence and assertiveness, disclosure of personal thoughts and feelings, and the open discussion of disagreements are valued forms of talk. As a result, individuals do not fear actions that call attention to the self. At the same time, however, they guard their privacy and value freedom to do and think whatever they choose.

Western individualism has been traced to the philosophy of liberalism. The fundamental assumption is that each human is a rational being capable of making well-reasoned choices and thus deserving the right to live his/her own life guided by the principles such as equality and non-interference. In a liberal society, people are free to pursue their own interest so long as they do not fringe on the rights of others, and laws, rules, and regulations are instituted to protect the equal rights of all citizens. Ideally, the good citizen is law-abiding and egalitarian in outlook, with a tendency to treat all others, regardless of virtue or rank, as equals. Of course, ideals and reality are not always consistent with each other.

Cultures with collectivist orientations place little value on individual identity but great value on group identity. They have been labeled as "we" cultures, because the basic unit is the in-group or collective. The survival of the group is more important than that of any individual member. Going one's own way is not valued as it may destabilize the group; instead, uniformity and conformity are stressed. Thus, collectivists are not socialized to draw attention to the self or to express unique opinions. On the contrary, they tend to view self-assertive behaviors as embarrassing and undignified, and potentially dangerous to group harmony. To them, conflict threatens social stability; the expression of contrary opinions risks face, potentially disgracing all involved; openly speaking one's mind appears distasteful. In collectively-oriented cultures, mutual aid and responsibility are stressed; the right to privacy in the sense of freedom from scrutiny or regulation is not recognized; one's business concerns that of the group; and friends should show concern for each other's personal affairs.

It goes without saying that we should recognize the complexity of these constructs. No culture is completely individualist or collectivist. Rather cultures vary in the mix of values they espouse, with some accepting more individualist notions, and others orienting more toward collectivist values. Nevertheless, most English speaking countries tend to view the world from a relatively individualist perspective, while China tends to be more collectivist.

---

① Alexis de Tocqueville (1805−1859): of all the books written about the United States and its institutions, perhaps none has been more significant than Alexis de Tocqueville's *Democracy in America*. For more than 150 years it has helped Americans to understand their government, their character, and the course of their history. Nearly as remarkable as the book itself is the fact that its clear-sighted analysis and prophetic vision were the achievement of a French citizen.

# 【Activity 17】

*Read the letter to a columnist with the reply and see how people differ in their values even within the same culture.*

Dear Mary,

We work in the typing pool of a large London store and are very concerned for the welfare of one of our young colleagues.

She is only 19, unmarried, and has become very friendly with a young man who works in one of the departments of the store. He pops into the typing pool to see her and they hold hands, whisper, and act as if we are not there. We know that he is engaged to a girl who lives near him.

We feel for the protection of the girl, that we should complain to the general manager. But we wouldn't like anybody to get the sack.

Four Worried Typists

The answer from the columnist:

My advice is simple—mind your own business. The girl is old enough to know what she is doing.

## Questions

1. If you were a friend of this girl, would you join the typists? Why or why not?
2. What do you think is the value orientation reflected by the behavior of the typists?
3. What value do you think is implied in the answer?

## Discussion

From the letter and the answer we see that the typists and the columnist differ greatly as to whether the girl should be protected or not. The columnist believes an adult is an individual who is held responsible for what he/she does. The value that the columnist upholds is independence and personal privacy, while that of the typists is otherwise. Here we see that even within the same culture where a lot are shared, people's opinions vary on the same issue. This helps us to know that cultures are complex, and there is diversity even within one culture.

# 【Activity 18】

*Here is a straightforward, everyday dialogue between Chinese businessman, Mr. Lau, and his Australian counterpart, Mr. Clarke.*

Mr. Clarke: Good day mate. I'm Robert Clarke. My friends call me Bob. Here's my card.

Mr. Lau: Hello Mr. Clarke. I am William Lau. Very glad to meet you. How was your trip? (*exchanges business cards*)

Mr. Clarke: Call me Bob. Good thanks. (*reading card*: "*Lau Wing-Leung*"). Oh it's Wing-Leung! Nice to meet you. I'll call you tomorrow Wing-Leung, OK?

Mr. Lau (*smiling*): Yes, I will expect your call. (*both men depart*)

(Adapted from *Scollon and Scollon*, 2001)

## Questions

1. How do people address each other when first time meet?

2. What would you suggest we should do when people exchange the business card?

3. What might be the inappropriate behaviors when people first time meet?

## Discussion

Meetings like these take place every day all over the world in offices, airports, restaurants, and in the street. But this apparent ordinary communication between members of different cultures is often full of unforeseen problems, which create tension and uneasiness, ultimately leading to intercultural miscommunication. According to *Scollon and Scollon* (1995), the reasons for this lie in the rules and regulations of the participants' own culture.

Mr. Lau prefers initial business meetings to be formal and polite, thus the use of "Mr. Clarke" and "Mr. Lau" would be a natural sign of respect for the occasion. The Australian, Mr. Clarke is uncomfortable with using formal titles, and also wishes to show his friendship by using first names. Mr. Clarke correctly distinguishes Mr. Lau's surname on his business card and then rashly uses his given name. In Chinese culture, use of given names is a complex process based upon kinship, past relationships and situations. Mr. Lau feels uncomfortable at being addressed as Wing-Leung and so smiles (an acceptable form of displaying embarrassment). Mr. Clarke however, feels secure in his cultural sensitivity and his egalitarian gesture of goodwill. Mr. Clarke also wants to show he is considerate of the Chinese culture and so avoids the English name in favour of the Chinese name. He is surprised when his follow-up telephone call is colder than he anticipated.

There are at least two intercultural problems in this short dialogue. The first concerns understanding the very real cultural differences involved in any intercultural communication exchange, while the second concerns how to deal with these issues successfully. In the above case, both parties make intercultural "mistakes" even though both men try to be culturally sensitive. Mr. Clarke's partial knowledge of Chinese culture leads to him making the situation more awkward, and if Mr. Lau wished to be addressed as William Lau, then perhaps his business card should have indicated this. Both men's expectations of the other was colored by their own cultural norms, which they could not escape.

# 【Activity 19】

### The Chinese Dinner Party

One of Canada's leading banks invited a Chinese delegation for dinner. The Canadian host chose to share his hosting responsibilities with a colleague.

The dinner was not a success. Both the Chinese and the Canadians remained relatively uneasy throughout the meal. During the dinner, no welcoming speeches or toasts to mutual good health were made. At the end of the meal, the Chinese stood up, thanked the bank officials, declined a ride back to their hotel, and left feeling slighted.

The Canadians also felt upset. They found the departure of the Chinese to be very abrupt, yet they did not know what they had done wrong. Despite planning the menu carefully (avoiding such foods as beef and dairy products), providing excellent translation services, and extending normal Canadian courtesies, the Canadians knew something had gone wrong; they were worried and somewhat hurt by the lack of rapport.

## Questions

1. What are the traditional practices when the Chinese host a welcoming dinner?

2. What are the expectations from the Chinese delegation in this welcoming dinner?

3. What might be the misunderstanding from the both parties in your view?

## Discussion

When the situation was analyzed, it was clear that the Chinese expectations had not been fulfilled. First, having two people share hosting responsibilities was confusing to the hierarchically minded Chinese. Second, because age is viewed as an indication of seniority, the Chinese considered the youth of their own status. Third, in China, it is traditional for the host to offer a welcoming toast at the beginning of the meal, which is then reciprocated by the guests; by not doing so, the Canadians were thought rude.

The specific incident that upset the Canadians—the abrupt departure of the Chinese following the banquet—was, in fact, neither unusual nor a problem: the Chinese retire early and it was getting late.

The Canadians' lack of understanding of the hierarchical nature of Chinese society and the Chinese ways of communicating respect clearly cost them in their business dealing with the visiting delegation. (Source: From G. Hofstede, *Culture's Consequences*, copyright 1983 by Sage Publications.)

## ■ Corporate Communication As a Form of Culture

## 【Activity 20】

*Work in groups to find the answers to the following questions and do the exercises in groups.*

1. On the Web and look up a well-known product brand such as Coca-Cola or McDonald's or a product such as jeans or joggers. Using Google, do a search for different countrys' websites, e.g.American sites, Australian sites and Japanese sites.

   How are the websites differently presented?

   What colors are predominantly used in different countries?

   Why do different nationalities create different looking websites for the same product?

2. When you are in middle of trip in a foreign country's, how much about that country's culture should you need to know?

   Conversely, how much of Australian culture should a new immigrant know when he/she arrives in Australia?

3. Are there any cultural practices, which are reprehensible to Australians?

   Are there any Australian cultural practices, which may be difficult for an foreigner to understand?

4. If someone comes to Australia to live, should they entirely give up their own culture? How much should they retain?

   Should a new immigrant to Australian be required to learn English?

5. Are there any universal cultural values, which transcend particular cultures?

6. If you are in a class with students from other cultures, ask different kinds of students if they have a word for "surfing" or "barbecue" in their language. Do they have more than one word for particularly important concepts in their own culture?

7. Describe the culture of the organization you work for, or the institution you are studying with?

## Discussion

Organizational cultural theory is an alternate way of describing and understanding companies, especially large, multinational corporations, which are prominent in our consumer society. In the 70's and early 80's several theorists began questioning the rational, goal-directed, systemic descriptions of modern organization. These scholars claimed that the traditional concepts of the organization did not capture the symbolic influences on the way that employees interpret their working lives. Drawing upon anthropology and sociology, these theorists say that organization are a form of culture, with their own history, worldview, myths, language and symbols.

It was the early ethnographic (modern day anthropologist) researchers who set the scene for contemporary theories. Studies of ordinary activities such as inner-city street gangs, patients in a mental hospital, and the rituals of factory workers showed that small groups of people have the same characteristics as large cultural groups, and that culture is just as important to these small groups as it is for whole societies.

Contemporary organizational culture theories can be categorized into two distinct but related schools. The first is the "cultural variables" approach, which says that key cultural elements influence an organisation's activities and outcomes. The second approach is rather more extreme, in saying that it is culture that is the lifeblood of the organization. Instead of being one aspect of an organization, culture is seen as the very thing that gives life and meaning to members' organizational reality. In other words, culture is the organization. There are several other slightly different approaches within these two categories, but we shall treat all these approaches as roughly the same from here on.

Early theorists, Deal and Kennedy (1982) categorized organizational culture into four dimensions:

1. Values are the shared philosophies and beliefs of the corporation, and include slogans such as Vidal Sassoon's "If you don't look good, we don't look good," Heineken's "It's all about the beer," or the University of Western Sydney's "Bringing knowledge to life."

2. Heroes are the standout members who best represent the organization's profile. Often these people are the founders of the company such as Colonel Sanders, Bill Gates of Microsoft, and Yataro Iwasaki from Mitsubishi. Sometimes they are elder managers or CEOs.

3. Rites and rituals are the ceremonial practices by which an organization celebrates or reinforces its daily activities. In higher education, the graduation ceremony, complete with gown, hood and mortar board is used to signify the passing from one kind of life (civilian) to another (academic) life.

4. Cultural communication networks are the informal channels of communication, which are used to indoctrinate new members into the prevailing culture. Students, for example, learn about assignment evaluation from fellow students who may have done the course in the past.

Although this approach is a useful method of describing organizational life, Kreps (1990) argues that it is too simplistic to simply assert that strengthening the four principles above will lead to a strong and profitable organization. An alternate set of categories is presented by Peters and Westerman (1982) who studied the traits of 62 highly successful organizations in the fields of technology, consumer goods, services, general industrial goods, and project management. Excellent organizations were discovered to embrace eight primary cultural themes: 1) a bias toward action rather than excessive planning, 2) closeness to the customer, 3) an emphasis upon autonomy and entrepreneurship, 4) people orientation akin to family,

5) a hands-on approach to management, 6) a focus on what the company does best, 7) a simple hierarchy and lean staff, 8) an ability to innovate and a unanimity of organizational spirit.

It should be noted that most of the theories of organizational culture originate from American researchers and use American companies as their source of data. An Italian-American organizational culture comparison study (Morley, Shockley-Zalabak, and Cesaria, 1997) showed that the cultural themes, values, activities and perceptions of staff were similar but not identical across the Atlantic. In particular, three additional dimensions were found to be important to a company's culture: 1) how success is defined, 2) the degree of expected conformity and 3. how expectations of work life should be defined.

The most recent research into organizational culture does not begin with the idea that culture is a universally shared set of symbols and beliefs. Hofstede et al's (1990) research showed that perceptions of organization culture may be affected by nationality and demographic characteristics. Keeton and Mengistu (1992) discovered that cultural perceptions vary across levels of management. Using just one health-related organization, Helms and Stern (2001) measured employee perceptions of 10 accepted cultural dimensions. They found significant differences between different organizational units, the age of the employee, gender and ethnicity, concluding that organizational cultures are not monolithic, but extremely flexible and subject to change.

# REVISION TASKS

1. *Review this chapter with the help of the following questions.*

(1) What does the core of culture include? Why should we be aware of it?

(2) What do you think of the theory of the Axial Age? Does it help the study of cultures?

(3) How do you understand worldview? In what way is it important?

(4) What is your worldview or outlook on the world? Dualistic, holistic,...? Can you list some other worldviews?

(5) What are the functions of values? What values do you carry with you? Make a list of your own values and compare them with others.

(6) Can you list some characteristics of values?

(7) Do different cultures have similar values? Why or why not?

(8) What traditional Chinese values do you cherish?

(9) What Western values appear to you as strikingly different? And why?

(10) What do you think of the cultural taxonomies devised by Kluckhohn and Hofstede? Do they help the study of cultures?

2. *Complete the tasks below.*

(1) If you want to work in some far away place after graduation, but your parents hope that you find a job near where they live, what would you do? Ask the same question of your parents: what would they have done when they were young in their 20s? Survey, if possible, some

young Western people as to what they would do in the same situation. Then compare the decisions and see if there is any difference. Try to offer some reasons for the difference, if any.

(2) When unhappy with a colleague or something else about the work environment, many Americans may complain directly to the "boss." Others may even complain directly to the colleague who is the source of the complaint. What would Chinese do in the same situation? Explain if there is any difference. The similar situation goes to roommates conflicts in college. Most of the college students would complain and gossip the misconceptions, misunderstanding among themselves, seldom seek help from the teachers or complain directly to the roommates who are involved in the affairs. Even worse , the lack of communication leads to the escalation of the conflicts. Explain, why if there is any difference.

(3) Do you feel comfortable with the idea that some people should have more power than others? For example, at home parents should have more power over children, or the president of a university should have more power over the faculty and students. Give at least three reasons for your position.

(4) Study the remarks of Alexis de Tocqueville that follow, and think about the questions: What kind of culture is talked about? Are there any characteristics of that culture revealed?

As social equality spreads there are more and more people who, though neither rich nor powerful enough to have much hold over others, have gained or kept enough wealth and enough understanding to look after their own needs. Such folk owe no man anything and hardly expect anything from anybody. They form the habit of thinking of themselves in isolation and imagine that their whole destiny is in their own hands.

Thus, not only does democracy make men forget their ancestors, but it also clouds their view of their descendants and isolates them from their contemporaries. Each man is forever thrown back on himself alone, and there is danger that he may be shut into the solitude of his own heart.

(5) Look at the following case and try to account for the difference reflected.

The American manager praises one Japanese employee in front of his group.

American: Mr. Sugimoto, I have noticed that you are doing an excellent job on the assembly line. I hope that the other workers notice how it should be done.

Japanese: (*He is uneasy.*) Praise is not necessary. I am only doing my job. (*He hopes that the other Japanese workers do not hear.*)

American: You are the best, most excellent and dedicated worker we have ever had at the Jones Corporation.

Japanese: (*He blushes and nods his head several times, and keeps working.*)

American: Well, are you going to say "Thank you," Mr. Sugimoto, or just remain silent?

Japanese: Excuse me, Mr. Jones. May I leave for five minutes?

American: Sure. (*He is annoyed and watches Sugimoto exit.*) I can't believe how rude some Japanese workers are. They seem to be disturbed by praise and don't answer you... just remain silent.

(6) Discuss in groups: The different orientations of the Chinese and Northern American toward family adapted from *Condon and Youself* (1975).

Try to think the suggested contents, do you agree or not agree? Why or why not?

| Family | China | the United States |
|---|---|---|
| Relational orientation | Lineal-orientation—characterized by a highly developed historical consciousness and a close association with extended families. Wife tends to be subordinate to husband and children must be obedient to parents in the family. | Individualistic-orientation—older and younger members of the family always share the same values. Wife and children are more equal to husband. |
| Authority | Authoritarian-orientation—reflects a strong orientation toward paternal authority. | Democratic-orientation—reflects a more even balance between paternal and maternal authority. |
| Positional role behavior | Specific-orientation—generation, age, and sex hierarchy is very strong, i.e., the older generation, elders, and males are superior. | Open-orientation—obligations are open to negotiation. |
| Mobility | Low-mobility-orientation—they family structure and an agricultural society made the Chinese settle in a fixed place and cultivate the land in an orderly fashion. | High-mobility-orientation—conjugal family structure, no kinship bondage and high degree of technology and transportation have produced a highly mobile society. |

# Chapter 4

# Verbal Communication

*By words the mind winged.* ( Aristophanes )

*The limits of my language are the limits of my world.* ( Ludwig Wittgenstein )

*The sum of human wisdom is not contained in any one language, and no single language is capable of expressing all forms and degrees of human comprehension.* ( Ezra Pound )

# I Warm-up: Read and Say

*Read the following passage and see how powerful words can be. Try to offer some more examples indicating the power of words and then share them with your partner.*

Fluorine in drinking water reduces tooth decay, especially in children. Certain fluorides are used in rat poisons. Newburgh, New York, voted to try fluoridation to improve the teeth of its children. The motion passed. Opposition to the project, despite a vigorous publicity campaign using the rat poison argument, was defeated. A day was announced when the chemical would be added to the water supply.

The day dawned, and before it was over, City Hall received hundreds of telephone calls complaining that the water causing dizziness, nausea, headaches, and general debility. City Hall replied that, owing to technical problems, no fluoride had yet been added—it was the same old water.

# II Understanding Language

The power of words is illustrated by the story above. You will find more of such incidents from media or people around you. Our life experiences alone can tell us that language is what we cannot do without for our survival. But language does not exist in isolation. It has a soil to be born and nurtured. That is what we call culture. In this chapter we will develop an understanding and appreciation of verbal language as it functions in intercultural communication. We will deal with the functions of language, its relationship with culture, communication styles in different cultures and thought patterns which exert great impact on communication.

What is language? Language, in its most basic sense, is a set of symbols and the rules for combining those symbols that are used and understood by a large community of people. In the following activities, you will learn more about language.

## 【Activity 1】

*Study in pairs the following two pictures and try to list at least two functions of language.*

"Your mum and I are worried, and we wish
you wouldn't chew so much gum."

## Discussion

The pictures show us that people transmit information, exchange ideas and feelings with language. In other words, language is what makes communication possible.

Communication theorists, linguists, psychologists, and anthropologists all agree that language has many functions. The basic one is for people to communicate with each other. Besides, language gives meaning to otherwise random experiences. It makes rational thought possible. It enables us to reason, to draw logical conclusions from the evidence of our senses, to generalize from one event to another, and to predict, create, and understand. It also enables us to exchange feelings, and then a certain relationship may be established between or among people concerned. It is the means of cognitive development for children and conceptual development for adults. It records, stores and disseminates knowledge.

Human beings are called "culture-bearing animals" because they have the capacity for symbolic communication, or language. Compared with human beings, other animals can communicate only in crude and limited ways. Dogs bark in warning, and birds sing to attract prospective mates. Bees and some other kinds of insects communicate only with body movements. More intelligent animals can also learn to respond to verbal signals like "sit" and "suppertime," but humankind has the unique ability to assign meanings to those sounds. Only people can invent words like "happy," "rain," "God," and "next week" and agree that they are symbols for certain thoughts and feelings. A human being can make almost any number of sentences including sentences he has never heard of before. The human ability to use words is indeed a remarkable gift.

Also from the pictures we see that there are more ways or "languages" other than verbal language that people use to send messages. The girl in the picture on the right, for instance, gives us a message about her through the way she dresses. This concerns non-verbal communication that we will address in Chapter 5. Moreover, there are other codes like painting and architecture that people use for communication. In this chapter our focus is the language, the most important symbolic system of communication.

# 【Activity 2】

*Study in pairs the short passage and the picture, and see what you can infer about language.*

Two Japanese who knew some Chinese were one day at a Beijing subway station. They saw a warning sign which read: 小心地滑! They were very much surprised to see that nobody around them was skating, though the floor was flat and somewhat slippery.

## Discussion

As Chinese we know perfectly what "小心地滑" means. The interpretation of the Japanese is amusing but not unreasonable. The humor of the laundry picture is easy to be enjoyed. From these examples we see that language is ambiguous. People may have different interpretations to the same words. Better understanding of the meaning of words requires us to take into consideration the context in which a certain word or group of words are used. Otherwise miscommunication may occur. Take the word "good". G.K. Chesterton (British author, 1874−1936) used it twice in one

sentence, each with a different meaning in different context: "If a man were to shoot his grandmother at a range of five hundred yards, I should call him a good shot, but not necessarily a good man."

In fact, language and context co-constitute one another: language contextualizes and is contextualized, such that language does not just function "in" context, language also forms and provides context. When context is involved, more often than not culture becomes indispensable.

# III Language and Culture

The relationship between language and culture may be better born out by some metaphors. One compares language and culture to a living organism—language is flesh, and culture is blood. Without culture, language would be dead; without language, culture would have no shape. Another takes communication into consideration. Communication is the swimming motion, language is the swimming skill, and culture is water. Without language, communication would remain to a very limited degree (in very shallow water); without culture, there would be no communication at all.

These metaphors point to the idea that language is part of culture and plays a distinct role in it. Some social scientists consider it the keystone of culture. Without language, they maintain, culture would not be possible. On the other hand, language is influenced and shaped by culture; it reflects culture. In the broadest sense, language is the symbolic representation of a people, and it comprises their historical and cultural backgrounds as well as their approach to life and their ways of living and thinking. It provides a window to the culture in which it is used. To sum up, language is both a means of communication and a channel of culture.

It is obvious that to communicate with people from different backgrounds we have to use a language, native or foreign. But we may not be quite aware that language alone does not ensure effective communication. To reach that end, cultural competence is necessary, because, as the above metaphors indicate, language and culture are inseparable. As a result, we cannot understand a language outside the culture in which it is used, and similarly, we cannot understand a culture without taking into account its carrier: its language.

The importance of cultural competence requires much more of our attention because it has not been adequately recognized. Please look at two kinds of errors in intercultural communication: linguistic and pragmatic errors. As the term indicates, linguistic errors refer to grammatical errors such as "He come yesterday." Pragmatic failure refers to the failure of communication caused by utterances made in an unsuitable manner or at an unsuitable time, by failing to keep close to the native speaker's expressive manner, and by lacking knowledge of the custom—lack of cultural competence. For example, years ago, a Chinese visiting scholar in America reacted to the compliment about her dress by saying: "No, no, it's just a very ordinary dress." This response, though appropriate in the Chinese context, would imply to the American that she doubted the speaker's ability to appreciate the style of dress. These two types of errors result in different consequences. Linguistic errors may at worst reflect upon the speaker as a less than adequate user of the language, while pragmatic failures may be taken in a more personal way and reflect poorly on the speaker as a person. It may lead to the judgment that the speaker is behaving badly— uncooperative, dishonest, impolite or even deceitful. It is obvious that the negative consequence caused by pragmatic failure is to some degree much more serious than that caused by linguistic errors.

But how are language and culture mutually affected? This is what we are going to deal with in the following section.

## Ⓐ The Influence of Language on Culture

It is in the very nature of language to be overlooked and disregarded. Language goes unnoticed because it's impossible for a culture to separate the sound-image and concept of something. A culture can't separate the entity and the name that they give that entity-it goes unseen. We don't think "that's the name we give that thing," instead we say "that's what it is." A tree is a tree to most humans, when it's actually just a representation.

Language isn't a system of naming things—it is, instead, a way to make our world possible for us to understand, by being able to differentiate between different concepts. There's more than just one way of looking at a concept and that we make assumptions by accepting what we're told and what we hear, hardly ever questioning or researching for ourselves. Each culture sees and understands things differently, and with that, each culture categorizes entities differently, having their own set of boundaries and spectrum, creating their own system of language. This is why language is difficult to translate.

Language is necessary for a culture, whereas it allows individuals to understand the world and communicate effectively. Languages don't work interdependently; instead they work dependently because each language relates terms in its own way.

Everyone interprets language differently. In any communication between two people, each person is going to interpret any linguistic message in a certain way—in accordance to their own experience, memory, environment, learning and the way they perceive stimuli. It's important to understand the origins of language, because language and culture are what forms the belief systems of the world. Donald's third stage of cognitive evolution, mythic intelligence, is based on the development of symbols and language which permits imitated cultural elements to be incorporated into verbal metaphors and stories.

Language acts as a way to represent culture. Outdated language, or meanings, becomes unused and as a society has more technological innovation and growth, new, updated language becomes necessary in order to articulate. For this reason, language is considered social because that's how it's constructed. It's similar to animals adapting to their surroundings. We adapt language to what's significant in our culture at that time, along with our experiences at a specific time period. Language therefore becomes a representation of a culture by representing our conditions at a specific time; this is where a culture's ideology comes into a language.

A culture decides upon a common viewpoint of the way things are—the way they see it and viewpoints change over time, which is why language adapts to the changes in time—changes in the way we see things and our perception. A society may even challenge language use because of the changing perceptions, corresponding to a change in language. This helps to support Sausseur's ideas, showing that because these concepts weren't pre-existing, that neither were these terms; we see that language is changeable. People see past language as a way to differentiate and comprehend and it's not viewed as something socially constructed based on what's socially signified.

Language varies. Like language, common sense also is dependent upon separate cultures—the time period, what's significant to that society and common perceptions / beliefs. The reason for this is that language and a culture's way of thinking goes hand-in-hand; since that way of thinking shifts over time, not only is language flexible and changeable, so is "common sense," if you could call it that. Thought, which makes up common sense, is the ability to create representations and symbols; it's the power to determine the signifier and signified.

Our thought is reflected in our language because it can be seen how we classify things and what's significant to us. People often believe they are superior to one another and are ethnocentric. People mistake that their culture is the "right" way of thinking. People believe that an idea is true because that's how they see it; if we were capable of understanding how others' can view ideas and customs, we would realize just how much we don't understand. How could we understand when we don't even know what else is out there or fully understand it? The problem lies within the fact we see and we believe; each person's perception is relative to their individual knowledge. A large part of seeing depends on habit and assumption.

## 【Activity 3】

*Read the following fictitious story and see what you can infer about the relationship between language, culture and thought. Discuss in small groups; the ideas of others may inspire you.*

When an old English lady hears some foreign words (meaning water) for the first time, she feels that foreign languages are odd and quite unreasonable. She says this is just plain water, but how strange that the Chinese call it "shui" (水), the French call it "de l'eau." Only we English give it the right name "water," because it is nothing else but water.

### Discussion

One possible interpretation is that we are usually ethnocentric and judge the behavior of people from other cultures against the background of our own cultural and language rules. One more interpretation may be that language not only gives us freedom to express ourselves, but also tends to confine our thoughts to a certain area. Out of what our language provides us, we feel confused. What we can safely say is that the difference does not lie in languages alone. German linguist von Humboldt (1767-1835) answered this when he wrote that "The difference in languages is not a difference in sounds and signs, but a difference in world views." The most well known theory relating to this is the Sapir-Whorf hypothesis.

### ■ Sapir[①]-Whorf[②] Hypothesis (SWH)

This hypothesis was formulated by Edward Sapir and his student Benjamin Lee Whorf. It deals with the relationship between thought and language. Sapir believed that language and thoughts are somehow interwoven, and that all people are equally being affected by the confines of their language. In short, he made all people out to be mental prisoners; unable to think freely because of the restrictions of their vocabularies. This is the foundation of the so-called linguistic determinism. It is informative to include the following quote from Sapir:

> Human beings do not live in the objective world alone, nor alone in the world of social activity as ordinarily understood, but are very much at the mercy of the particular language which has become the medium of expression for their society.... The real world is to a large extent unconsciously built up on the language habits of the group. No two languages are ever sufficiently similar to be considered as representing the same social reality. The worlds in which different societies live are distinct worlds, not merely the

---

① Edward Sapir (1884−1939), anthropologist, born in Germany, emigrated to the US in 1889 and lived in NY.

② Benjamin Lee Whorf (1897−1941), American linguist and anthropologist.

same world with different labels attached.

Whorf developed this idea of Sapir's. He stated:

> … that the linguistic system (in other words, the grammar) of each language is not merely a reproducing instrument for voicing ideas but is itself the shaper of ideas, the program and guide for the individual's mental activity, for his analysis of impressions, for his synthesis of his mental stock in trade… We dissect nature along lines laid down by our native languages. The categories and types that we isolate from the world of phenomena we do not find there because they stare every observer in the face; on the contrary, the world is presented in a kaleidoscopic flux of impressions which has to be organized by our minds—and this means largely by the linguistic systems in our minds. We cut nature up, organize it into concepts, and ascribe significances as we do, largely because we are parties to an agreement to organize it in this way—an agreement that holds through our speech community and is codified in the patterns of our language. The agreement is, of course, an implicit and unstated one, but its terms are absolutely obligatory; we cannot talk at all except by subscribing to the organization and classification of data which the agreement decrees.

Two principles can be inferred from the passages above: linguistic determinism that what one thinks is fully determined by their language; and linguistic relativity which states that the differences in languages reflect the different views of different people. The following is an example of this hypothesis:

> If my language has only one term—brother-in-law—that is applied to my sister's husband, my husband's brother, and my husband's sisters' husbands, I am led by my language to perceive all of these relatives in a similar way. Vocabulary, through what it groups together under one label and what it differentiates with different labels, is one way in which language shapes our perception of the world.

This hypothesis can be summed up this way that different languages determine or shape the ways in which their users view the world. Do you agree with this hypothesis? You may have read the Chinese classic *The Red Chamber Dream*. How did "林黛玉" and "贾宝玉" relate to Grandma Jia? Did the old lady love both of them? Did she treat them as if they were equally important to her? If differently, why? Can you find the English equivalents for "孙" and "外孙"? The answer is of course "no." Do you think that language plays a role here?

In addition, Martin Luther King, Jr.'s remark about the connotations of the color whiteness and blackness may serve as another example. In his speech *Where Do We Go from Here*, he said:

> In *Roget's Thesaurus* there are some 120 synonyms for blackness and at least sixty of them are offensive, such words as blot, grim, devil and foul. And there are some 134 synonyms for whiteness and all are favorable, expressed in such words as purity, cleanliness, chastity and innocence. A white lie is better than a black lie. The most degenerate member of a family is the "black sheep." Ossie Davis has suggested that maybe the English language has to be reconstructed so that teachers will not be forced to

teach the Negro child sixty ways to despise himself, and thereby perpetuate his false sense of inferiority and the white child 134 ways to adore himself, and thereby perpetuate his false sense of superiority.

Dr. King talked about racial segregation and discrimination, and in order to do away with this inequality he suggested reconstructing the language his people use. This suggestion of Dr. King's may be based on the assumption that language affects thoughts.

The impact of language on culture can also be found in the verb tenses of some languages. For instance, English has tenses built into their verb forms, so native speakers automatically think in terms of time (being "punctual," "time is money," "make the time," etc.). But Algonquian Indian languages do not have tenses (not that they cannot express time if they wish), but rather have "animate" and "inanimate" verb forms, so they automatically think in terms of whether things around them have a life essence or not. So when Chippewa Indians do not show up for a medical appointment, Anglo health care workers may explain this as being "present oriented," since English native speakers normally cannot think except in terms of time frames.

But up to now there has not been enough evidence to show that language actually determines a culture's pattern of thought. Some scholars question that if the world view and behavior of people are affected so severely by the structure of their language, and languages have radically different structures, then how can cross-cultural communication and understanding be a realistic goal for the modern world?

Although few modern sociologists fully accept the notion that people's view of reality is entirely constructed by the language they speak, they do generally agree there are differences in the way languages represent experience, and these differences influence how people perceive the world, and then how they behave. Therefore, we can safely say this hypothesis does contain some useful insights. It suggests that language is more than a way of communicating, and it offers hints to cultural differences and similarities among people.

## B  The Influence of Culture on Language

Now we should turn to the other side of the issue: how culture affects language. This impact works at various levels. In verbal communication there are differences at phonemic, lexical, syntactical, and discourse levels. In this part we examine those aspects where, we think, more confusion may appear when it comes to communication with people from other cultures. The aspects concern the word meanings and the use of language, especially the differences in the ways people express themselves in spoken and written forms.

It is widely believed that culture is created but language is partly innate and to a certain extent, instinctive. They are both developed through the journey of life and have different and open areas of study. Cultural differences and language variations also play a significant role in bringing about other meanings of the same word or expression. That is the reason why our understanding of them may contradict or coincide.

There are certain aspects of life that require a socially appropriate use of language and that tell us that the impact of society on language cannot be ignored. Language does not constrain people's ability to think although sometimes people claim they cannot express what they feel or think. It rather reflects personal perceptions and cultural preoccupations.

If thought is controlled through cultural taboos, there would be fewer words in the language to express an action or event. Cultural inhibitors, concerning what is proper and improper to talk about, can serve to narrow the range of thought. As a result, when a Kurdish talks about sex, they refer to the action indirectly; for example, "they are/were in bed together." Needless to say, this sentence deals with association, and does not quite match with sex, a term which is established in English culture.

Some words will fade away with the passing of time and others will be replaced. Kurdish people expect to be greeted with a handshake and a warm reception, while Americans may be satisfied with a smile. In face-to-face greetings, a Kurd mostly asks questions and tends to forget the answer. Consider the following:

A: How are you?

B: How are you? How is your family? How is your health?

A: How is everyone? How are your parents? How are your wife and children?

After asking each other many questions, they will then come to answer the questions. When asking an American "How are you?" s/he would normally say, "I am fine. Thank you. How are you?" Such language use is influenced by culture and could bear many interpretations. Kurdish people generally may be described as people-centered, friendly and truly want to engage into the conversation and appeal to the listener's emotions. By contrast, they may be described as chatty by a foreigner. An American might be accused of being unsociable or insensitive by a Kurd. Nevertheless, the same American may be described as direct and to the point by a Kurd who has information about American culture. Culture and cultural knowledge here determines the way our language is observed and used.

After all, humans are endowed with the ability to speak but they learn cultural conventions through imitation and cultural rules. To address sensitive subjects, there seems to be a need to use several words to represent one action or concept. But that does not necessarily impose curbs on the proliferation and growth of vocabulary, dictionary, and language.

To conclude, language is not free of its cultural influence but with the current technological revolution and the expansion of media, the language will surely adopt, embrace, and has the flexibility to absorb new words and there seems to be no cultural frontier when it comes to the Internet.

## ■ Word Meanings: Source

## 【Activity 4】

*We all know that words have meanings. But where do their meanings come from? Read the following movie story The Gods Must Be Crazy and think about this question.*

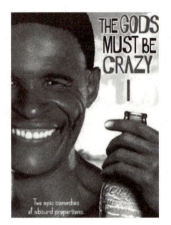

In a desert somewhere in Africa, Jingo, a tribesman, picked up an object dropped from a passing plane. What was it? Jingo and his fellow tribesmen activated their world knowledge and reached an interpretation of the object, namely it must be something from their God. Since kids all tried hard to own it and started fighting, which never occurred before, the tribal head thought that their God had sent a message of some sort to warn them that something bad was going to befall them. A decision was made that Jingo must go to the edge of the earth and throw the object away. In fact, it was only an empty Coca-Cola bottle.

### Discussion

This story may be a joke. But it tells us that what a word or an object means to us is actually an interpretation we give it, and that our interpretation relies on our knowledge about the language and the world. Two points about word meanings may be arrived at here. One is that words do not mean anything by themselves; people attribute meaning to them. The other concerns the process by which people generate a meaning: we look at the word, activate the knowledge about the word in our mind and reach an interpretation or meaning for that word.

A question may follow. If a word meaning is our interpretation, can we say that no word has a steady and fixed meaning, since different people may have different interpretations? What we have to know is that the meanings of words are usually conventionalized (约定俗成). For example, you may know the story about the kangaroo, a well-known Australian animal. Many years ago a Western explorer saw an animal in Australia. He asked an aboriginal there what it was. The answer sounded like kangaroo. Although the aboriginal meant in his mind "I don't know," the explorer took it to be the name of that animal and recorded it. Within a short time people accepted that the term kangaroo refers to any of various herbivorous marsupials of Australia and adjacent islands, having short forelimbs, large hind limbs adapted for leaping, and a long, tapered tail. This meaning is thus conventionalized.

## ■ Word Meanings: Types

## 【Activity 5】

*Conventional meaning has at least two kinds of interpretation. Study the case about* "终身大事" *and try to identify this term's two kinds of meanings.*

In a CCTV quiz program hosted by Wang Xiaoya (王小丫), an American guest who could speak some Chinese was to choose the correct meaning of 终身大事 from the following four choices: 工作,事

业,婚姻,生死. Although he fully understood the literary meaning of this term (the most important thing in one's life), he didn't work out the meaning we Chinese attach to it until the host gave him some hint. Why did he have difficulty figuring out the implied meaning?

## Discussion

The problem the American met is that he knew the term's denotation (the primary, surface meaning, or explicit meaning, or conceptual meaning), but not its connotation (the socio-cultural and "personal" association, or the implicit meaning, the implication of a word). For many words there are both denotations and connotations. Another example is the English term "politician", whose denotation is "a person whose business is politics," but its connotation is "a person who doesn't usually keep his promises, often cheats for his own selfish purpose," which is derogative. What determines the connotations of words? Culture does.

It is inevitable that one will encounter misunderstanding and misinterpretation even within the same culture, however much interlocutors share, for one word may mean different things to different people. But in general, when communicating with someone from one's own culture, the process of using words to represent their experiences is much easier because within a culture people share many similar experiences. The process is more problematic when communication is performed between people from distinct cultures, because their experiences, beliefs, values, customs, traditions, and the like are different. Part of the problem concerns the associative meaning of words. So in intercultural communication, we have to be careful about the connotations words may have. We may hurt our partners' feelings without knowing how we did that.

## ■ Word Meanings: Equivalence in Different Languages

## 【Activity 6】

In the 1990s, the return of Hong Kong to China was a heated topic in many media. But the Chinese term 香港回归 has two versions in English. The term which was used in English newspapers published in China was "return," while in the West the chosen term was "revert." For example:

1. The report was divided into several parts... ensuring the smooth return of Hong Kong and promoting the reunification of the motherland. (*Beijing Review*. Mar. 17—23. 1997. p.7)

2. He will officially take office on July 1, 1997, the day Hong Kong reverts to China. (*Times*. Dec. 23, 1996. p.47)

*How do you account for the difference in the choice of words?*

## Discussion

Besides their denotations, both "return" and "revert" have political implications. According to *Oxford English Dictionary*(1998), one of the definitions of "return" is the recovery of something taken by others, especially illegally. "Revert," however, can be a legal term that refers to the return (of property) to (the original owner) by reversion①.

Therefore, in the special context of Hong Kong in 1997, "revert" has a specific political implication that Britain's occupation of Hong Kong and its return to China was based on the "agreement" between the British government and the Chinese government (Qing Dynasty), and so Britain has been law-abiding.

This activity just reminds us that we have to be very careful about the associative meanings or connotations of words when we engage in communication, especially when we use a foreign language.

# 【Activity 7】

Whether expressing ourselves in the foreign language or translating, we have to find appropriate words. We naturally hope to find words whose meanings are equivalent in both our native language and the target one. But pitfalls often result when we are doing so, because many words are culturally loaded. Exact equivalent terms in any two languages are rare.

In order to see the differences of words in distinct languages, some researchers identify five categories of words based on the degree of equivalence. This study also contributes to our linguistic competence and cultural competence.

*Now study the following categories and try to give more examples to each category. Team work is recommended.*

1. Terms in one language that have equivalents (or near equivalents) in the other language. Comparatively there are fewer such words. Fox, for example, is one of them. In both languages its denotation is an animal, and its connotation cunning. One more example is dove and gezi (鸽子), both of which are often related to peace. In addition, many terms for natural substances as well as scientific and technological terms are of this kind: water, rain, snow, computer, clone, etc.

2. Terms in one language that find no counterparts in the other language. For example, in Chinese there are 三伏 and 三九, for which you find no equivalents in English. And the other way round is also true. English words like democracy, science, tank, privacy, brunch, car pool, commuter, splashdown etc. don't have any equivalents in Chinese.

3. Terms in two different languages that appear to refer to the same objects or concepts on the surface, but may actually refer to quite different things or have different connotations. Words in this category demand our special attention. For they appear to refer to the same things on the surface, we are likely to overlook their connotations. For example, 爱人 and Lover are not at all the same. We know what 爱人 means. But if a Chinese man introduced his wife as my lover, English people would stare in surprise. How could Chinese, who are known to be so circumspect(谨慎的) in such matters, be so open

---

① reversion: The return of an estate to the grantor or to the grantor's heirs or successors after the grant has expired. 在赠予期满后,将财产返回给赠予者或赠予者的继承者。

about having a lover? The word for a person's spouse in English is simply: husband, wife, fiancé or fiancée, not "lover" which refers to a man in love with or having a sexual relationship with a woman outside of marriage.

4. Terms in one language that seem to have equivalents in the other, but these so-called equivalents are only partly equivalent. Let's look at family and 家庭 whose meanings are similar when referring to people connected by blood or marriage, but the following example tells us that there is some difference between them.

An American (A) attended her Chinese friend's (B) wedding. Two years later, the two met again.

A: Have you started a family?

B: Oh, yes. You attended my wedding, remember?

A: I mean if you've had children.

Here we see that family means more than 家庭, though they seem to be equivalents.

5. Things or concepts that are represented by one or perhaps two terms in one language, but by many more terms in the other language; that is, finer distinctions exist in the other language. The proportionately high number of terms in a particular domain is an important index to the focus of a culture. In other words, this analysis helps us see to what extent a particular culture attaches significance. Take the word "Grandmother" as an example. In Chinese there are two sets of names zumu/nainai(祖母/奶奶), wai zumu/waipo(外祖母/外婆) for one English word "grandmother". Here each Chinese name contains the meaning of the precise relationship between the user and the person addressed. This reflects the emphasis of kinships in China, but not in English speaking countries. Wan (湾) can be another example. As the UK is an island country, there are a lot of words describing different wan: bay (in the shape of a half circle), gulf (deep and long), bight (small and shallow), cove (small with rocks on both sides of the entrance), creek (narrow), fiord (long and narrow with cliff on both sides), etc. In Chinese, some explanation has to be added to the word wan when a specific wan is to be rendered into Chinese.

## Discussion

Here are some more examples of the second category: culturally unique terms or terms in one language that find no counterparts in the other. In Chinese there are 阴,阳①,气功,武术,纸老虎,气节,节气,中医的经络,肾虚,肝火,湿症,热症,etc.; in English there are parent, sister, brother, uncle, aunt, niece, nephew, wake-up call②, etc.

Try to render this simple sentence into English: Linda's brother married Michael's sister. Is it easy or difficult? Why?

The following are more examples of the third category: terms in two languages that seem to be equivalent but in fact not. 干部 and 单位 are two interesting terms. 干部 is most commonly rendered in

---

① The explanation is "two forces/principles through whose essences, according to Taoist cosmology, the universe was produced and cosmic harmony is maintained. Yin is dark, female and negative, and yang is light, male and positive."

② Wake-up call: hotel service to wake the client by phone at the required time.

English as cadre. But a cadre is not the same as a 干部. Furthermore, cadre is not a common word. Many English-speaking people don't know what it means; those who do know pronounce it in different ways—it has three or four common pronunciations. Other terms have been suggested as substitutes: official, functionary, administrator, etc. But none of these is exactly the same as 干部.

In English there is no such general term as 单位 to refer to a place where one works. If you translate it as a school, a company, a factory or any other institution, it doesn't mean the same as a 单位 which in China takes care of almost everything we are to encounter in our life and work. None of the organizations in America or other Western European countries do the same. As changes are universal, the meaning of 单位 in China has changed in recent years.

农民 and peasant. Among the definitions of peasant we find "a usually uneducated person of low social status," "a countryman; rustic," "an ill-bred person." Imagine how English-speaking people would react to this sentence: The poor peasants talked about their happy life today.

政治 and politics. 政治, an often used term in China, is hard to render into proper English. In most cases, politics would not convey the proper meaning, for one of its English connotations is "... political activities characterized by artful and often dishonest practices."

宣传 and propaganda. 宣传 is a neutral term in China, meaning to explain to the people in order to convince them, and then ask them to take actions accordingly. But in Western countries, propaganda is seen as quite a biased term, meaning to influence decisions by way of over-stating or exaggerating facts and circumstances in a self interest way.

唯物主义者 and materialist. The following quote tells the meaning of materialist: "Quite frankly, I'm a materialist. I've got a good-paying job and I want to keep it. I've bought a home near Westlake, and my wife and I want to enjoy the comforts of life. I had a hard time when I was a kid and I don't want to go through all that again." And 唯物主义, being fearless, dauntless in the Marxist sense commonly used in China today, denotes something quite different from what is implied in the quote above.

The following examples belong to the fourth category: terms in two languages that are only partly equivalent.

知识分子 and intellectual. In China, the term 知识分子 generally includes college teachers, college students, and such people as medical doctors, engineers, interpreters—people who have had a college education—and middle school teachers. In many Chinese rural areas, even middle school students are considered 知识分子. In English speaking countries, however, intellectuals would include only people of high academic status such as college professors, but not ordinary college students. So the term covers a much smaller range of people. Another difference is that intellectual is not always a complimentary term in English. It is sometimes used in a derogatory sense.

社会科学 and social science. They are not completely equal. The Chinese term covers all the fields not in the natural and applied sciences. This would include what are called the humanities in English: language, literature, philosophy, etc., the branches of learning dealing mainly with the cultural aspects of civilization. The English term, however, covers a smaller area of learning—political science, economics, history (which is often classified under the humanities), sociology, etc., branches of learning that study human society, especially its organization and relationship of individual members to it.

玩 and play. An American teacher was stunned when more than one male student said to her: "I played with my girl friend yesterday." According to the American teacher, play here means sex relationship. It doesn't have the same meaning as in "play football, basketball" etc.

同事 and colleague. In China 同事 is used to refer to those who work together in an office, in a company, in a school or in a factory. But colleague in English includes those who are in the same profession whether they work for the same organization or other organizations inside or outside the country. In this sense, colleague should contain the meanings of the two Chinese terms: 同事 and 同行. The following are more examples of the fifth category: things or concepts in one language that have fewer or more terms in the other. In the sense of a teacher, Chinese has many more synonyms: 教师, 老师, 教员, 导师, 师长, 先生等.

骆驼: In Chinese this is the only term for the animal; in English there is camel. But in Arabic, it's said that there are more than 400 words for the animal. The camel is of far greater importance as a means of travel with most Arabic-speaking people.

雪: In English and Chinese, there is only one word to describe all of the possible kinds of snow. But Eskimos have as many as thirty-two different words for snow. They have different words for falling snow, snow on the ground, snow packed as hard as ice, wind-driven snow, and so on. In contrast, cultures that rarely experience cold weather and snow have only one word to express several concepts that are differentiated in English or Chinese. For example, the ancient Aztec language of Mexico used only one word to mean snow, cold and ice.

副: In Chinese there is only one term expressing this meaning, while in English there are more terms showing the position below the highest rank, such as vice, associate, assistant, deputy, lieutenant, and under①.

# 【Activity 8】

Colors have both similar and different meanings in different languages. For example, black is the color of mourning; red symbolizes danger, violence, or bloodshed; if you're afraid of something, you're yellow. But none of these sayings is true outside the English-speaking world. In China and other Eastern Asian countries white is the color of mourning. In Russia red stands for beauty and life. In Italy and Germany you're yellow with anger, not with fear.

*Work in small groups and discuss what connotations red, white and yellow have in Chinese and English cultures respectively.*

## Discussion

RED is usually associated with celebrations and joyful occasions in both cultures. So in English we find, for example, red-letter days—holidays such as Christmas and other special days. "To paint the town red" means to celebrate, to go out to drink and have a good time. "Roll out the red carpet for someone" means to give a lavish welcome, as in: He was the first European head of state to visit their country, and they rolled out the red carpet for him. In Chinese we have 红双喜, 开门红, 红利, 红运, 红榜, 红娘, 红火, 又红又专 etc. (But 红眼病 in English is green eyed, because green has the connotation of jealousy or envy.) However, in English RED also has some negative connotations. For example, the thief

---

① Instances of these words: vice-chairman, vice-president, vice-chancellor; associate professor, associate director; assistant manager, assistant secretary; deputy director, deputy chief-of-staff; lieutenant governor, lieutenant general; under secretary (of State, U.S.).

was caught red-handed. Other examples are "get or go into the red（be in debt），" "see red（lose control of oneself through anger or indignation），" and "red-light district" （a part of a town where one can hire prostitutes, so the modern Chinese Beijing opera *The Red Lantern Story* was often misunderstood by native English speakers）.

WHITE has certain similar connotations in both languages：purity, innocence, 洁白无瑕, 清白无辜. But there are differences. For example, in English there are white lies that refer to trivial, harmless, or well-intentioned untruths. In Chinese we have a lot of terms containing the color white. The following are just a few of them that may be confusing when we attempt to express them in English. One is 红白喜事. Its proper translation would be "weddings and funerals." This is because white is the traditional color for brides at Western weddings. To have white at funerals would be offensive; and to have funerals described as happy occasions would be absolutely shocking to Westerners, although the expression reflects a certain philosophic attitude of the Chinese toward death. Another is 皮肤白/黑. In English neither white nor black is used to describe one's complexion. Fair/dark may be the choice.

YELLOW appears in such Chinese expressions as 黄色书刊, 黄色电影, 黄色音乐, 黄色网站. Originally in China yellowness was the symbol of nobility and authority. This obscene meaning derives from the English terms：yellow press, yellow covered literature, and yellow journals etc. which are vulgar and sensational publishing, not something obscene. 黄色 in the above sense should be translated into English as pornographic, trashy, obscene, filthy, or vulgar, as in pornographic pictures, obscene movies, filthy books, or vulgar music. In English yellow carries the connotation of caution and cowardice.

# 【Activity 9】

Words for animals and plants usually have the same denotations in different languages, but very often have distinct connotations. One of the authors of this book went to Canada on a study tour in 1999. On the departure, one Canadian friend gave each member of the group a gift：a sculpture of an animal. One member was quite puzzled when she received an owl. She didn't feel happy until she got the explanation.

*Why was she unhappy about the gift? Did the Canadian mean to hurt her? Discuss the questions in groups.*

## Discussion

This is because Chinese and English native speakers assign different associative meanings to the same bird—owl. Owl in China is the sign of bad luck. The mere sight of an owl or the sound of the creature's hooting is enough to cause people to draw back in fear. But in English it is associated with wisdom. In children's books and cartoons, whenever there is a dispute among birds or beasts, it is the owl that acts as judge. In moments of crisis, it is the owl that they go for advice. The above mentioned Chinese lady who got the "strange" gift felt quite satisfied when she got the explanation. Other animals have different connotations too.

The term dog elicits different feelings in these two cultures. In China gou（dog）often has derogative meanings, such as 狗急跳墙, 狗仗人势, 狼心狗肺, 狗腿子 etc. But the animal "dog" in the West is considered the best friend of man, which is well established in their cultures. So they feel disgusted at eating dog meat. In most cases dog is positive in its connotations. Mohamed ElBaradei, Director General of International Atomic Energy Agency (IAEA), said when interviewed① by Mr. Shui Junyi (水均益) that the function of IAEA is a watchdog that barks when it senses some danger. Other examples include: "You lucky dog." "Every dog has its day." "Love me, love my dog." "He worked like a dog." "You can't teach an old dog new tricks."

Long (龙) is a symbol of the emperor in ancient China. It has been almighty to us Chinese. Today long is often identified with China or Chinese. For example, we compare China to a massive dragon soaring high. We often refer to ourselves as the descendant of the long. Many Chinese parents 望子成龙—longing to see their sons become longs, that is, be successful. The Chinese long has been rendered in English as "dragon." This translation is inappropriate, because to the English-speaking people, dragon is a fire-spitting monster, cruel and fierce that destroys and therefore must be destroyed. That is why the English version of 亚洲四小龙 is "The Four Tigers of Asia" instead of "The Four Dragons of Asia."

Phoenix, in Western mythology, is associated with rebirth and resurrection. According to Greek legend, the phoenix lives a certain number of years—500 by one account. At the end of the period, it makes a nest, sings a death song, then sets fire to its nest by flapping its wings. The phoenix is burned to ashes, but from these ashes emerges a new bird. Thus, when a town, a place, or the headquarters building of an organization is destroyed by fire or other form of disaster, well-wishers may express the hope that it will, like the legendary phoenix, rise from the ashes in new splendor. In Chinese

mythology, the phoenix was regarded as the king of birds. The male was called feng (凤), the female Huang (凰). It is considered by Chinese as a creature of good omen.

The bat is usually associated with negative qualities in the West. "As blind as a bat," "crazy as a bat," "he's a bit batty," "have bats in the belfry" are typical expressions of negative associations. Mention of the word bat often evokes the image of an ugly, sinister, blood-sucking creature. The emotions aroused in English speaking people are similar to those that the dreaded owl arouses among Chinese: fright and revulsion. To Chinese, however, the bat is a symbol of good fortune, well-being, and happiness—all positive qualities. The reason for such associations is probably because the name of the creature is pronounced the same as the word 福 (happiness), thus the popularity of the traditional design that shows the bat and the deer

---

① Top Talk, program of CCTV Channel 1, broadcasted on Jan. 7, 2007.

together, 蝠鹿, pronounced as 福禄—good fortune, happiness, wealth and position.

The peacock in China is the symbol of luck. But in English it has the connotation of being proud of oneself and showy, as in the phrase: as proud as a peacock.

"'You chicken!' he cried, looking at Tom with contempt." Here chicken means a coward, a person without courage. In Chinese timidity is associated with the rat. Sometimes this is also true in English.

The beaver is chiefly a North American animal. Its constant activity, its habit of gnawing down trees and building complex "homes," and its skill and ingenuity in doing this have earned for the animal the name "eager beaver." In metaphor, an eager beaver is a person who is anxious to get things done, works hard, and is somewhat impatient.

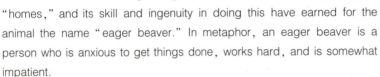

To most Westerners, "the king of the beasts" is the lion. The lion enjoys high prestige, as can be seen from such expressions as "regal as a lion," "majestic as a lion." In his poem, Shelley calls on the oppressed to "rise like lions." But to Chinese, it is the tiger that more likely evokes such associations, which can be seen in phrases like 虎将, 虎虎生威, 虎老雄心在, etc.

In Chinese there are many metaphors with the ox: 执牛耳, 初生牛犊不怕虎, 牛刀小试, 老黄牛, 牛鬼蛇神, 钻牛角尖 etc. In English, the horse, instead, is used in a lot of metaphors: a dark horse (unexpected winner), a willing horse (a helpful person who often gets all the work to do), put the cart before the horse, you may take a horse to the water, but you can't make him drink (don't ask others to do what they find difficult or what they don't want to), horse sense (common sense), talk horse (boast), etc. In Chinese there is a phrase 力大如牛, meaning "as strong as an ox." But in English the similar meaning is expressed by "as strong as a horse."

The same ordinary insect cricket is in English a happy insect, as in the phrase "as merry as a cricket," but in Chinese it signifies the coming of autumn, so there is always a feeling of sadness attached to it.

In Chinese, 松, 柏, 鹤, 桃 stand for longevity. In Chinese paintings and art designs, 松 and 鹤 often appear together with the motto 松鹤延年. But their equivalents in English pine, cypress, crane and peach do not have such connotations. Pine, bamboo and plum blossom (松, 竹, 梅, 岁寒三友) are admired in China because they are believed to possess a quality that is highly valued—resisting coldness (wickedness). In English they are just plants.

Daffodil in English signifies spring time and merriment as can be found in some English poems. But in Chinese, it is just a flower with no associative meaning attached to it.

## C Styles of Discourse

Discourse is a term with many definitions. Within linguistics, discourse is used to refer to language and linguistic structure above the sentence level. In spite of the variety in understanding discourse, one thing is clear: there is a concern with extended texts and the use of language and structures above the level of the sentence. Examples of discourse forms include letters, jokes, stories, chapters, sermons, speeches, arguments, interviews, business dealings, instruction, and conversations. Some of them are spoken, some are written. A spoken discourse represents the joint product of all the participants in the situation, while a written discourse represents the one-sided product of a discourse by the participants who compose the text. Discourses are conditioned by cultural factors.

Chinese and English are quite different languages used in quite different cultures. So we naturally expect different styles of discourse. Our concern here is not the grammatically correct use of language, but the cultural differences that affect the getting across of meaning. Neglect of this aspect may result in unexpected, even shocking, responses from the listener or reader, while the response to mere grammatical errors is usually that of understanding.

## 【Activity 10】

*The following is taken from a handout (in both Chinese and English) about a Dragon Boat Festival celebration held in a Chinese city. Compare the Chinese original with its English version, and then tell whether you think the versions are acceptable in either language.*

中华大地,江河纵横;华夏文化,源远流长……轻快的龙舟如银河流星,瑰丽的彩船似海市蜃楼,两岸那金碧辉煌的彩楼连成一片水晶宫,是仙境? 是梦境? 仰视彩鸽翩飞,低眸漂灯流霓,焰火怒放火树银花,灯舞回旋千姿百态,气垫船腾起一江春潮,射击手点破满天彩球,跳伞健儿绽空中花蕾,抢鸭勇士谱水上凯歌……啊,××城是不夜城,龙舟会是群英会!

The divine land of China has its rivers flowing across; the brilliant culture of China has its root tracing back long...

The lightsome dragon-boats appear on the river as though the stars twinkle in the milk-way. The richly decorated pleasure boats look like a scene of mirage. The splendid awnings in green and gold chain into a palace of crystal. Is this a fairyland or a mere dream? Looking above, you can see the doves flying about; looking below, you can see the sailing lamps glittering. Crackling are the fireworks, which present you with a picture of fiery trees and silver flowers. Circling are the lantern-dancers, who present you with a variation of exquisite manner. Over there, the motorboats are plowing the water, thus a wash stirs up. Over there, the marksmen are shooting at their targets, thus colorful beads whirl around, ... all claim a strong appeal to you. Therefore, we should say: ××× is a city of no night; its Dragon-Boat Festival a gathering of heroes.

## Discussion

Professor Duan Liancheng thinks that the Chinese version seems acceptable, but the very "faithful" translation in English sounds odd. The American journalist, who Professor Duan invited to read the English version and give his comments and sentiments, wrote:

My first reaction was unfortunately laughter because it is so full of mistakes. It omits some necessary information about the Dragon-Boat Festival, including its historical origins and when it actually takes place. These things are important... The copy seems to try to "snow" the reader with fanciful, overblown assertions about how terrific it all is, but in unintentionally hilarious language that leaves the reader laughing out uninformed... The brochure also suffers from lack of background material, the taking-it-for-granted that the reader already is familiar with many aspects of Chinese history and culture... It doesn't tell you where to go, how to get there, when things are open and closed, how much they cost, and so forth. All these are things people visiting an area want to know.

Why is it that many Chinese travel guides read basically the same, no matter what region is being written about, and are so packed with indiscriminate hyperbole? Less exaggeration would actually be more convincing.

This reaction may indicate that there is some difference in the discourse style. According to some researchers, this difference is that there are more adjectives, proverbs and allusions in Chinese writing than in English writing. This is at least partly true, considering that the wide use of well-known "four-character expressions" is usually approved, and even encouraged by Chinese. Some Western scholars name this style "flowery," stating that its aim is to give a more fanciful impression than information, and the impression is usually of beauty, fragrance, happiness, and any other "goodness" aspects so as to attract people. We think that this style does appear in some Chinese discourses, but of course not in all!

This feature seems confusing to Westerners. Why? One interpretation could be that Westerners are generally low-context communicators who tend to lay emphasis on information instead of on impression. So their discourse pattern is different in that it is more direct with objective information. To them, much-repeated words may mean less after a while. Clichés are an example. A cliché is an expression that loses its punch through overuse. Used sparingly, "That's really great!" may get a listener's special attention. If it's used too often, however, it does not mean much to most listeners. Common expressions of courtesy often lose meaning. Chances are that a casual acquaintance who asks "How are you?" doesn't really want to know. Therefore, a native English speaker would frown on this sentence: He slept like a dog and woke up at the crack of dawn, fresh as a daisy, as it contains three clichés: "slept like a dog, " "at the crack of dawn," and "fresh as a daisy." In order to make this difference clearer, we may term the two styles as impression-oriented and information-oriented.

Another case in point is the difference in the use of proverbs. While English proverbs are part of the oral culture in the United States, they are not used in writing as often as those in Chinese. Good writers in Chinese often begin an essay with a Chinese proverb. It shows knowledge of the past, an important Chinese value. But Americans do not value the past as much as the Chinese do. They think it is more important to think of something new and original. So a good writer in English will try to explain ideas in a new way and not use proverbs if possible.

To conclude, what we should remember is that adjectives are necessary in good writing. But if overused, they can have an opposite effect—quickly kill interest and produce boredom. This is true of both Chinese and English. But one problem remains: how many adjectives in one piece of writing are thought to be too many? The appropriateness varies from language to language. Therefore, the remark by the American journalist about the English version of the handout is just made from the perspective of his own home culture. It tells us something about the English communication style. And it alerts us to the fact that we have to take culture into consideration when we use a language other than our own.

# 【Activity 11】

*Study the following two versions of the same spoken discourse presented at a business meeting between Hong Kong Chinese and Anglo-North American businessmen. Decide in small groups which one might have been given by a Chinese and which by an American, and what is the reasoning behind your decision.*

A. Because most of our production is done in China now, and uh, it's not really certain how Hong Kong will be like after 1997, and since I think a certain amount of caution in committing to TV advertisement is necessary because of the expense. So, I suggest that we delay making our decision until after Legco makes its decision.

B. I suggest that we delay making our decision until after Legco makes its decision. That's because I think a certain amount of caution in committing to TV advertisement is necessary because of the expense. In addition to that, most of our production is done in China now, and it's not really certain how Hong Kong will be like after 1997.

## Discussion

This concerns the way in which ideas are organized. The message of both versions is the same but the way it is expressed is different. The first version is the speech in English by a Chinese. There is little difficulty in understanding at the level of the words and sentences which are clear enough. Listening to it, however, English natives may have a feeling that it is not quite clear what the speaker's main point is. The second version is what the Westerner might expect. The reason lies in the different discourse patterns which Chinese (and other Asians) and native English speakers use respectively. The deductive (topic-first) pattern is prevalent in the West. Chinese and other Asians tend to favor the inductive (topic-delayed) pattern. Therefore, some people maintain that Westerners are in the habit of directly expressing themselves, while Chinese employ an indirect way when presenting their ideas.

This feature is also displayed in sentences. Linguist Zhao Yuanren suggested that half of Chinese discourses use a "topic-comment" structure. In a sentence with such a structure, the topic part lists person(s), object(s) or concept(s) and the comment part develops the topic part. That is to say, the conclusion usually comes in the end part. In English the "subject-predicate" structure is prevailing. The "topic-comment" and "subject-predicate" are two different terms. The former describes information structure, while the latter describes grammatical structure.

We find from the above that the way people organize their ideas is very important, and that native Chinese and English speakers differ greatly in this aspect. However, we are not usually aware of this important fact. So it is worthwhile to spend a little more time on this point. You will find different aspects of the same issue in Activities 11-14.

# 【Activity 12】

*From Activity 11 we know that Chinese and Westerners have different spoken discourse patterns. Chinese favor the inductive or indirect way while Westerners prefer the deductive or direct style. Here are two examples of written discourse, one by a Chinese student and one by an American. Read them and decide whether the same difference in spoken discourse is also found in written discourse.*

A. Why Is English Important to Scientists

Today English has been the most wide-used language. When a scientist draws a conclusion after a long period of study, he wants to let other people know his discovery. How should he do? If he writes the paper in his native language, only some persons understand it. If he writes in English, then more people will know it. So other scientists may discuss it and draw different conclusions. It is good for the development of the science field. To other scientists, they can get news about their study. English, as a useful tool, it is helpful for the scientists to communicate the information. If every scientist knows about English, he can see other's opinions without difficulty. So English is important to scientists.

B. Synonyms

Synonyms, words that have the same basic meaning, do not always have the same emotional meaning. For example, the words "stingy" and "frugal" both mean "careful with money." However, to call a person stingy is an insult, while the word frugal has a much more positive connotation. Similarly, a person wants to be slender but not skinny, and aggressive, but not pushy. Therefore, you should be careful in choosing words because many so-called synonyms are not really synonyms at all.

## Discussion

Wang Moxi and Li Jin from Shanghai Science & Technology University conducted a survey on the writing pattern of Chinese students. One conclusion from the survey is that when doing narration Chinese students and English students have the similar thought pattern (problem—solution). But when it comes to exposition and argumentation, the difference is distinct.

In exposition and argumentation, writing in English has often been characterized as based almost entirely on a deductive thought pattern. In this pattern, one properly begins with a general topic sentence and then systematically restricts its meaning by presenting more specific details at several levels of generality. This pattern is also referred to as a direct or linear approach. The Chinese pattern, however, is the inductive format (moving from specific details to generalities). It is also thought of as the pattern of indirection. Its feature is that at the beginning, the author presents the relevant situation, with the topic in his mind. He develops around the hidden topic until the last when the topic finally appears. He may expect that the reader will infer the main idea from signals such as necessary, must, want, have to, if, difficulty, if not, etc.

Other Asians display the similar style of writing. Kyeongja Kim (1996), Professor Hu Wenzhong's graduate student in the USA, compared passages written by Korean students and American students. She found that Korean students tended to place the main idea near the end, while American students tend to state their main idea at the beginning.

To sum up, native English speakers tend to be deductive (topic-first) in organizing ideas while Asian people seem to prefer the indirect (topic-delayed) way. Each is reasonable in its own cultural context.

## 【Activity 13】

*Activities 11 and 12 suggest that Westerners prefer the deductive pattern of discourse while Chinese favor the inductive pattern of discourse. Do Chinese never use the deductive pattern or English native speakers never use the inductive pattern? When you talk with your friends, will you be direct or indirect? Explain.*

*Then read the letter written by a talented and promising American musician to his agent, and try to figure out what discourse pattern is employed and why.*

Mr. David Bashaw

Beautiful Noise Industries

485 Wilcox Street

Los Angeles, CA 90087

Dear Mr. Bachaw,

I appreciated very much the work you've done on my behalf during the past four years. You have contacted most of the major recording studios, introduced me to some very influential people in the business, sent out dozens of demo tapes that I recorded, and widely publicized my music in other ways as well. I don't doubt that you have done your job quite thoroughly. However, after all this time, I still have not been able to get a recording contract. I will have a hard time paying my bills if I continue to try to make a living as a musician. Because I feel that it's time to move on with my life, I hereby notify you that I must terminate my association with your agency. Thank you for all of your help. I wish you better luck with your other clients.

Sincerely,

Chris Jenkins

## Discussion

Our own experiences tell us that Chinese students usually feel entirely free to just call up a friend and say, "Let's go to a movie," or "Let's go play a game." when they come across a friend on campus. They are quite direct in introducing the topic. Another exception to this so-called Eastern inductive pattern is the situation such as calling a taxi, paying an electricity bill, or buying a bus ticket. In such cases, the pattern appears to be simply topic, without any preliminary communication. In other words, in the East where people are in a close relationship to each other and of relatively equal status, the normal pattern is the deductive pattern. This shows that the Chinese do use a deductive style of communication.

This letter above is obviously in the pattern of induction. It tells us that Westerners do not exclude the use of the inductive pattern. The letter writer may feel that he and the other party have been close, so he has to be polite by delaying the topic until much later. Let's consider the situation in which one is going to a friend with the intention of borrowing a large sum of money or asking for some big or embarrassing favor. In such a situation the person would understandably be reluctant to come out with his/her topic at the outset of the conversation. This is because the request carries too much "weight of imposition". In another situation where the superior and the subordinate are involved, the superior tends to be deductive while the subordinate person is more likely to be inductive in their spoken or written communication. To sum up, when communication is conducted between people of unequal status, the person in a higher status tends to use the deductive pattern in introducing the topic, while the person in a lower status tends to use the inductive pattern in doing so. This is true of both east and west.

Therefore, we can conclude (from what has been discussed in the above activities) that both inductive and deductive patterns are used in Chinese (Asian) and Western communications, though it is also true that comparatively speaking the deductive pattern is more often used in the West while the inductive style is more prevalent in the East.

## 【Activity 14】

*Read the following short essay and identify the respective characteristics of the written discourse in English, Arabic and Persian, Spanish and Asian languages.*

Culture, Logic and Rhetoric

 Logic, which is the basis of rhetoric, comes from culture; it is not universal. Rhetoric, therefore, is not universal either, but varies from culture to culture. The rhetorical system of one language is neither better nor worse than the rhetorical system of another language, but it is different.

English logic and English rhetoric, which are based on Anglo-European cultural patterns, are linear—that is, a good English paragraph begins with a general statement of its content and then carefully develops that statement with a series of specific illustrations. A good English paragraph may also use just the reverse sequence: it may state a whole series of examples and then summarize those examples in a single statement at the end of the paragraph. In either case, however, the flow of ideals occurs in a straight line from the opening sentence to the last sentence. Furthermore, a well-structured English paragraph is never digressive (wandering away from the main topic). There is nothing that does not belong to the paragraph, and nothing that does not support the topic sentence.

A type of construction found in Arabic and Persian writing is very different. Whereas English writers use a linear sequence, Arabic and Persian writers tend to construct a paragraph in a parallel sequence using many coordinators, such as "and" and "but." In English, maturity of style is often judged by the degree of subordination rather than by the degree of coordination. Therefore, the Arabic and Persian styles of writing, with their emphasis on coordination, seem awkward and immature to an English reader.

Some Asian writers, on the other hand, use an indirect approach. In this kind of writing, the topic is viewed from a variety of angles. The topic is never analyzed directly; it is referred to only indirectly. Again, such a development in an English paragraph is awkward and unnecessarily vague to an English reader.

Spanish rhetoric differs from English rhetoric in still another way. While the rules of English rhetoric require that every sentence in a paragraph relate directly to the central idea, a Spanish-speaking writer loves to fill a paragraph with interesting digressions. Although a Spanish paragraph may begin and end on the same topic, the writer often digresses into areas that are not directly related to the topic. Spanish rhetoric, therefore, does not follow the English rule of paragraph unity.

In summary, a student who has mastered the grammar of English may still write poor papers unless the rhetoric of English is also mastered. Also, the student may have difficulty reading an essay written by the rules of English rhetoric unless he/she understands the "logical" differences from those of his/her own native tongue.

## Discussion

Rhetoric, or the concept of organizing words, sentences, and paragraphs in a particular way in order to achieve a particular end affects how credible an audience will perceive a given oral or written discourse. Rhetoric could be worked as a Persuasive Tactic. Rhetoric is normally employed to convince people to think something in particular, or to take a certain side in a debate or discussion. The main value of rhetoric for an advertiser, for example, is to convince potential buyers that a certain product is superior to those of the competitors. Politicians also use rhetoric to convince the public that they are going to be better at running the country or state than their competitors.

A person in ordinary life can also use rhetoric to do things like convince friends and coworkers of certain thoughts, allegiances, or ideals. Newspaper column writers also use it to convince readers to take their view on a particular issue or event. The tactic is particularly common in the editorials section, for instance.

Specific uses of rhetoric can be partially determined by the rhetorical device itself. For example, metaphor is one commonly used form of rhetoric, in which two different things are compared by referring to one as if it were the other. Metaphor can be used by a politician to insinuate that his or her opponent shares characteristics with anything of their choosing. An example of this would be a politician who isn't currently in power referring to the White House as his opponent's "playground," to suggest that the incumbent is childlike and therefore unsuited to power. Likewise, an advertiser might use metaphor to insinuate that its product is superior or an opponent's is inferior by associating it with something else, ideally something with a commonly negative association.

But unfortunately, there is no single, universal rhetorical standard. Rather, human rhetorical expectations and preferences vary from group to group and culture to culture, as is indicated by the above passage. Moreover, these cultural rhetorical differences can occur on a variety of levels (from the choice of words, the sentence to the overall discourse). The point is that when reading or speaking in another language, the reader or speaker usually unconsciously prefers the rhetorical patterns of their native culture and even judges the effectiveness of other language discourses according to their own cultural rhetorical expectations. This is what we should be aware of.

## D Discourse Patterns and Thought Patterns

As the Sapir-Whorf hypothesis suggests, language and thoughts are closely related. The reason why people have different discourse patterns is probably due to the differences in their modes of thinking. And the mode of thinking is connected with the worldview, which influences all aspects of our perception and consequently affects our belief and value systems, as well as how we  think and act. Scholars like Humbold and Ji Xianlin (季羡林) maintain that the difference in languages is not just a difference in sounds and signs, but a difference in worldviews. (For detailed study of worldviews, see Chapter 2.)

From Chapter 2 we know that generally speaking Westerners tend to be dualistic in their outlook while Chinese are inclined to believe in holism. Accordingly, with regards to modes of

thinking, people nurtured in Western culture tend to dissect things into parts and analyze their relationships in order to understand them properly. Their emphasis is upon the parts rather than upon the whole of things. People brought up in Chinese culture are likely to synthesize elements into a unit, with the emphasis on the "whole," the systematic and synthetic perceptions of objects.

When it comes to problem solving, the Western mind is generally trained to think in terms of cause and effect, that is, in a linear line. If something is wrong, they find the cause and fix it. However, the Chinese tend to think in terms of webs of thoughts and relationships, or in a circular way. They usually make a comprehensive survey of the overall situation, and then think over details.

As analytical thinking prevails in the West, people in that culture tend to be good at classification and categorization and to pursue dichotomies such as good and bad, God and the devil, the individual and the whole, in a word, "A" or "not-A." This may lead to the fact that they prefer making use of concepts for logical judgment and reasoning. Another trait results: abstraction. Abstraction is synonymous with precision and clarity. This characteristic can be found in Western languages.

The Chinese synthetic mode of thinking has its own traits. It usually leads to the emphasis on gaining intuitive insight and thinking in terms of images. Precision and accuracy is not emphasized.

The following activities are on different modes of thinking.

## ■ Synthetic Thinking and Analytic Thinking

## 【Activity 15】

*Think about the layouts of a Western hospital and a Traditional Chinese Medicine ( TCM) clinic. How do a Western doctor and a TCM doctor treat patients respectively? What are the differences? Discuss in groups and try to offer some interpretations.*

### Discussion

The differences in the modes of thinking are clearly reflected in the unlikeness between Western medicine and TCM. Western medicine divides the human body into different parts and treats them accordingly. In a Western hospital, patients have to go to different departments to get treated. A doctor treats his patient by examining parts of the body through tests ( detailed analysis) and X-rays before making a diagnosis. Chinese medicine, however, takes the patient as an organic whole, requiring the consideration of the connections of all parts of the body. A

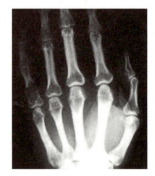

TCM doctor treats his patient by looking at his complexion and the coating on his tongue, feeling his

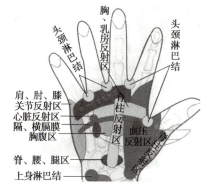

pulse and eliciting his complaints in order to form a correct judgment of his general physical condition. He tries to get at the root of the trouble and aims at a permanent cure rather than apply a palliative remedy. As a result, a patient suffering from severe headache may get some foot treatment, as some xuewei①, are believed to be connected with certain parts of the head. Although such xuewei are hard to prove by means of modern scientific instruments, the treatment has worked for thousands of years in China.

## 【Activity 16】

*Study the following paintings. Discuss in groups and try to find some differences between the Chinese and Western paintings.*

## Discussion

The differences in the modes of thinking can also be found in the art of painting. First, it can be seen from the pictures here that the Chinese painting is a synthesis of different art forms: calligraphy, painting, poetry and stamp. In the West, however, painting is painting and poetry is poetry. They are quite different and therefore are treated accordingly. Second, in Chinese painting the eye of the viewer is assumed to move across the surface of the painting, while in the Western painting there was only one focal point, one spot from which the viewer looks at the painting. Third, Western paintings seem to be more true to life, precision being obvious. But the Chinese painter seeks close resemblance in spirit instead of accurate likeness in appearance. In addition, landscapes are conventional themes in Chinese painting, through which artists express both inner harmony and harmony with the natural surroundings.

---

① xuewei: 穴位, some invisible but crucial points in the body.

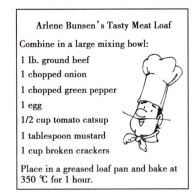

**Arlene Bunsen's Tasty Meat Loaf**

Combine in a large mixing bowl:

1 lb. ground beef
1 chopped onion
1 chopped green pepper
1 egg
1/2 cup tomato catsup
1 tablespoon mustard
1 cup broken crackers

Place in a greased loaf pan and bake at 350 ℃ for 1 hour.

Even in cooking, differences in thought patterns can be seen. The Western style of cooking is relatively more scientific: you are told exactly how much water, how many grams of salt, sugar and other ingredients are needed for a certain dish, how many minutes, how strong the heat, etc. the food takes to be cooked. But what a Chinese recipe tells you is roughly a little oil, a little salt, etc. You have no idea exactly how much each of the ingredients is. A Chinese cook usually senses how much by their experience and produces delicious dishes. An apprentice learns cooking not by following recipes with precise quantitative descriptions, but by intuitively acquiring his master's technique after repeated imitations.

## ■ Concrete Thinking and Abstract Thinking

## 【Activity 17】

*A. The ways of the ancient Chinese and Greeks to prove the theorem of triangle are different. One is found in the Zhou Bi Suan Jing①. The other is Euclid's② Proposition 47 next page.*

*Compare them and see which one can be understood intuitively and more easily, and which one cannot be so understood and why.*

*B. Compare one Chinese idiom with its English translation. What differences can you find between them?*

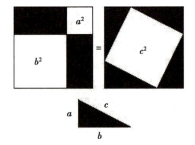

Chinese idiom: Zuo chi shan kong (坐吃山空, "Sit eat mountain empty")

English translation: If you only sit and eat and do nothing, even a fortune as big as a mountain will vanish.

### Discussion

These examples to some degree illustrate the different modes of thinking between the Chinese and the Westerners. Case A tells us that the Chinese thinking tends to be concrete or intuitive. The relationship of the lines of a triangle is made clear by the diagram itself, thus no abstract reasoning is necessary. In contrast, the Euclid's Proposition is to be understood by abstract deduction. This example provides some evidence to show the preferred modes of thinking of Chinese and Westerners: concrete/intuitional thinking and abstract/rational thinking. Case B reflects the difference in thought patterns. It seems that Chinese thinking depends more on images, metaphors and analogies, while Western thinking tends to be more circumspect, depending more on concept, judgment and reasoning.

In conclusion, Western thinking tends to be more analytical, statistical, rational, and circumspect,

---

① *Zhou Bi Suan Jing*:《周髀算经》,据认为成书于汉代,约公元前 100 年,提出了"勾三股四弦五"定理, a work on astronomy and mathematics, assumed to be written in 100 B.C.

② Euclid: a Greek mathematician, about 325 B.C.–265 B.C.

laying more emphasis on objectivity, specificity and precision. Chinese thinking, however, is more likely to be synthetic, intuitive, and concrete, valuing subjectivity and wholeness. The Western thinking is characteristic of the Aristotelian modes of reasoning. It views man as a rational being capable of factual and sound reasoning. In the Taoist view, however, man is not a rational being, nor is truth to be conceived in terms of reason and logic. Taoist philosophy states that human life is conditional and not free, and only when man recognizes this limitation and makes himself dependent upon the harmonious and beneficent forces of the cosmos does he achieve success. Tao teaches the wisdom of being foolish, the success of failure, the strength of weakness, and the futility of contending for power—all of which might be seen as irrational by the traditional Western mind. The basic philosophy of Taoism is based on the need to achieve harmony with the cosmos. Thus this relationship  is what it pursues. According to the Western way of thinking, something is generally either "A" or "not-A." But the Taoist easily combines these two by seeing a rational relationship between them. There are endless examples that can be observed from nature. A tree limb that is strong and does not bend eventually breaks under the increasing weight of winter snow, but the weak limb—the one that is limber and bends—gives way to the weight of the snow and lets it fall to the ground before enough can accumulate to break the limb. Weakness is perceived as strength; strength is seen as weakness. In terms of Tao, this is rational.

Sure enough, there is no absolute distinction between cultures. Exceptions are numerous and counter-evidence exists due to the extreme complexity of culture. In fact, the Chinese and the Western cultures do share quite a lot in spite of their differences. These observations are intended to facilitate a global understanding of the main historic trends in our home culture and the Western culture, the culture of English speaking countries in particular.

## REVISION TASKS

1. *Review this chapter with the help of the following questions.*

(1) How do you usually communicate with other people? Can you communicate with others without language? If yes, how much?

(2) What does language mean to you?

(3) How is language related to culture? How would the change of language over time reflect, facilitate, and perpetuate cultural change?

(4) Do you sometimes experience the difficulty in finding the counterpart of a Chinese word in English and vice versa? If so, why?

(5) Do you agree that most words in a language are culturally loaded?

(6) How do you understand the Sapir-Whorf hypothesis?

(7) What is thought to be the Chinese discourse pattern and the Western discourse pattern? How

do you look at them?

(8) How does the Chinese way of writing an address on the envelope differ from that of the English? Can you offer an interpretation for the difference?

(9) Comment on the analysis of synthetic thinking vs. analytic thinking and concrete thinking vs. abstract thinking. Give some examples to further analyze your comments.

(10) Can you offer your own interpretations for the Chinese and the Western modes of thinking?

## 2. *Complete the tasks below.*

(1) Study the statement by Ralph Ellison. "If the word has the potency to revive and make us free, it has also the power to blind, imprison and destroy." What does it tell you about his view on the relationship between language and thought? Do you agree with him?

(2) Read the paragraph about word meanings and see what conclusion you can draw from it on this point. Then compare the denotations and connotations of duty/责任 and family/家庭 and see how they are similar and different.

> A strong belief in democracy unites us;... However, look beneath the surface of our collective faith in democracy, and you'll find that we understand it in very different ways. Some say that democracy means government by the people, or the right to vote, or equality under the law. Others say it's the freedom of choice, or unlimited economic opportunity. Still others argue that democracy means the active participation of all citizens in shaping public policy, or economic as well as political justice.

(3) Read the quotation that follows and try to find out what language difference it reveals.

> The author of an Arab-English dictionary said to Hall: "I have spent the entire afternoon trying to find the Arab equivalent of the English word 'rape.' There is no such word in Arabic. All my sources, both written and spoken, can come up with no more than an approximation, such as 'He took her against her will.' There is nothing in Arabic approaching your meaning as it is expressed in that one word."

(4) How would you describe your mother or grandmother? Then study the remarks made by Linell Davis. Do you agree with them or not? Why? Give your detailed comments.

> Native English speakers teaching writing in China often comment that their students' writing is rich in visual and other sensory images, but at the same time they also say that it is too sentimental. What they mean is that Chinese students tend to idealize what they are writing about. The writer is presenting a person, memory, or situation as he or she thinks it should be rather than how it is observed to be. The writer may not intend to portray a realistic picture of the world. Foreign teachers cautioned one another, "Don't ask them to write an essay about their mothers or grandmothers. All you get is stereotypes about devotion and sacrifice. They will all sound alike."

(5) Study the case and then try to answer the questions that follow.

> Wu had just started working for a Swedish company that had extensive business commitments in China. A large part of his work concerned advising his expatriate colleagues on Chinese business practices. This involved both writing reports and recommendations and addressing meetings.

As he was very anxious to succeed, Wu always researched his topics thoroughly and tried to make his presentations as clear as possible. However, he gradually became aware that something was wrong. It often seemed that nobody listened to him and his advice was ignored. When he spoke at meetings, he felt that people were impatient and uninterested in what he had to say. He got more and more unhappy and began to feel that his colleagues were not interested in his opinions because he was Chinese. This, he thought, was racism.

The company had a policy of annual review, which meant that every staff member met with the managing director once a year to discuss his or her progress. When the time came for Wu's review, the managing director gave him a copy of the company's assessment of his performance. The assessment praised his hard work, but made the following, very serious criticisms: ① When speaking at meetings, arguments are often unfocused and speeches lack clear direction. ②Written reports contain too much irrelevant material. ③ In both speaking and writing, material is poorly organized, with important recommendations often appearing only at the end of the report. ④We often appears uncertain about the points he wants to make.

Wu was shocked by these criticisms. He could not understand why they had been made and he was not sure what to do about them.

## Questions

a. Why do you think the company criticized Wu in this way?

b. Do you think he is correct to conclude that the problem is racism?

c. What cultural expectations about presenting information orally and in writing may account for the negative evaluation of Wu's work?

d. Give advice to Wu on dealing with each of the specific criticisms the managing director made.

(6) In the traditional Chinese family, usually the wife's status is subordinate to her husband. The household is the wife's domain, and she actually manages the family business only when her husband is weak and incapable. Please discuss the following sayings that show the typical relationship between a husband and wife, and also a wife's subordinate status in the Chinese family of the feudal society.

"Follow the man you marry, be he a fool or a crook."

"The husband sings, the wife accompanies."

"Follow her father before she marries; follow her husband after she marries, follow her son after her husband dies."

(7) Traditionally, Chinese parents have enjoyed the freedom to decide their children's future. The basic difference in the relationship between parents and children in Chinese and American families is that Chinese as what children should do for their parents, and Americans ask what parents should do for their children. The communication between Chinese parents and children is one-way-from parents to children. Please discuss the following sayings that show the typical relationship between parents and children.

"Have ears but no mouth."

"Filial piety is the chief of the hundred virtues."

"Parents are always right."

(8) Positional role behavior within the traditional Chinese family is decided by three factors: in order of priority, generation, age and sex. Three features characterize the family structure: ① in the sex hierarchy, the maternal system is subordinate to the paternal line; ② age is the locus of power; and ③ males are superior to females. Please discuss the following common expressions of these cultural values in the daily life.

"A boy is better than two girls."

"An elderly man at home is like jade in the hand."

"Men rear sons to provide for old age."

"A married daughter is like water bursting its banks."

"Daughters must not be kept at home unmarried, if they are forcibly kept in this condition, it is sure to breed enmity."

"A virtuous woman cannot marry two husbands."

"Ignoring the old man's advice makes one stupid."

"A grown daughter cannot be kept unmarried for long."

"A girl will doll herself up for him who loves her."

"It is virtue for women to be without talent."

(9) Ancestor worship is one of the most distinctive features of the Chinese family system. It is one of the main components of Chinese family life. In the Chinese family, ancestor worship implies that the physical bodies of ancestors die, but their souls continue to live an watch over the life of their descendants with a supernatural power. In China, the function of ancestor worship is to reinforce the unity of the family and to enhance the generation-age-sex scheme of authority in the family.

## Questions

a. What are the common places do most of the Chinese worship their ancestors?

b. When do the Chinese worship their ancestors?

c. What do the Chinese do when they worship their ancestors? ( the food offerings, the rituals and etc.)

# Chapter 5

# Nonverbal Communication

*There's language in her eye, her cheek, her lip.* (William Shakespeare)

*Nobility and dignity, self-abasement and servility, prudence and understanding, insolence and vulgarity, are reflected in the face and in the attitudes of the body whether still or in motion.* (Socrates)

*While we speak with our vocal organs we converse with our whole bodies.* ( Author Unknown)

# I  Warm-up: Look and Say

A. Look at the picture on the right. How do you think the two people are related? How do you get that information, through verbal or nonverbal expressions? What are the ways other than language that also communicate?

B. What do you think of the following statement? "Your body doesn't know how to lie."

# II  Understanding Nonverbal Communication

From the Warm-up part we know something about nonverbal communication. It is obvious that the two people in A are very likely in love with each other. We know this from their physical touch, the way they stand, their eye contact and so forth. All of us have adopted those and many other means to communicate, consciously or unconsciously. We sometimes wave our hands when saying good-bye to somebody. We sometimes greet guests when they are introduced to us at a formal occasion. We let the speaker know that we are listening carefully in class by having eye contact with that speaker. In these cases we successfully communicate by using our hands, our eyes or by giving a smile. We may have wondered why we sometimes take an almost immediate liking to a person we have just met. We may have worried about why someone we were talking to suddenly became cold and distant. The chances are that it wasn't anything that was said, but something that happened: a gesture, a movement or a frown. In short, we convey a whole variety of information and emotions to others with our bodies. All this is non-verbal communication.

## A  Nonverbal Communication: Definition

As for culture and communication, there are a host of definitions of nonverbal behavior. We shall just select one that is consistent with the aim of this book. "Nonverbal communication involves all those nonverbal stimuli in a communication setting that are generated by both the source and his/her use of the environment and that have potential message value for the source or receiver." (Samovar, 2000:149) In other words, non-verbal communication refers to any form of communication that is not directly dependent on the use of language.

## B Nonverbal Communication: Importance

Nonverbal communication is a silent infiltrator, having broad influence over our social environment. It provides us with a mode for conveying messages without the use of verbal language. It may enhance or detract from a verbal communication. It regulates relationships by affecting the likelihood of introduction and continued interaction. We are able to infer emotion through nonverbal communication and influence other's perception of our competence, power and vulnerability. It also plays a role in the perception of the actual message we are trying to convey. It affects our lives in a myriad of ways from childhood throughout adulthood, and as long as we intend to communicate with others.

You may believe that in face-to-face communication your words carry the majority of the meaning of the message. But what some researchers have shown is otherwise. Anthropologists estimate that language accounts for only 35% of communication, while such cultural factors as nonverbal communication, basic cultural assumptions, and values affect the other 65%. Whether this estimation is right or wrong, it at least tells us that nonverbal behaviors are so important that they deserve much of our attention.

Nonverbal communication is important because we use the actions of others to learn about their affective or emotional states and to form impressions of others. And as the statement "Your body doesn't know how to lie" indicates, the messages sent by body behaviors tend to be more believable when they contradict the verbal messages, because many of our nonverbal actions such as blushing are not easily controlled consciously. As Greek philosopher Heraclitus remarked over two thousand years ago, "Eyes are more accurate witnesses than ears."

Nonverbal communication is especially important to the study of intercultural communication. Although a great deal of nonverbal behavior speaks a universal language, differences are found in nonverbal expressions of different peoples. More often than not, what is perfectly acceptable in one culture may be rude, or even obscene, in other cultures. By understanding important cultural differences in nonverbal behavior, you will be able to gather clues about underlying attitudes and values. Smiling and shaking hands tell us that a culture values amiability. Bowing tells us other values such as formality, rank, and status. You will also be conscious of your own ethnocentrism which you will try to isolate. You might, for instance, feel less critical about someone's body odor if you realize that the meanings attached to smell are culturally based. The following activity helps us see what problems may arise when the differences are not recognized or otherwise neglected.

## 【Activity 1】

*Read the passage next to the picture. What caused the indignation of the American people?*

When he visited the United States in 1959, the former Soviet Premier Nikita Khrushchev once used the clasped-hands-over-the-head gesture. The next day American newspapers printed it on first page, which shocked the whole country, and American people became indignant.

## Discussion

This is a famous example of how nonverbal behavior can be misunderstood. The gesture that Khrushchev used is for Russians a sign of friendship, of international goodwill, but was interpreted by most Americans as an arrogant gesture usually used by prizefighters after defeating an opponent. So the misunderstanding is obvious: the Soviet Union would defeat the United States.

This story illustrates how important it is to learn at least the basics of nonverbal communication.

## 【Activity 2】

*Read the following passage, and think what caused the misunderstanding between the man and the waiter.*

Meaning of Gestures in Different Cultures... Complimentary or Offensive?

In Greece, an American visited a local restaurant. He didn't speak their language. He ordered something indecipherable off the menu. When the waiter brought him a plate of delicious looking fried noodles, he smiled and made an OK sign at the waiter with his thumb and forefinger linked in a circle. Looking angry, the waiter then picked up the dish and thrown it to his lap. What he did wrong, he wondered. Well, nothing is quite as it seems when it comes to using hand gesture in another country.

## Discussion

If you are an English-speaking Caucasian and under the sea scuba diving around the world, it means "OK," "good," or "spot on." In fact, it was believed that this "OK" sign has been popularized by divers.

French understands it as "zero" or "worthless."

Japanese would read it as "money."

Don't show this to a Northern Greek. About 2000 years ago, ancient Greek vases have been found showing this gesture as a sexual insult. It is still thought the same way today. So, if you use this sign in northern Greece to tell a person that he is "ok," he will feel insulted.

Other regions where this sign can be sexually insulting are parts of Central and Mediterranean Europe, Germany, Turkey, Malta, Sardinia, Tunisia, Greece, Russia, Middle-East, Paraguay, Brazil.

## Ⓒ Nonverbal Communication: Functions

Nonverbal communication is thought to comprise six functions in human communication. These functions consist of complementing verbal messages, substituting for verbal messages, accenting verbal messages, contradicting verbal messages, repeating verbal messages, and regulating verbal messages. Each of these functions of nonverbal communication are, for the most part, missing during the course of using the Internet as a communication tool.

The complementing function of nonverbal communication includes nonverbal cues—such as tone of voice, facial expression, gestures, or distance between people—often serving to complement the verbal message and add to, clarify, or reinforce the meaning. The term "complement" indicates that the behavior alone would not communicate the intended message. "A complementing nonverbal message changes the meaning of the verbal message by adding additional insights or information." This function of nonverbal cues on the Internet is missing in any message sent by e-mail or chat. If a person writes "I hate college" on the Internet, we can't make an assumption on the truth of the statement without more information. They could be laughing when they say it, or frowning, or crying—all of those nonverbal cues would make a difference in determining the meaning behind the words. Some Internet users try to duplicate these nonverbal cues with "netiquette"—by using smiley faces or words describing their feelings in parentheses. The message sender can reflect some of the missing nonverbal cues by sending the cues as written words.

It's kind of like the terrible two's. Where children are discovering what they can do with their own kinesthetics. This is a time where children like to touch everything they see. It doesn't matter what it is. If they see it, they want to have the experience of touching it. Often times you can find them totally lost in the moment, fully absorbed in whatever kinesthetic experience they are indulging in at that moment. It's

like a moment frozen in time. As they sit there manipulating that object, time passes, but for them there is no awareness of time, only the moment.

Communication is a complex dynamic system. It involves all modes of sending receiving and feedback. It appears at a young age and decoding ability increases with age. At times nonverbal cues may be used to emphasize a message we are trying to convey. On other occasions it replaces verbal communication. Communication is used in everyday life, from greeting a stranger to touching a lover. The nonverbal behavior an individual uses is a product of characteristics endowed at birth and socially learned norms.

Knowledge of the effects nonverbal communications is needed, because our awareness may enhance favorable communication. Nonverbal cues may be unconsciously acted and reacted upon, regulating proximity, gestures, eye gaze and touch. Each component of nonverbal behavior affects our relationship and interpersonal environment in intricate ways. Nonverbal cues provide insight into affect states, influence another's perception of an individual's competence, persuasiveness, power, sincerity and vulnerability. In a new age where increasing population is decreasing personal space, it is imperative to understand cultural and personal communication differences and similarities.

Nonverbal communication has its own unique functions in interpersonal and intercultural communication. The following activity deals with some of the important ways that nonverbal behavior regulates human interaction.

# 【 Activity 3 】

*Nonverbal communication encompasses more than one activity, and it is not limited to one set of messages. This multi-dimensional aspect of our nonverbal behavior also carries over to the many uses and functions of nonverbal communication. Study the following situations and try to figure out some basic functions of this form of communication.*

1. When we say "The new museum is south of that building," we usually point in a certain direction.

2. You tell someone that you are pleased with his/her performance, and at the same time you pat the person on the shoulder.

3. If people in a group are boisterous, you might place your index finger to your lips as an alternative to saying, "Please calm down so that I can speak."

4. In conversation we nod our head in agreement to indicate to our partners in communication that we agree and that they should continue talking.

5. Just before an important examination, you tell someone you are relaxed and at ease, yet your voice quavers and your hands shake.

## Discussion

The first situation in which the gesture and words have a similar meaning and reinforce one another demonstrates the function of repeating. People often use nonverbal messages to repeat a point they are trying to make.

The second one tells us that nonverbal communication has the function of complementing, which generally adds more information to messages. Physical contact places another layer of meaning on what is being said. This is also referred to as a type of accenting because it accents the idea the speaker is trying to make.

The third one is a case of substituting. If you see a very special friend, you are apt to enlarge the size of your smile and throw open your arms to greet him or her, which is a substitution for all the words it would take to convey the same feeling.

The fourth is an example of exercising regulation. We often regulate and manage communication by using some form of nonverbal behavior. Motioning someone to come closer means we want to talk to them and having direct eye contact with someone is to let them know that the channels are open.

The fifth indicates contradicting. On some occasions, our nonverbal actions send signals opposite to the literal meanings contained in our verbal messages.

In a sense, all body language should be interpreted within a given context; to ignore the overall situation could be misleading. When one communicates in a certain language, it is generally advisable to use the nonverbal behavior that goes with that particular language. Observation shows that a truly bilingual person switches body language at the same time as the language switches.

# III Nonverbal Communication and Culture

As with verbal communication, nonverbal communication is also closely associated with culture. People from different cultures have diverse means of sending messages without the use of verbal language. Understanding the cultural differences in nonverbal behavior helps us to communicate successfully with members from other cultures. To do so, we must be aware of two things. First, we must pay attention to our own nonverbal actions. Second, learn the nonverbal ways of the other language. But both are difficult to do because of the way deep culture works. Most people are not aware of their own nonverbal communication because it is so much a part of them; it just feels like the only natural way to act. As Andersen says "Individuals are aware of little of their own nonverbal behavior, which is enacted mindlessly, spontaneously, and unconsciously." To learn about another culture, we must watch carefully how the people act and how they react to us. In doing so, we may learn as much about our own culture as about theirs.

# 【Activity 4】

*Read the following case and answer the questions that follow. Discuss the questions in small groups.*

Eva came to the United States from Peru to study at an American college. She wanted to live with an American family to find out more about the American way of life. And she wanted to improve her English.

The foreign student office of her college found the Larsen family for Eva to live with. Eva spoke with Mrs. Larsen on the telephone. She sounded very warm and friendly to Eva. She told Eva she could move in the next day. Eva was very happy about it.

Eva arrived the next day with all her luggage. She was excited to meet the Larsens. She rang the doorbell.

A tall, blond woman answered the door with a big smile on her face. She said, "Oh, you must be Eva! I'm so glad you're here! Let me help you with your bags. Come on in. I'm Hilda Larsen." She took one of Eva's bags into the house.

When they got inside, Mrs. Larsen put the bag down and stood across from Eva, about 3 feet away. She crossed her arms in front of her and asked Eva, "Tell me about your trip. I'd love to go to Peru someday."

Just then, her teenaged son walked in, hands in his pockets, "Jimmy, meet Eva. Maybe she can help you with your Spanish this semester," said his mother.

Jimmy said, "Hi, glad to meet you." His hands stayed in his pockets while he nodded his head.

Eva didn't know what to do with her hands. She felt uncomfortable. But she smiled and said, "Hi, nice to meet you."

The Larsens showed Eva her new room. Then they left her alone to unpack. Eva felt a little disappointed, but she didn't know exactly why. She thought Mrs. Larsen seemed so friendly on the phone. But now she wasn't sure. Jimmy also seemed a little cold, but maybe he was just shy.

Eva tried to decide what was wrong. She thought to herself: if an American girl came to stay with me in Peru, she would get a warmer welcome than that. My mother would give her a big kiss, instead of just standing there, on the other side of the room. And my brother would give her a proper greeting. Well, people told me that Americans are cold. I guess they're right.

## Questions

1. How did Mrs. Larsen and Jimmy greet Eva respectively?

2. Why did Eva feel that the Larsens were cold?

3. If you were Eva, would you think that Mrs. Larsen was cold? Why or why not?

## Discussion

Many Americans shake hands when they meet someone. To them, the important things are the words and tone of voice. But in other cultures, such as Eva's, a greeting is not a real greeting if there is no physical contact. A handshake or a kiss is a way of showing respect. Asian greetings are different, too. In most traditional Asian cultures, there is no physical contact at all in a greeting. Respect is shown by not touching the other person.

Eva used the "rules" of her own culture to understand Mrs. Larsen. But she misunderstood her. To Eva, Mrs. Larsen seemed cold because in Eva's culture a woman who greets another woman without giving her a kiss is cold. But Mrs. Larsen was not cold by the rules of American culture: she gave a warm smile and asked friendly questions. In fact, in Mrs. Larsen's culture, to kiss another woman when meeting for the first time would seem very strange.

Another reason why Mrs. Larsen seemed cold to Eva was that she stood so far from her. (For personal space, see Activities 19 and 20 in this chapter.)

## IV Elements of Nonverbal Communication

Up to now there has been a lot of research on nonverbal communication. Though what constitutes the subject matter of this study has not met with widespread agreement, most classifications divide non-verbal messages into two comprehensive categories: those that are primarily produced by the body (appearance, movement, facial expressions, eye contact, touch, smell, and paralanguage); and those that the individual combines with the setting (space, time and silence). Some facets of the two categories are studied in the following activities.

## A Body Language

### ■ Gestures

Gestures are an important component of nonverbal communication. Some gestures have come to be widely accepted and understood, such as handshaking, a gesture that goes with greeting. But many gestures vary in meaning from culture to culture, as is illustrated by the clasped-hands-over-the-head gesture. Some can be particularly troublesome, for a slight difference in making the gesture itself can mean something quite different from that intended.

## 【Activity 5】

*Read the case story and discuss in small groups the questions asked.*

Vu Nguyen was a Vietnamese student studying English in the United States. He often visited his local public library. One day he found a book he wanted to read at home. So he asked the librarian, "Excuse me, may I borrow this book?"

The librarian answered, "Why, of course. Just give me your card."

Vu smiled at her and nodded his head politely. The librarian kept talking. "That book is wonderful. Isn't that author great?" Vu had never read anything by the author. But he smiled and nodded again to show his interest. Finally, he said, "I would like to borrow this book today. Could you please tell me how to apply for a library card?" The librarian looked confused. "Oh! I thought you said you already had one. I'll give you a temporary card for today. We'll send you your regular card in the mail. It will be about two weeks. Come right this way to fill out the application." The librarian held out her hand, palm up, moving her index finger to get Vu to follow her.

Now Vu was confused. He did not understand why the librarian had suddenly become so rude. Vu smiled to cover up his confusion. As the librarian gave Vu the application, she said to him, "You look so happy. You must be glad about your new library card."

## Questions

1. Do you think Vu was happy? Why did the librarian think he was?
2. Why did Vu nod his head? What did the librarian think it meant?
3. Why did Vu think the librarian was rude?
4. How do you account for the differences shown in this passage?

## Discussion

Some scientists believe that no single gesture has the same meaning everywhere in the world. Even a smile means different things in different cultures. Vu smiled to cover up his confusion. And there are other meanings of a smile in his culture. It can also mean anger, happiness, politeness, or embarrassment. But his smile confused the librarian, because a smile usually means happiness to an American.

In a similar way, the librarian's gesture with her finger confused Vu. In his culture, this gesture with the palm up is used only to call an animal. To call a person with the same gesture is very bad, because it means that you think the person is like an animal. Yet in the United States, this "beckon with the index finger" gesture is not rude.( The dog call is a gesture where you curl your finger and summon someone towards you. It's mostly seen to be carried out by a tempting woman to her man. However, it should be avoided in Philippines as this is one of the worst forms of hand gesture which is used only for dogs. It could get you arrested or maybe even punishable by breaking your finger, so that you never attempt to do this gesture again. In countries like Japan, it's considered a rude gesture In Singapore, it's indication of death. )

Another problem involved here is that the librarian thought that Vu had a library card because he nodded his head when she told him to take it out. In Vu's culture, you nod your head to show that you heard someone, to be polite. But in American culture, when you nod your head, it means you agree with the person, and it often means that you will do as they say.

Now we know that if we expect people from other cultures to act according to the same "rules" as we do, then their manners and behaviors can be extremely confusing, and may even cause unhappiness.

# 【Activity 6】

*Study the gestures and try to figure out the meaning of each one.*

## Discussion

All the gestures could be understood by speakers of English except those in Pictures 7 and 10. Number 1 is used together with the verbal message "Let's keep our fingers crossed" in the United States, England, and Sweden to mean that the person is hoping for good luck. But in Greece and Turkey it means the breaking of a friendship, and in parts of Italy it means "OK." Crossing of fingers is considered as a sign of wishing for good luck or fortune. It also may interpret that someone is hoping for something good to happen. The cross may have originated from the Pagan symbols that means to ward off evil. Many times people cross their fingers before telling a lie, as it is believed to countervail the evil that comes of the lie. It is a positive and negative symbol as it interprets both luck or lies.

Number 2 is normally used when talking privately about a third person, meaning that person is crazy, often in a joking way.

Number 3 indicates "I have no idea." or "I don't know."

The gesture in Picture 4 means that "Would you speak louder? I can't or didn't hear you."

Number 5 means "That's enough. It's all over for me."

In Picture 6 the "thumbs down" sign indicates "rejection" or "refusal," "defeat" or "no good" or "bad news" to Americans. It is an indication of something that is bad or something that you do not approve of. It also indicates that something or someone has failed. The thumbs down sign is not used as often as the thumbs up sign. This is a rude and an arrogant way to indicate failure.

Number 7 is used in some parts of the world to mean "Something is a bit suspicious or odd here."

Number 8 means "Come here."

The ring gesture in number 9 is widely used in the US to mean "Great, perfect, acceptable, O.K." But in Belgium and France, it means "zero"; in Turkey, Brazil, Greece, and Malta, it has an obscene meaning; in Japan it means money; and in Tunisia, it is used as a threat.

Number 10 is used in Italy to say "Hello." For Indonesians, Malaysians, and some speakers of Arabic, it signals "Come here."

Number 11 means "Oh, I forgot." or an expression of surprise.

The gesture in Number 12 means "Slow down", "Relax" or "Wait a second".

## ■ Some More Gestures

Shaking hands is a gesture of friendship widely used in many cultures. And this is done with the right hand. One origin of such a practice is that it symbolized a peaceful gesture, in that the right hand was the hand which held weapons, and these weapons would have to be set aside in order to shake hands. But styles of handclasps can definitely vary around the world. In the United States, a firm grip has long been an indicator of strength of character and a limp hand, one of timidity or weakness. If you're in a Muslim or Orthodox Jewish environment, you must be highly sensitive to touching the opposite gender.

The "V for victory" sign is now accepted in a number of cultures. A well-known case is a gesture made by Winston Churchill, the Prime Minister who led Britain through WWII. As he appeared before a large crowd, he was greeted with cheers and applause. Churchill flashed the "V for victory" sign — with the forefinger and middle finger raised to form a "V." Whether by mistake or ignorance, instead of facing the palm of his hand to the front, he made the "V" with the back of his hand toward the audience. Some in the crowd applauded; some gasped; some broke out into laughter. The Prime Minister's gesture, as given, meant quite something else. Instead of "V for victory," it meant something dirty; it was an obscene gesture!

The thumbs-up sign in most American and European cultures meaning things are OK and going according to your plans or something you approve of. However, the going good sign translates into a rude and offensive gesture in Islamic and Asian countries. In Australia, it means OK, but if you move it up and down, it is considered as a grave insult.

Based on 1,200 informants from 40 different locations from all over the world, the meanings of "thumb-up" were interpreted as follows:

| | |
|---|---|
| O.K. | 738 |
| One | 40 |
| Sexual Insult | 36 |
| Hitch-hike | 30 |
| Directional | 14 |
| Others | 24 |
| Not used | 318 |

The speaker or performer clapping at the same time when the audience applauds is acceptable in China. This hand-clapping is understood as conveying thanks to the audience. However, it is considered improper or immodest in English-speaking countries, for oneself to do so is thought to be applauding oneself.

Both hands are used in China and some other Asian cultures when one hand would be enough in offering something to a visitor or another person. Both hands together show respect.

Pointing at something in the room using index finger. It is impolite to point with the index finger in the Middle and Far East.

Pat a student on the head. This is very upsetting to students from Asia. The head is the repository of the soul in the Buddhist religion. Children from cultures which are influenced by Buddhism will feel uncomfortable if their head is touched.

## ■ Postures

Postures and sitting habits, too, offer insight into a culture's deep structure. In Japan, for example, bowing is much more than a greeting. It signifies that culture's concern with status and rank. In the U.S., where being casual and friendly is valued, people often fall into chairs or slouch when they stand. In the office, an American sometimes put his feet on his desk, signifying a relaxed, informal attitude. In the classroom the teacher sometimes sits on the desk while speaking to the students.

## 【Activity 7】

*Study the following case and try to explain why the students became so angry.*

While lecturing to his poetry class at Ain Shams University in Cairo, a British professor became so relaxed that he leaned back in his chair and revealed the bottom of his foot to the astonished class. The next day the Cairo newspapers carried headlines about the student demonstration that resulted, and they denounced British arrogance and demanded that the professor be sent home.

### Discussion

This is an example of misunderstanding due to the lack of knowledge of each other's culturally determined nonverbal behavior. In Muslim society revealing the bottom of one's foot to others is the worst kind of insult. Similarly, in many other cultures like Thailand, Japan and France this "sit with shoe-sole showing" behavior also sends a rude message. Showing the soles of the feet demonstrates disrespect. You are exposing the lowest and dirtiest part of your body, so this is insulting. But such behavior in the English culture is quite common.

## ■ Eye-contact

Eye contact is an important aspect of body language. In different cultures there have developed a variety of uses for the eyes in the communicative process. The Arabs, for example, look directly into the eyes of their communication partner, and do so for long periods. They believe such contact shows interest in the other person and helps them assess the truthfulness of the other person's words. While in Japan, prolonged eye contact is considered rude, threatening, and disrespectful.

## 【Activity 8】

*Read the following story and discuss in small groups whether the principal's judgment is correct and why. Think about how Chinese people have eye contact in communication.*

A teenage Puerto Rican girl in a New York high school was taken with a number of other girls to the principal for suspected smoking. Although there was no proof of any wrongdoing and although she had a good record, the principal decided she was guilty and suspected her. "There was something sly and suspicious about her," he said in his report. "She just wouldn't meet my eye. She wouldn't look at me."

## Discussion

When she was questioned by the principal it was true that she kept looking at the floor and refused to meet his eyes. Her response was interpreted by the principal as being guilty. An English saying "Don't trust anyone who won't look you in the eye" helps explain why. But according to Puerto Rican culture, a good girl "does not meet the eyes of an adult." The behavior of that girl is "a sign of respect and obedience." Fortunately, one of the teachers of that high school had a Latin American background. He went to the principal and explained the difference in culture. And then the principal accepted the explanation, admitted his mistake and the matter was settled properly.

From the above case study, we see rules for eye contact are not universal. American customs demand for eye contact to apply to both the speaker and the listener. For not to look at the other person could imply a number of things: fear, contempt, uneasiness, guilt, and indifference. In public speaking, if a speaker "buries his nose in his manuscript," or reads a speech instead of looking at and talking to his audience, he/she would be regarded as inconsiderate and disrespectful. In conversation, there is plenty of eye contact too. This shows that the listener is interested. And the listener will occasionally make sounds like "Hmm," "Ummm," or nod his/her head to indicate attention. A nod or smile may show agreement, while tilting or slanting of one's head to one side, and raising an eyebrow at the same time may mean disagreement or reservations.

However, staring at people or holding a glance too long is considered improper in English-speaking countries. Even when the look may be one of appreciation—as of beauty—it may make people uneasy and embarrassed.

Like the Puerto Rican girl, African American children are taught to look down at the ground when they are talking to elders or when elders are talking to them. This is to show respect.

To look at someone in the eye in Japan is rude, because it is invading someone's space. The Japanese may sit close together in an office, but they seldom look at each other in the eye. On the crowded subways and trains, nobody makes eye contact. When greeting someone, one bows and looks past the other person. They are taught to look at the neck.

## ■ Facial Expressions

Human beings are animals full of emotions. For example, young people feel happy when they fall in love and old people sometimes can't help feeling sad when they think that their good old days are gone forever.

Some psychologists argue that there are six basic emotions: surprise, fear, disgust, anger, happiness, and sadness. Shock, horror, revulsion, fury, ecstasy and grief are strongly-felt variants of each of these. Combinations of the six basic emotions give rise to others, such as embarrassment, shame, pride, shyness, boredom, suspicion, and confusion.

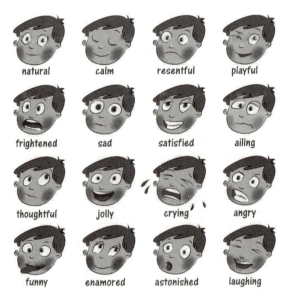

natural    calm    resentful    playful

frightened    sad    satisfied    ailing

thoughtful    jolly    crying    angry

funny    enamored    astonished    laughing

Our emotions are expressed both verbally and nonverbally. One of the nonverbal channels is facial expression or the look. The emotions expressed by one's looks carry other messages, like character and attitude. A typical example is the mask shifting performance in Sichuan opera, where one mask represents one type of character. In Beijing opera, actors and actresses often wear heavy make-up that demonstrates each performer's character and attitude. The different masks and make up arouse different reactions from the audience, thus contributing to their entertainment. In a sense we all are actors because we wear a variety of "masks"—we have a host of facial expressions. We "put on a face to meet the faces that we meet" (T.S. Eliot).

But our facial expressions are often culturally dictated. In many Mediterranean cultures, people exaggerate signs of grief or sadness. It is not uncommon to see men crying in public. Yet in the United States, white men suppress the desire to show these emotions. In China too, men never shed tears unless in extremely strongly-struck occasions (男儿有泪不轻弹). Japanese men even go so far as to hide expressions of anger, sorrow, or disgust by laughing or smiling. In the latter cultures men are trained not to cry because crying is considered not manly. It is usually identified with childishness, weakness and dependence.

## ■ Wink

A wink is made by either briefly closing one eye or by rapidly blinking both eyes. Like the smile, the wink can have several meanings. It can be a flirtation, especially if made to a person of the opposite gender, a means of mute communication between two people or a signal of a shared joke or experience. If accompanied by words, a wink can also be used to take "the sting" out of what has actually been said.

## ■ Puppy Face

Making a puppy face can be a very efficient means of body language communication. The head is slightly tilted downward, the lower lip protrudes and the eyes look straight up at the other person. The purpose is to make one look slightly vulnerable and childlike with the intent of getting out of having to do what one does not really want to do or to plead forgiveness. The person making a puppy face might also simply want to gain sympathy by looking "cute." It can also signal shyness and to a certain degree or be used as a plea not to expect too much. The puppy face is often pulled to provoke a smile in the other person and thus "to break the ice." Perhaps the most well-known puppy face maker was Lady Diana-at least in her younger days-and at the beginning of her career as Crown Princess.

## ■ Wrinkled Brow

Wrinkling the brow can indicate that a person is deeply in thought. It can also express concern, doubt, frustration or disbelief.

## 【Activity 9】

*Work in small groups and find out what messages smiles and laughters usually convey. Study the following three cases and explain why the people in each case smiled or laughed.*

A. In a Chinese classroom a girl was asked to answer a question. She stood up and smiled, without making any sound.

B. When an American is parking his bicycle and the bicycle accidentally falls over, he feels embarrassed at his awkwardness, and is quite angered and humiliated when Chinese onlookers laugh.

C. In the dining room, an American drops a plate quite by accident and feels bad, and Chinese onlookers laugh, compounding his discomfort thus causing anger and bad feeling.

### Discussion

Smile is a powerful tool of body language. It can be used to express a great variety of meanings. In the U.S. a broad smile exposing the teeth is the strongest form, showing joy, friendliness, politeness and approval. If the smile does not reach the eyes, however, it expresses insincerity. Historically, exposing the teeth when smiling was construed as unfriendly. In ancient times, man snarled when angry, exposing his canine teeth. Legend has it that many a missionary lost his life when smiling at indigenous tribes with his lips parted, because it was construed as a sign of hostility and pending attack.

A lopsided smile with only one corner of the mouth drawn up, expresses doubt and even cynicism or sarcasm. A smile can also be motivated by fear or to hide nervousness. A not so friendly smile is one where the smiler makes fun of the other person and ridicules him or her. A certain belief holds that one should not smile at or expect a lot of smiles from Russians, because they only smile at people they know or if they have a distinct reason for a smile.

But very often Westerners are confused at the smile or laughter of the Asians, which does not necessarily mean happiness or friendship. In case A, the girl smiled to cover her embarrassment resulting from not being able to answer the question. In cases B and C, the laughter is, of course, not at the person or his misfortune—whether he be a foreigner or a Chinese. It can convey a number of feelings: don't take it so seriously; laugh it off, it's nothing; such things can happen to any of us, etc. But a smile usually means happiness to an American who tends to appear open and friendly.

While a smile is generally part of an introduction, smiles aren't always the universal signal for friendship. Although smiles invite communication in much of the Western Hemisphere, in the Far East, a smile can be used to cover up embarrassment, dismay or fury. The Japanese smile can be used to mask an emotion, or to avoid answering a question, or even to hide embarrassment. A Japanese woman may smile when there is bad news, the purpose being to cover up her sadness. In the French frame of reference, a person who grins too much can be regarded as simple. And in Germany, smiles are often reserved for family, friends and social situations, but not displayed freely in business settings. One saying goes "Life is serious and there is very little to smile about."

A new study has suggested that different facial expressions may vary with the shift of cultures.

Some prior research has supported the notion that facial expressions are a hard-wired human behavior with evolutionary origins, so facial expressions wouldn't differ across cultures. But this study challenges that theory and used statistical image processing techniques to examine how study participants perceived facial expressions through their own mental representations.

"A mental representation of a facial expression is the image we see in our 'mind's eye' when we think about what a fearful or happy face looks like," Jack said. "Mental representations are shaped by our past experiences and help us know what to expect when we are interpreting facial expressions."

The study published by the American Psychological Association says that though facial expressions are seen as "universal language of emotion," people from different cultures perceive happy, sad or angry facial expressions in unique ways.

"By conducting this study, we hoped to show that people from different cultures think about facial expressions in different ways," said lead researcher Rachael E. Jack, PhD, of the University of Glasgow.

"East Asians and Western Caucasians differ in terms of the features they think constitute an angry face or a happy face," she added.

Fifteen Chinese people and fifteen Caucasians living in Glasgow took part in the study. After showing them randomly altered facial expressions on a computer screen the study found that the Chinese participants relied on the eyes more to represent facial expressions, while Western Caucasians relied on the eyebrows and mouth.

(The study was published online in APA's *Journal of Experimental Psychology: General.*)

## ■ Dress

Concern over how one appears is universal. You can find lots of evidence to prove this, from the ornaments our ancestors made and wore to what modern people are doing to make them look beautiful. Every culture gives special meaning to clothing. For example, in the United States, brides wear white, the color of purity, while in China brides are traditionally married in red, the color of good luck.

## 【Activity 10】

A Korean student in an American university was telling one of his teachers about the arrival of new students from Korea. "There are many things I have to tell them," he said. "I have to explain to them about girls wearing shorts. They will be confused because in Korea if a girl goes out on the street wearing shorts, she can be arrested by the police." The American teacher laughed. "I can imagine that it will be quite a shock for them," she said, "when they see women in shorts out jogging." The Korean student agreed. "Jogging is popular in Korea now, but women do not jog. In the United States everybody jogs— young people, old people—everybody. I can look out of my dorm window any time of day or night and see somebody out jogging."

*Try to explain the difference and think about how things are in China.*

### Discussion

What people wear reflects their values and attitudes. In Korea girls are not supposed to wear shorts. The possible reason is that the Oriental tradition treats men and women differently and demands that women not expose too much of their bodies. In contrast, in the U.S. where egalitarianism prevails, women enjoy more freedom in many aspects, including what to wear.

In the Western world, different occasions require different clothing. Formal and informal occasions ask people to dress accordingly. In some Asian cultures, the distinction is between public and private occasions. In public people are required to wear dress in a formal way.

In general, when deciding whether to ask the way or strike up a conversation with a total stranger, we are usually influenced by the way that person looks. We often make inferences (often faulty) about another's intelligence, gender, age, approachability, financial well-being, class, tastes, values, and cultural background from attractiveness, dress, and personal artifacts.

## ■ Physical Contact

Physical touch varies from culture to culture. One classification made by some researchers is that world cultures fall into two categories: high-contact culture and low-contact culture. People in high contact cultures evaluate "closeness" as positive and good, and "further away" as negative and bad. People in low contact cultures are just the opposite. They evaluate "closeness" as negative and bad, and "further away" as positive and good. Cultures in most of the Arab world, Mediterranean countries (including France, Greece, Italy), and those of the Jews in Europe and Middle East, East European nations, Russians, Indonesians and so on tend to be more high contact. However, cultures in most Northern European countries, Germany, Britain, the United States (Anglo-Saxons) and Japan are likely to be more low contact. The Australians are somewhere in between.

## 【Activity 11】

*Read the following passage and the dialogue. Then have a discussion in small groups.*

A. Parfait Awono (a Cameroonian teaching French in the U.S.) wrote: "In my French class... I introduced handshaking. I asked them how often they shake hands with their friends. The answer was rarely to never. I then explained to them how friends in Cameroon would shake hands several times during the same day. Whenever they would meet, they would shake hands. Students said they would really be uncomfortable to be touched.... To make things worse, I told them that friends, brothers, sisters walk hand in hand—literally—in Cameroon, without having any connotation. When they heard this, most students were shocked, except for a Korean-American student. He said that on a trip to South Korea he noticed people holding hands everywhere, and he thought everybody was gay. He said he refused to hold hands with his cousins, and they thought he was just a weird American kid..."

B. Sun Mei: Nice to see you here, Sarah.

Sarah: So he's got on the train?

Sun Mei: Yes... (choked with sobs)

Sarah: You puzzle me. Now you're crying, but just now you seemed so calm. You simply let him go without a kiss.

Sun Mei: He wanted to kiss me goodbye but I stopped him. I felt embarrassed.

Sarah: Why? He is your boyfriend and you don't see each other very often.

Sun Mei:...

Sarah: How strange!

## Questions

1. Why were the students in the French class unwilling to hold hands with others?

2. Why did Sun Mei behave as she did?

3. If you are parting from your boyfriend or girlfriend, will you hug and kiss each other? Why?

4. How do you look at other behaviors such as hand-holding between members of the same sex and between members of different sexes, fondling other people's babies, and parents kissing in front of their children?

*Ask some Westerners you know how they look at these actions. Think about what values underlie their different behaviors.*

## Discussion

Physical contact between members of the same sex in English-speaking countries is a delicate matter. Once past childhood, the holding of hands, or walking with an arm around another's shoulder is not considered proper. The implication is one of homosexuality. That is why Parfait Awono's students would be uncomfortable to be touched, especially by the same sex.

DON'T TOUCH ME!

American always struggle with personal space, but also physical contact. Other than shaking hands, physical contact, such as holding hands or hugging, is reserved for people we are close with. It's pretty awkward with a stranger. In most Western countries physical contact can mean social dominance. People with a higher status tend to exert more physical contact, whereas lower status individuals receive more of the physical contact. For example, your boss might pat you on the back or maybe grip your shoulder as they're leaning over you to look at your work. This is not uncommon, yet it can still make employees feel uncomfortable. On the flip side, you would never pat your boss on the back, it's a superiority thing.

Men in much of Eastern Europe, Spain, Italy, Portugal, and the Arab world will kiss when they meet their friends. But this is not done in English-speaking countries where physical contact is generally avoided in conversation among ordinary friends or acquaintances. Between male and female, however, hugging and kissing is appropriate.

So, what cultures tend have more physical contact? Very similar to personal space, the Middle East, Latin America and southern Europe prefer a lot more physical contact during normal conversations. A common greeting is kissing on the cheek. In Spain, I noticed many conversations with men clasping each other's arm or placing a hand on the other person's shoulder. In Northern Europe, you have to apologize if you accidentally brush by someone. If one touches another person accidentally, they usually utter an apology such as "Sorry." "Oh, I'm sorry." They do not appreciate touching at all. The Japanese though, are culturally most opposed to the touch of a stranger. If you think about it, they greet each other with a bow, not a kiss or handshake.

Muslims also have strict cultural rules about touching. Men and women cannot touch, even casually, in public. You will not see couples, even married, walking down the street holding hands. Now, two women often walk holding hands and men can be seen walking arm in arm with one another. We might do a double take if we see two men casually walking with their arms linked. Remember, the appropriateness of touching varies by culture. Don't make the mistake of touching someone's arm during a conversation in a culture where it is not appropriate or be horrified if someone from Latin America places their hand on your shoulder during a discussion. Be aware of different culture's comfort toward touching, as well as your own. Does anyone have an example of being uncomfortable with certain physical contact in a different culture?

Chinese tradition teaches us not to show our affection for adults in public. So hugging and kissing openly is usually not allowed. But as you may have noticed, in our country today there have been changes in this kind of behavior. It is no longer rare to see young people hug and kiss in public, especially on campus. However, the interesting thing is that husband and wife seldom, if ever, kiss before others in spite of the change. They never do so in front of their children. But couples in Western cultures hug and kiss openly as well as in private. One author of this book has a Canadian friend who, when talking about this subject, said: "We kiss in front of our children to teach them how to express love."

Hugging and embracing in public is fairly common among women in many countries. But in most of the Western countries this practice is done frequently between husband and wife and close members of the family when meeting after a period of absence.

In China adults are often seen to fondle other people's babies and very small children to show their affection and friendliness. But such behavior by people other than their relatives and close friends—whether touching, patting, hugging or kissing—can be quite embarrassing and awkward for the mothers from Western cultures. The reason may be that in their cultures such actions would be considered rude, intrusive and offensive, and thus could arouse a strong dislike and even repugnance. In the early 1990s, a Western couple told one author of this book that they didn't like other people to touch their baby. Of course, these "other people" don't include family members and very close friends.

Another aspect of tactile (触觉的) communication concerns the location of the touch. In Thailand, it is offensive to touch the head as this part of the body is considered to be sacred. It is advisable to avoid touching all Asians on the head including small children's heads. In the Middle East, the left hand is not used to touch others because the left hand is thought to be unclean. While Muslims hug another around the shoulder, in Korea younger people do not touch the shoulders of their elders. To sum up, in foreign cultures we should inquire to make sure what touching behavior is appropriate before we act.

# B Paralanguage

A voice may tell whether the speaker is sick or healthy, sleepy or awake, drunk or sober. It can cry or laugh, moan, groan, or giggle apart from pronouncing the words. They are sounds that go along with language. This kind of sounds is called paralanguage.

Paralanguage involves the linguistic elements of speech; how something is said, not the actual meaning of the spoken words. In other words, loudness and tone of voice reflects psychological arousal, emotion, and mood. It may also carry social information, as in a sarcastic, superior, or submissive manner of speaking. Sometimes it carries more than the words of language. This is the aspect of communication that cannot be neglected.

Most classifications divide paralanguage into three kinds of vocalization: (1) vocal characterizers (laughing, crying, yelling, moaning, whining, belching, yawning); (2) vocal qualifiers (volume, pitch, rhythm, tempo, resonance, tone); (3) vocal segregates ("uh huh," "shh," "oooh," "mmmh," "humm"). As silence also sends messages, it is usually included in the study of paralanguage.

## ■ Silence

## 【Activity 12】

*Work in small groups. Discuss why silence should not be neglected in communication. What messages can silence convey? Do Chinese audiences usually ask questions after a lecture?*

## Discussion

Silence cues affect interpersonal communication by providing an interval in an ongoing interaction during which the participants have time to think, check or suppress an emotion, encode a lengthy response, or inaugurate another line of thought. Silence also helps provide feedback, informing both sender and receiver about the clarity of an idea or its significance in the overall interpersonal exchange. Silence cues may be interpreted as evidence of agreement, lack of interest, injured feelings, or contempt. But we have to remember that silence is interpreted differently in different cultures, and even in the same culture there can be alternative interpretations about silence.

Generally speaking, silence is not a meaningful part of the life of most members of the dominant culture in the United States. Talking, watching television, listening to music, and other sound-producing activities keep them from silence. Compared with the American view of silence, the Eastern one is much different. There is often a belief among many Eastern traditions that words can contaminate an experience and that inner peace and wisdom come only through silence.

An American speaker in China often feels uneasy about the silence shown by the Chinese audience, because in their culture the more questions the audience ask after a speech, the more interested they are, and therefore more successful the speaker is. But in China there is no such custom. It is good manners for students to listen to the teacher or other speaker without asking any questions. Today things are changing in China, and some students have begun to ask questions. Still, silence is there after many lectures.

This, however, doesn't mean that Chinese people are always quiet. In proper occasions they love Renao (热闹), which means literally "heat and noise." It is the Chinese word for "good fun," in which noise and movement are essential.

To have a global view of the cultural differences in the use of silence, the division of high/low context cultures in Chapter One will be of help.

In low-context cultures where ideas are explicitly encoded into words, silence does not fit with the emphasis on precision and clarity. People in low-context cultures usually view silence as lack of communication and are generally uncomfortable with it. They would think of something to say to avoid awkwardness. But this does not mean that silence carries no meaning in low-context culture. There are cultural codes for observing silence. In a church when a preacher is preaching, people are supposed to keep quiet. At a funeral, people are supposed to remain silent. High-context cultures, however, hold a different attitude toward the use of silence. People in some Asian countries, for example, consider that silence is an integral part of social discourse, not a failure of communication. It may mean that the audience or listener is angry at the message and needs time to think, or is embarrassed. We Chinese like periods of silence and do not like to be hurried. The Japanese can put up with long silence in communication and do not hurry to fill it up with speech. They believe that through silence one can discover the truth inside oneself. Contemplation and meditation take place in silence. In the Indian culture silence plays a dominant role, too.

The Hindu believes that self-realization, salvation, truth, wisdom, peace, and bliss are achieved in a state of meditation and introspection when individuals are communicating with themselves in silence.

## Ⓒ Environmental Language

### ■ Our Use of Time

What is time? We cannot hold or see time, but we respond to it as if it had command over our lives. When the bell rings at a certain time, students and teachers begin their classes. Some people set the alarm clock to wake them up at a certain time. If we arrive 30 minutes late for an important appointment and offer no apology, we send a certain message about ourselves. Although time is universal, people in different cultures respond to time in different ways.

## 【Activity 13】

*Read the following passage by Huxley about time and answer the questions below. Discuss the answers in small groups.*

Time, as we know it, is a very recent invention. The modern time sense is hardly older than the United States. It is a byproduct of industrialism...

Time is our tyrant. We are chronically aware of the moving minute hand, even of the moving second hand. We have to be. There are trains to be caught, clocks to be punched, tasks to be done in specified periods, records to be broken by fractions of a second, machines that set the pace and have to be kept up with. Our consciousness of the smallest units of time is now acute. To us, for example, the moment 8:17 a.m. means something—something very important, if it happens to be the starting time of our daily train. To our ancestors, such an odd eccentric instant was without significance—did not even exist. In inventing the locomotive, Watt and Stephenson were part inventors of time.

Another time-emphasizing entity is the factory and its dependent, the office. Factories exist for the purpose of getting certain quantities of goods made in a certain time. The old artisan worked as it suited him; with the result that consumers generally had to wait for the goods they had ordered from him. The factory is a device for making workmen hurry. The machine revolves so often each minute; so many movements have to be made, so many pieces produced each hour. Result: the factory worker (and the same is true of the office worker) is compelled to know time in its smallest fractions. In the hand-work age there was no such compulsion to be aware of minutes and seconds.

Our awareness of time has reached such a pitch of intensity that we suffer acutely whenever our travels take us into some corner of the world where people are not interested in minutes and seconds.

The unpunctuality of the Orient, for example, is appalling to those who come freshly from a land of fixed mealtimes and regular train services. For a modern American or Englishman, waiting is a psychological torture. An Indian accepts the blank hours with resignation, even with satisfaction. He has not lost the fine art of doing nothing. Our notion of time as a collection of minutes, each of which must be filled with some business or amusement, is wholly alien to the Oriental, just as it was wholly alien to the Greek. For the man who lives in a pre-industrial world, time moves at a slow and easy pace; he does not care about each minute, for the good reason that he has not been made conscious of the existence of minute.

## Questions

1. Where did the Western time sense come from according to the passage?
2. According to Huxley, what's the difference in the time sense of East and West? Do you agree?
3. Why did the author say that Watt and Stephenson were part inventors of time?
4. Do you think that Chinese people's time sense has changed? If yes, what are the manifestations and why?

# 【Activity 14】

*Read the following case story and answer the questions below.*

Martha was an American high school student who was chosen to spend a summer in Indonesia as part of a student exchange program. When she got her letter of acceptance, she felt very lucky. She was sure it was going to be the most exciting experience of her life. She did not even feel a bit sad about leaving behind her busy schedule back home: her piano lessons, the diving team, her church youth group, and her baby-sitting job.

The first few days after her arrival in Indonesia were filled with meeting her new Indonesian exchange family, trying new foods, walking around the neighborhood, and getting to know her Indonesian exchange sister, Ketty. It was just as exciting as Martha had hoped. But by about her second week in Indonesia, Martha began to feel as if something was wrong.

One morning, after breakfast, she looked at her watch and asked Ketty, "So, what are the plans for today? What are we going to do?"

Ketty replied, "Oh, I didn't really make any plans. My mother might want us to go shopping with her later. Then we'll see what we feel like doing. Maybe we could go downtown." Martha answered, "What time is your mom going shopping?"

"Oh, whenever she's ready. Are you getting bored, Martha? Maybe we should sign up for one of those guided tours of the city. The downtown hotels have them for American tourists. Would you like that?"

"Oh, no, I don't want to be a tourist. I want to do just what you do. I guess I'm just used to being busy all the time. It's hard for me to get used to not having plans," said Martha.

"Doesn't it bother you to rush around so much?" asked Ketty.

"No, I love it when I'm busy. Sitting around wasting time makes me nervous. Let's go do something, Ketty. I'm only here for two months, after all. I don't want to leave Indonesia feeling that I haven't experienced as much as I can." Martha looked down at her watch again and said, "Goodness, it's almost 11 and all we've done is sit around talking!"

## Questions

1. What was Martha's life like at home?
2. Why did she begin to feel as if something was wrong?
3. What can you tell about the Indonesian concept of time?
4. What can you tell about Martha's concept of time?
5. What could make Martha feel better again?

## Discussion

In many ways, Martha's concept of time is typically American. Many Americans believe that time should be "used wisely" as much as possible, that is, used to accomplish certain goals. In Martha's case, her goal was to experience everything she could. To her, experiencing Indonesia meant running around doing many things. But she may have missed some important experiences of Indonesian life because she could not slow down and relax.

It is easier to understand how people think about time by using some concepts from anthropology, the study of the cultural development of human beings. Anthropologists ask: Which is more important to each culture: the future, the present, or the past? Most Americans act as if they think that the future is most important. They are future-oriented. (For time-orientation, see Kluckhohn's cultural dimensions in Chapter 2.) Part of the American orientation toward the future is the value placed on accomplishing goals. Americans rush through the present in order to accomplish some goal for the future. Another example of Americans' orientation toward the future is the way they value change. In the American way of thinking, new is better than old, just as youth is valued more than maturity.

Other cultures are more oriented toward the present or toward the past. For example, Ketty's idea of waiting until later to "see what we feel like doing" shows a present orientation. It can be said that she is situation-oriented (do things when something needs to be done) rather than being sensitive to clock-time. Filipinos and Latin Americans are present-oriented, too. They emphasize living in the moment. These cultures tend to be more impulsive and spontaneous than others and have a casual, relaxed lifestyle.

The Chinese with their tradition of ancestor worship and strong pride in their culture's persistence for thousands of years is a culture that uses the past as a guide as to how to live in the present, as a Chinese proverb advises, "Consider the past and you will know the present." Other such cultures are the British, Greek, French, and some other Asian ones.

The Chinese, like most Asians, "walk around the pool" in order to make well-considered decisions, but they also have a keen sense of the value of time. This can be noticed especially in their attitude toward taking up other people's time, for which they frequently apologize. At the end of a meeting in

China, it is customary to thank the participants for contributing their valuable time. Punctuality on arrival is also considered important—more so than in many other Asian countries. Indeed, when meetings are scheduled between two people, it is not unusual for a Chinese to arrive 15 to 30 minutes early "in order to finish the business before the time appointed for its discussion," so not stealing any of the other person's time! It is also considered polite in China to announce, 10 or 15 minutes after a meeting has begun, that one will soon have to be going. Again, the worthy aim involved is to economize on their use of your time. The Chinese will not go, of course, until the transaction has been completed, but the point has been made.

This is indeed a double standard. The Chinese penchant for humility demands that the other person's time be seen as precious; on the other hand, the Chinese expect a liberal amount of time to be allocated for repeated consideration of the details of a transaction and to the careful nurturing of personal relationships surrounding the deal. They frequently complain that Americans, in China to do business, often have to catch their plane back to the U.S. "in the middle of the discussion." The American sees the facts as having been adequately discussed; the Chinese feel that they have not yet attained that degree of closeness—that satisfying sense of common trust and intent—that is for the Chinese the bedrock of the deal and of other transactions in the future.

This point can be made clearer by the comparison between Korean culture and American culture in the time orientation. An American businessman visiting Korea for the first time is almost certain to be told that Koreans have a "5000-year history" and to be shown Namdaemun and Dongdaemun[1], the "new" gates to the city of Seoul, built before the United States was established as a country. The American, on the other hand, is likely to have little consciousness of his own cultural roots. He is more likely to focus on the newness of his culture and the rapid change and progress of ideas. Although Martha's goal was to "experience" as much as she could in Indonesia, she didn't seem to think "sitting around" was an important experience. That is because Americans value doing, or action, more than simply being. They are "action-oriented," not "being-oriented." Why do so many Americans feel they must be busy to be happy? Perhaps the idea comes from the Protestant religion of the Puritans, the first English people to live in America. The Puritans believed strongly in the "work ethic," the idea that work is morally good. The Puritans believed doing nothing was a sin. These ideas may help explain how uncomfortable many modern Americans feel about "wasting time."

To avoid wasting time, Americans plan their time as much as possible, and measure it carefully. In the case study, Martha looked at her watch twice, even though she had no worry of being late. She felt uncomfortable without a planned schedule of things to do, as she had back home. Many busy Americans carry a small calendar around with them, to help them remember their daily schedule. They only see friends when they have made an appointment to do so.

The Japanese have a keen sense of the unfolding or unwrapping of time—this is well described by Joy Hendry in her book *Wrapping Culture*. People familiar with Japan are well aware of the contrast between the breakneck pace maintained by the Japanese factory worker on the one hand, and the unhurried contemplation to be observed in Japanese gardens or the agonizingly slow tempo of a Noh

---

[1] Namdaemun is one of the four main gates of the old city wall. Completed in 1398. Dongdaemun, originally called Heunginjimun ("Gate of Uplifting Mercy"), first built in 1397, once served as the main eastern gate in the wall surrounding Seoul.

play on the other. What Hendry emphasizes, however, is the meticulous, resolute manner in which the Japanese segment time. This segmentation does not follow the American or German pattern, where tasks are assigned in a logical sequence aimed at maximum efficiency and speed in implementation. The Japanese are more concerned not with how long something takes to happen, but with how time is divided up in the interests of properness, courtesy and tradition.

For instance, in most Japanese social gatherings, there are various phases and layers—marked beginnings and endings—for retirement parties, weddings, parent-teacher association meetings and so on.

In Japan's conformist and carefully regulated society, people like to know at all times where they stand and where they are at: this applies both to social and business situations. The mandatory, two-minute exchange of business cards between executives meeting each other for the first time is one of the clearest examples of a time activity segment being used to mark the beginning of a relationship. Another example is the start and finish of all types of classes in Japan, where the lesson cannot begin without being preceded by a formal request on the part of the students for the teacher to start. Similarly, they must offer a ritualistic expression of appreciation at the end of the class.

Other events that require not only clearly defined beginnings and endings but also unambiguous phase-switching signals are the tea ceremony, New Year routines, annual cleaning of the house, cherry blossom viewing, spring "offensives" (strikes), midsummer festivities, gift-giving routines, company picnics, sake-drinking sessions, even the peripheral rituals surrounding judo, karate and kendo sessions. A Japanese person cannot enter any of the above activities in the casual, direct manner a Westerner might adopt. The American or Northern European has a natural tendency to make a quick approach to the heart of things. The Japanese, in direct contrast, must experience an unfolding or unwrapping of the significant phases of the event. It has to do with Asian indirectness, but in Japan it also involves love of compartmentalization of procedure, of tradition, of the beauty of ritual.

To summarize, when dealing with the Japanese, you can assume that they will be generous in their allocation of time to you or your particular transaction. In return, you are advised to try to do the "right thing at the right time." In Japan, form and symbols are more important than content.

In other cultures, the concept of time is more flexible. Things happen when they are ready to happen, rather than when the clock says so. People see their friends when they feel like getting together, not when their calendar or watch tells them it is time. This more flexible concept of time is common in agricultural rather than industrialized cultures. There, it is nature, not the clock, that sets the schedule by which people work. In contrast, the modern factory system of urban, industrialized societies may have forced people to become slaves to the clock.Edward T. Hall advanced another classification of time as a form of communication. Hall proposed that cultures organize time in one of two ways: either mono-chronic time (M-time) or poly-chronic time (P-time). They represent two variant solutions to the use of both time and space as organizing frames for activities. M-time emphasizes schedules, segmentation, and promptness. P-time systems are characterized by several things happening at once. They stress involvement of people and completion of transactions rather than adherence to preset schedules.

M-time is characteristic of people from Germany, Austria, Switzerland and America. People in most Asian countries, Latin America, the Arab world and African countries tend to take time in a polychronic way. They deal with time historically. They can interact with more than one person or do more than one thing at a time. The caution, however, is that the differences in the use of time are relative and cannot be taken as extremes.

# 【Activity 15】

*Find as many expressions and proverbs as possible relating to time in English and Chinese respectively. Examples are: "Time is money," "不着急,慢慢来。" Then try to find out what attitudes toward time are reflected, and see whether there are any differences.*

## Discussion

The English language is preoccupied with time. Time can be killed, redeemed, spent, wasted, saved, divided, bought, sold, lost, measured, made up etc. Moreover, words like "schedule" and "agenda" are widely used. The following phrases are often heard: have a full schedule, map out a schedule, fill in the schedule, behind the schedule, accomplish something according to schedule, place... on the agenda, my agenda for today starts with.... Proverbs like "Time is money" and "He who hesitates is lost" reflect their concept of time. Chinese terms and expressions concerning time are not listed here, for we assume that you are very familiar with them.

From the above terms and expressions and the case in Activity 14, we see that the dominant culture in English-speaking countries greatly values time. Time is looked upon as a present, tangible commodity, something to be used, and something to be held accountable for. People there live in the present and the near future. They always plan their time as much as possible and measure it carefully. For them, the smallest set of time is 5 minutes. One may be 5 minutes late for a business appointment, but not 15 and certainly not 30 minutes late, which is perfectly normal in Arab countries. Any consistently tardy person is taken to be undependable, untrustworthy, and disrespectful vis-à-vis the audience, message, or occasion. They usually feel offended with the last minute notice. When they plan to get something done, there is usually a deadline.

Accordingly, Americans tend to exercise control over their own time. They don't want their arrangements—that is what they are doing at different moments of time—be interrupted. Hence they have appointments for any visits, even for friends and relatives. A visit without prior notice is unimaginable. And when they don't want to be disturbed, they hang up a sign "Please don't disturb" on the door to protect themselves or their privacy.

In fact, time is the most expensive, as anyone who has had to deal with American doctors, dentists or lawyers will tell you.

For an American, time is truly money. In a profit-oriented society, time is a precious, even scarce, commodity. It flows fast, like a mountain river in the spring, and if you want to benefit from its passing, you have to move fast with it. Americans are people of action; they cannot bear to be idle. The past is over, but the present you can seize, parcel and package and make it work for you in the immediate future. The following two pictures could vividly tell you how Americans view time, and how they use it.

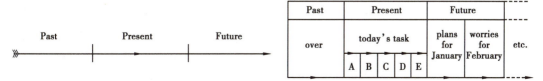

As the Americans value time so much, they can't wait to get things done. Their pace of life is fast. They always seem to be in a hurry, to be on the run—for them, there is always one more thing to do. There are fast-food restaurants, drive-in banks, processed food, microwave ovens which help get things done quickly. A friend of the authors, who has lived in the United States since the end of 1980s and is presently having two jobs, said that her time is calculated in terms of minutes.

It follows that punctuality is greatly stressed by the Americans. In their language there are many terms expressing this idea, such as punctual, on schedule, on time, on the minute, to the minute, on the hour, at the appointed time, at the stated time, in time, in good time, timely, well-timed etc.

# 【Activity 16】

*There are two stories about the use of time. One is the experience of a Chinese student in Germany. The other is the experience of the Psychologist Robert Levine while he was a visiting professor at a university outside Rio de Janeiro, studying time norms. Read these two passages and find out the differences, and then discuss with your classmates why there are differences.*

A. A Chinese student told of his experience of house renting in Germany. After deciding the place he wanted to rent, he talked with the landlady over the phone that he was to look at the house at 10 o'clock the next morning. Then the next day he arrived by car at the place at 9:40. He pressed the doorbell, expecting the warm reception of the landlady. Quite unexpectedly, the landlady said behind the door: "Why have you come earlier than 10 o'clock as we agreed yesterday?" leaving the surprised Chinese student waiting for 20 minutes. In fact, the elderly landlady was not busy with anything when he knocked. When it was time, the landlady opened the door and welcomed the guest, as if nothing happened. The end of the story is that the student rented the house and became friends with the landlady.

B. My first day of class was scheduled from 10 until noon. As I left home, I asked someone the time. It was 9:05 a.m., which allowed me time to relax and look around the campus before my lecture. After what I judged to be half an hour, I glanced at a clock I was passing. It said 10:20! In panic, I broke for the classroom, followed by gentle greetings from unhurried students, many of whom, I later realized, were my own. I arrived breathless to find an empty room.

Frantically, I asked a passerby the time. "Nine forty-five" was the answer. No, that couldn't be. I asked someone else. "Nine fifty-five." Another said: "Exactly 9:43." The clock in a nearby office read 3:15. I had learned my first class about Brazilians: their timepieces are consistently inaccurate. And nobody minds.

Many students came late, some very late. Several arrived after 10:30. A few showed up closer to 11. Two came after that. All of the latecomers wore relaxed smiles... Each one said hello, and although a few apologized briefly, none seemed terribly concerned about lateness. They assumed that I understood.

Back home in California, I never need to look at a clock to know when the class hour is ending. The shuffling of books is accompanied by strained expressions that say plaintively, "I'm starving... I've got to go to the bathroom...I'm going to suffocate if you keep us one more second." When noon arrived in my first Brazilian class, only a few students left immediately. Others slowly drifted out during the next 15 minutes... When several remaining students kicked off their shoes at 12:30, I went into my own "starving/bathroom/suffocation" routine. Apparently for many of my students, staying late was simply of no more importance than arriving late in the first place.

## Discussion

Not only Americans, but also Northern Europeans emphasize punctuality a lot. The Germans and the Swiss are admired by other Westerners because of their ability to "make the trains run on time". The first passage seems to have clearly epitomized this characteristic. But other cultures like the Brazilian culture place a very different value on punctuality. Terms like late, early, or on time are not universal. Psychologist Robert Levine noted that Brazilians have much more flexible conceptions of time and punctuality than Northern Europeans and Americans do. In addition, some other South American cultures and some Arab cultures are also noted for their apparent disregard for timeliness.

Such cultural differences in time are not merely amusing or trivial. They tell us a great deal about the nature and values of a particular society. Brazilians tend to believe that a person who is consistently late is probably more successful than one who is consistently on time. Lack of punctuality is a badge of success. Appreciating such cultural differences in conceptions of time becomes increasingly important as modern methods of communication put greater numbers of people in daily contact.

## ■ Our Use of Space

The study of man's use of space is called proxemics（空间关系学）which is another silent language that people use to convey messages. Territoriality is an important concept concerning people's use of space. It is known that animals usually have their own territories. Once their territories are invaded, they will make a response by either retreating or attacking to safeguard their own space. Human beings too have a sense of territory, very often unconsciously though. But how large one's territory is varies with culture.

## 【Activity 17】

When a North American and a Mexican stand together to converse, the Mexican will nudge slightly closer to the North American. The North American will step back an inch or two. Then the Mexican will move closer. These two will create a kind of dance in which they will move across a considerable amount of space in the course of a brief conversation. If the space is crowded with people, they will end up moving around and around in a circle.

*How do you account for this?*

## Discussion

This is because each person has a "bubble" of space (territory). Studies show that people from South America, Arab countries, and many Asian countries have a smaller personal territory than do

North Americans, British and Germans. In Mexican and Arab cultures, physical distance between people when engaged in conversation is very close. In order to feel comfortable while talking, what the Mexican does is to move closer, while what the North American does is to step back a little.

In Western countries, personal territory is highly valued. Each one has his/her own space at home or in office which should not be invaded. In public places, they have "temporary territory," not be intruded upon either. For example, if in a park you want to sit on a bench which another person has occupied, you are obliged to ask for their permission before sitting down. This shows that you recognize their "temporary territory." This territoriality extends to the territory of private properties. For example, things on a certain person's desk should not be touched, let alone taken away without permission. The concept of privacy has a lot to do with the sense of territoriality. (For "privacy," see Activity 11 in Chapter 3.) As is in the case of human behavior, the use of space is directly linked to the value system of different cultures. The Americans whose culture stresses individualism generally demand more space than do people from collective cultures and tend to take an active, aggressive stance when their space is violated.

## 【Activity 18】

*West European countries and North America share significant portions of each other's cultures, but still at many points their cultures clash. The following is what E. T. Hall wrote about cultural differences in the use of space. Read the passage and discuss with your classmates the questions that follow.*

Public and private buildings in Germany often have double doors for soundproofing, as do many hotel rooms. In addition, the door is taken very seriously by Germans. Those Germans who come to America feel that our doors are flimsy and light. The meanings of the open door and closed door are quite different in the two countries. In offices, Americans keep doors open; Germans keep doors closed. In Germany, the closed door does not mean that the man behind it wants to be alone or undisturbed, or that he is doing something he doesn't want someone else to see. It's simply that Germans think that open doors are sloppy and disorderly. To close the door preserves the integrity of the room and provides a protective boundary between people...

The open-door policy of American business and the closed-door patterns of German business cultures cause clashes in the branches and subsidiaries of American firms in Germany. The point seems to be quite simple, yet failure to grasp it has caused considerable friction and misunderstanding between American and German managers overseas. I was once called in to advise a firm that has operations all over the world. One of the first questions asked was, "How do you get the Germans to keep their doors open?" In this company the open doors were making the Germans feel exposed and gave the whole operation an unusually relaxed and unbusinesslike air. Closed doors, on the other hand, gave the Americans the feeling that there was a conspiratorial air about the place and that they were being left out. The point is that whether the door is open or shut, it is not going to mean the same thing in the two countries... .

Germans get very technical about intrusion distance, as I mentioned early. When I once asked my students to describe the distance at which a third party would intrude on two people who were talking, there were no answers from the Americans. Each student knew that he could tell when he was being intruded upon but he couldn't define intrusion or tell how he knew when it had occurred. However, a German and an Italian who had worked in Germany were both members of my class and they answered without any hesitation. Both stated that a third party would intrude on two people if he came within seven feet! Many Americans feel that Germans are overly rigid in their behavior, unbending and formal. Some of this impression is created by differences in the handling of chairs while seated. The American doesn't seem to mind if people hitch their chairs up to adjust the distance to the situation—those that do mind would not think of saying anything, for to comment on the manners of others would be impolite. In Germany, however, it is a violation of the mores to change the position of your chair. An added deterrent for those who don't know better is the weight of most German furniture. Even the great architect like Ludwing Mies van der Rohe①, who often rebelled against German tradition in his buildings, made his handsome chairs so heavy that anyone but a strong man would have difficulty in adjusting his seating position. To a German, light furniture is anathema (curse), not only because it seems flimsy but because people move it and thereby destroy the order of things, including intrusions on the "private sphere."...

The middle-class American growing up in the United States feels he has a right to have his own room, or at least part of a room... .

The middle-and upper-class Englishman, on the other hand, is brought up in a nursery shared with brothers and sisters. The oldest occupies a room by himself which he vacates when he leaves for boarding school, possibly even at the age of nine or ten. The difference between a room of one's own and early conditioning to shared space, while seeming inconsequential, has an important effect on the Englishmen's attitude toward his own space. He may never have a permanent "room of his own" and seldom expects one or feels he is entitled to one. Even Members of Parliament have no offices and often conduct their business on the terrace overlooking the Thames. As a consequence, the English are puzzled by the American need for a secure place in which to work, an office. Americans working in England may become annoyed if they are not provided with what they consider appropriate enclosed work space. In regard to the need for walls as a screen for the ego, this places the Americans somewhere between the Germans and the English.

The contrasting English and American patterns have some remarkable implications, particularly if we assume that man, like animals, has a built-in need to shut himself off from others from time to time. An English student in one of my seminars typified what happens when hidden patterns clash. He was quite obviously experiencing strain in his relationships with Americans. Nothing seemed to go right and it was quite clear from his remarks that we did not know how to behave. An analysis of his complaints showed that a major source of irritation was that no American seemed to be able to pick up the subtle clues that

---

① Ludwig Mies van der Rohe (1886−1969): Ludwig Mies van der Rohe, along with Walter Gropius and Le Corbusier, is widely regarded as one of the pioneering masters of modern architecture. "Less is more" and "God is in the details" are his best-known remarks.

there were times when he didn't want his thoughts intruded on. As he stated it, "I'm walking around the apartment and it seems that whenever I want to be alone my roommate starts talking to me. Pretty soon he's asking 'What's the matter?' and wants to know if I'm angry. By then I am angry and say something."

It took some time but finally we were able to identify most of the contrasting features of the American and British problems that were in conflict in this case. When the American wants to be alone he goes into a room and shuts the door—he depends on architectural features for screening. For an American to refuse to talk to someone else present in the same room, to give them the "silent treatment," is the ultimate form of rejection and a sure sign of great displeasure. The English, on the other hand, lacking rooms of their own since childhood, never developed the practice of using space as a refuge from others. They have in effect internalized a set of barriers, which they erect and which others are supposed to recognize. Therefore, the more the Englishman shuts himself off when he is with an American the more likely the American is to break in to assure himself that all is well. Tension lasts until the two get to know each other. The important point is that the spatial and architectural needs of each are not the same at all.

## Questions

1. Why do Germans keep doors closed and Americans leave doors open?
2. Would you mind your guests moving their chairs at your home?
3. What do Americans and English usually do when they want to be alone according to the passage?
4. How do the Chinese use their space? Different from or similar to the ways the Germans, English and Americans use their space?

## 【Activity 19】

*Read the passage about personal distances in the United States, and then make some tentative statements about distances in Chinese social and business relations ( observations on the campus and in other places preferred).*

Various cultures have accustomed their peoples to feel comfortable at different distances in personal conversation situations. According to studies by the anthropologist Edward Hall, it seems there are four main distances in American social and business relations: intimate, personal, social, and public. Intimate distance ranges from direct physical contact to a distance of about 45 centimeters; this is for people's most private relations and activities, between man and wife, for example. Personal distance is about 45 ~ 80 centimeters and is most common when friends, acquaintances and relatives converse. Social distance may be anywhere from about 1.30 meters to 3 meters; people who work together, or people doing business, as well as most of those in conversation at social gatherings tend to keep a distance of about 1.30 ~ 2 meters. Public distance is further than any of the above and is generally for speakers in public areas and for teachers in classrooms. Generally speaking, most Americans ( and other English speaking people) do not like to be too close. Being too far apart, of course, may be awkward, but being too close makes people uncomfortable, if there is not a reason.

PUBLIC SPACE

SOCIAL SPACE

PERSONAL SPACE

INTIMATE SPACE

1.5 ft
(0.45 m)

4 ft
(1.2 m)

12 ft
(3.6 m)

25 ft
(7.6 m)

# 【Activity 20】

*Discuss in small groups when you feel crowded in a bus: when all the seats are occupied or when there is no more standing room. What is your attitude toward crowdedness?*

## Discussion

Generally speaking, you feel crowded when your personal space bubble is violated and you cannot act freely. But crowdedness means different things to people from different cultures. In Montreal, when there is still room for twenty more passengers in a subway car, people prefer to wait for the next train. On buses, passengers have the habit of standing in front of the doors, but they move automatically when they see someone getting off or on. They hate to be touched or pushed. When they unavoidably touch others or are touched, they will usually apologize, and take it for granted that others will apologize.

In general, North Americans feel much more ill at ease in crowded places such as buses and trains than do some of the people from Asian or Mediterranean lands.

# 【Activity 21】

*Study the following three pictures and try to discuss the relationship between the two people on each picture: and think which countries these people are from.*

## Discussion

Based on Hall's categorization of cultures, Richard Lewis further expanded the types of cultures based on the communication styles adopted by each culture type. This cultural classification is called the "The Lewis Model." It also includes a test that individuals can take to determine their own cultural style of communication. In the model, Lewis outlined three categories, of which one represented the contact culture, whereas the other two were a bifurcation of the non-contact cultures. They are as follows.

Linear-active (Pic.1)

It is a subset of non-contact cultures, and is characterized by cool, logical, and decisive actions of the individuals. People of this type of culture tend to be direct and to the point, and are often perceived as being impatient. Their general demeanor is reserved, and they mostly deal with facts rather than speculations. They include cultures like the North American, and Northern European cultures.

Reactive (Pic.2)

It is the other subset of non-contact cultures. The people belonging to it are accommodating and non-confrontational. They are mostly calm and collected and do not instigate or encourage an aggressive behavior. They value decorum and diplomacy over facts and emotions in order to conduct everyday activities in a harmonious fashion. They are very patient listeners, and exhibit neutral body language and expressions. This type includes cultures of Vietnam, China, and Japan.

Multi-active ( Pic.3)

This sub-type represents the contact cultures, where the people are warm and impulsive. Individuals are enthusiastic and readily express emotion in an extravagant display. They prefer personal stories and emotional accounts over cold hard facts. Their enthusiasm is evident in the way they interrupt each others flow of conversation. These type of people are impulsive and openly impatient. Examples of these cultures are those of Brazil, Mexico, and Greece.

Despite the usefulness of the study of proxemics, the theory suffers from extensive criticism on account of it offering sweeping generalizations and cultural stereotypes. While these claims may be partially true, the fact that these studies help in enhancing cross-cultural communication and non-verbal behavior cannot be overlooked.

## REVISION TASKS

1. *Review this chapter with the help of the following questions.*

(1) Is nonverbal behavior important in communication? Why?

(2) What are the functions of nonverbal communication?

(3) Why should we take culture into consideration when we study nonverbal behavior?

(4) List some Chinese gestures that may be misunderstood by Westerners.

(5) What messages do you think silence can communicate in China?

(6) What does time mean to you?

(7) How do people in the world use time differently according to E. T. Hall?

(8) Do you think Chinese people are past-, present- or future-oriented? Why?

(9) Do you agree that everybody carries a "space bubble" with him/her? If yes, do you think people from different cultures have "bubbles" of different size? Why?

(10) How do you think the arrangement of furniture can affect people's behavior?


## 2. *Complete the tasks below.*

(1) Study the four statements and think about which you agree with more and why. Then compare your ideas with your classmates.

> Life should be carefully scheduled.
>
> Life should be free and flexible.
>
> Slow pace of life contributes to health.
>
> Fast pace of life and punctuality lead to success.

(2) Read the passage about the Japanese house and think about what cultural features are reflected in the interior design of a Japanese home. Compare the Japanese house with the Chinese house. Are there any similarities and differences?

During his stay in Japan, Boon, an American student, found that with the exception of a few one-and two-room apartments every house he ever visited in Japan was designed to incorporate three common elements: tatami, fusuma (sliding screens made of paper and light wood) and sboji (a type of even simpler sliding screen). In the houses of rich people the tatami might last longer, the fusuma decorations might be more costly, but the basic concept was the same. It was not surprising to find certain similarities in the behavior and attitudes of the people who lived in them.

The most striking feature of the Japanese house was lack of privacy, the lack of individual, inviolable space. In winter, when the fusuma were kept closed, any sound above a whisper was clearly audible on the other side, and of course in summer they were usually removed altogether. It is impossible to live under such conditions for very long without a common household identity emerging which naturally takes precedence over individual wishes.

There was no such thing as the individual's private room, no bedroom, dining-or sitting-room as such, since in the traditional Japanese house there was no furniture determining that a room should be reserved for any particular function. A person slept in a room, for example, without thinking of it as a bedroom or as his room. In the morning his bedding would be rolled up and stored away in a cupboard; a small table known as the kotatsu, which could also be plugged into the mains to provide heating, was moved back into the center of the room and here the family ate, drank, worked and relaxed for the rest of the day. Although it is becoming standard practice in modern Japan for children to have their own rooms, many middle-aged and nearly all older

Japanese still live in this way. They regard themselves as "one flesh", their property as common to all; the uchi (household, home) was constituted according to a principle of indivisibility. The system of moveable screens meant that the rooms could be used by all the family and for all purposes: walls were built round the uchi, not inside it.

(3) Read the following short passage and answer the questions.

During his presidency, Bill Clinton traveled to China and, at one stop during the trip, spoke to university students in Beijing. His remarks were generally well received and were followed by a lively question and answer session.

When interviewed by an American reporter, one student remarked, "During the question and answer period, I did not understand why the President pointed his finger at us to select a person. We would not use such a rude gesture." Puzzled, the American reporter asked the student what gesture the President should have used.

## Questions

a. What do you think was the gesture that the student recommended①?

b. Can the gesture recommended by the student be applied universally? Why or why not?

(4) Read the following paragraph about physical contact. Do you agree that young people are more likely to touch each other than older people do today? Will you conduct a survey to find out the changes in physical touch between the younger and the older generations in the past 30 years since the opening of China? Try to explain the possible reasons for the change, if any.

The appropriateness of physical contact varies between different cultures. One study of the number of times people conversing in coffee shops over a one-hour period showed the following interesting variations: London, 0; Florida, 2; Paris, 10; and Puerto Rico, 180. Not only does it vary between societies, however, it also varies between different sub-cultures within one society. Young people in Britain, for example, are more likely to touch and hug friends than the older generation. This may be partly a matter of growing older, but it also reflects the fact that the older generation grew up at a time when touching was less common for all age groups. Forty years ago, for example, footballers would never hug and kiss one another on the field after a goal as they do today.

(5) Look at the diagram—Conceptual Site Layout for Drive-through Restaurants. What values are reflected by the kind of drive-through something: drive-through restaurants, drive-through banks, drive-in movies, etc.?

---

① The student answered using a sweep of the open hand—palm upward.

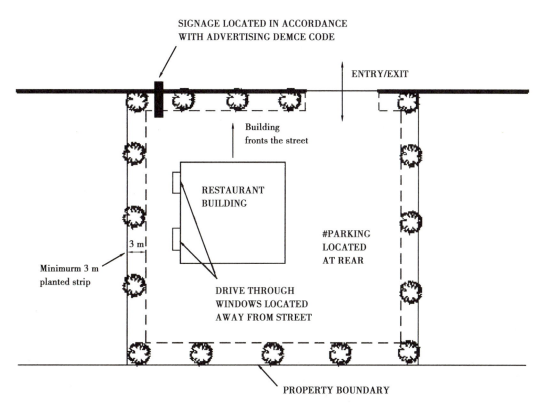

SIGNAGE LOCATED IN ACCORDANCE
WITH ADVERTISING DEMCE CODE

ENTRY/EXIT

Building
fronts the street

RESTAURANT
BUILDING

#PARKING
LOCATED
AT REAR

3 m

Minimurm 3 m
planted strip

DRIVE THROUGH
WINDOWS LOCATED
AWAY FROM STREET

PROPERTY BOUNDARY

(6) When someone sends you a mixed message in which the verbal and nonverbal messages contradict each other, which one do you place more meaning on? Why?

(7) Our personal presentation, style of dress, and surroundings such as a dorm room, apartment, car, or office send nonverbal messages about our identities. Analyze some of the nonverbal signals that your personal presentation or environment send. What do they say about who you are? Do they create the impression that you desire?

# Chapter 6

## Interpersonal Relationships

*I don't care how poor a man is; if he has family, he's rich.* (Colonel Potter)

*I don't need a friend who changes when I change and who nods when I nod; my shadow does that much better.* (Plutarch)

*All human beings have social needs which cannot be satisfied except in association with their follow human beings.* (Francis L.K. Hsu)

# I Warm-up: Read and Say

Professor Zhu Yongtao tells a story in his book *American Values* of an old Chinese lady in America. She lived with the family of her daughter and her son-in-law who is an American, looking after her grandson. One day she fell seriously ill and needed an operation. Hospitalization expenses were high and she had no

medical insurance. The husband said to his wife: "We could not afford the expenses." Extremely surprised and angry, the wife told him that she would save her mother even at the cost of her own life.

*Work in pairs. Offer some possible reasons for the husband, explaining why he said that and some possible reasons for the wife, explaining why she reacted so strongly.*

# II Understanding Interpersonal Relationships

People who learn how to develop interpersonal relationships with most everyone they meet certainly experience more success in life than those who don't. Effective and personal communication stands at the heart of every relationship, whether you are interacting with a friend, a significant other, a family member, a professional colleague or the sales clerk at the local coffee shop. You may ask yourself, what are interpersonal relationships and how can I enjoy more of what they offer?

Two people that share communication in any form have an interpersonal relationship. The types of interpersonal relationships are many and some have lasting consequences. Interpersonal relationships can be brief, such as when you interact with the pharmacist at the local pharmacy, such as the relationship you enjoy with a spouse, friend or family member. Professional interpersonal relationships, such as those with work colleagues, doctors or clients, take on a different tone than the relationships you share with your friends or family members. Any person with whom you share communication, whether face-to-face, anonymously over the Internet, a stranger you pass on the street or the neighbor next door, defines the meaning of interpersonal relationship.

The development of interpersonal relationships is the keystone in building what you want to achieve in life. How you interact with others, your body language, the tone of your voice and the expressions on your face are just as important as what you say, if not more important. Interpersonal relationships involve more than just the verbal communication between people. People communicate as much with their gestures and body language as they do with their voice and words.

When you learn to communicate effectively, people gravitate toward you naturally and interact with you because they sense this quality in you. Your ability to make a person feel comfortable in your presence, no matter their station in life, is a measure of your effectiveness in the development of interpersonal relationships.

In a world where everything is moving at lightning speed, and new forms of communication are changing the face of communication itself, the development of interpersonal relationships becomes increasingly more important. This is evident with the popularity of social networking and the need to "connect" with others electronically. This represents a deep-seeded, but often misunderstood need for interpersonal relationships with other people.

The importance of interpersonal relationships cannot be denied. Whether you interact with a colleague, a stranger who shares your likes or dislikes on your favorite social network, your boss, your wife or your friend—learn to listen, learn to care about what the other person has to say and you will find yourself at the center of several interpersonal relationships that define and give meaning to your life. Making connections with other people starts with your ability to listen to them, your ability to validate them and your ability to let them know that what they say is important to you.

Personal relationships are universally important. As nobody is culture free, peoples of different cultural backgrounds carry different expectations about relationships. The problem is that most of them expect people everywhere to develop relationships in similar ways. This is where misunderstandings and even conflicts may arise. Communications will then be affected. For example, in the warm-up part, the conflict between the husband and wife is mostly due to different values. The Chinese value (filial piety) holds that it is the children's obligation to try their best to help their parents, especially when their parents are old and in trouble. But the American value is that it is up to the father-in-law, not the daughter, let alone the son-in-law, to pay for the medical cost.

Of the many aspects of interpersonal relationships, we will focus on two sets of relationship that every one of us are involved in: family and friendship. It is from the family that one learns their relationships with the world. And friendship, which is related to family life, is what all people value wherever they live. Both are universally significant. However, the manners in which people are related are not the same among different cultures.

# III Family Relationships

## A Family Types

What does family mean to you? What do you know about family? Galvin and Brommel said "We are born into a family, mature in a family, form new families, and leave them at our death. Family life is a universal human experience." It is also an experience that helps shape the manner in which each individual sees the world and their place in it. The importance of family cannot be overemphasized in the development of culture and society.

We can look at family from three different perspectives. First, it is the primary or basic institution of any society—charged with transforming a biological organism into a human being (physiological view). Second, it is the primary caretaker of a culture's core values and worldview and transmits them to new members of the culture (cultural view). Finally, it supplies a person with a part of their identity (personal view).

Traditionally, all people encounter two families during the course of their life. Firstly, the family they are born into, or the family of orientation, being members of which are bonded by blood. Secondly, the family that is formed when, and if, they take a spouse, or the family of procreation, in which the kinship bond comes from marriage.

## 【Activity 1】

*The following two pictures represent two types of family. Can you tell which type each one belongs? Are there other types of family that you know of? Discuss with your classmates and try to list some.*

Parents          Baby

## Discussion

Families can be divided, on the basis of generations, into extended families in which three or more generations live together and nuclear families in which there are only parents and children. But in recent years in some countries, Western ones in particular, definitions of family have begun to include different configurations: live-in couples, heterosexual or homosexual, with or without children, who are unmarried but have a binding relationship; single-parent families, in which the parent—married, never married, widowed, or divorced—lives with their biological or adopted children; blended families, consisting of two adults and their children, all, some, or none of whom may be the offspring from their union; and DINK families, meaning "double-income-no-kid" families.

## B Family Structures

## 【Activity 2】

*Read the passage below concerning family structure, which may help you have a better understanding of the cultural differences between family structures. Then think about the questions that follow.*

Family structure and their inherent relationships and obligations are a major source of cultural difference.

The family is the center of most traditional Asians' lives. Many people worry about their families' welfare, reputation, and honor. Asian families are often extended, including several generations related by blood or marriage living in the same home. An Asian person's misdeeds are not blamed just on the individual but also on the family—including the dead ancestors.

Traditional Chinese, among many other Asians, respect their elders and feel a deep sense of duty toward them. Children repay their parents' sacrifices by being successful and supporting them in old age. This is accepted as a natural part of life in China. In contrast, taking care of aged parents is often viewed as a tremendous burden in the United States, where aging and family support are not honored highly.

Filipinos, the most Americanized of the Asians, are still extremely family-oriented. They are dedicated to helping their children and will sacrifice greatly for their children to get an education. In turn, the children are devoted to their parents, who often live nearby. Grown children who go away and leave the country for economic reasons typically send large parts of their salary home to their parents and the rest of the family.

The Vietnamese family consists of people currently alive as well as the spirits of the dead and of the as-yet unborn. Any decisions or actions are done for family considerations, not individual desires. People's behavior is judged on whether it brings shame or pride to the family. Vietnamese children are trained to rely on their families, to honor elderly people, and to fear foreigners. Many Vietnamese think that their actions in this life will influence their status in the next life.

Fathers in traditional Japanese families are typically stern and aloof. Japanese college students in one study said they would tell their fathers just about as much as they would tell a total stranger. The emotional gap and communication barrier between children and fathers in Japan appear very strong after children have reached a certain age.

Traditional Latin Americans are as family-centered as the traditional Asians. The family is the number one priority, the major frame of reference. Latin Americans believe that family members must help each other. Children in Latin America are taught to respect authority and are given many responsibilities at home. The Latin American family emphasizes authority with the males and older people being the most important. The family in most parts of Latin America includes many relatives who remain in close contact. Family connections are the main way to get things done; dropping names (mentioning the names of important people the family knows) is often necessary to accomplish even simple things.

Although there has been much talk about "family values" in the United States, the family is not a usual frame of reference for decisions in U. S. mainstream culture. Family connections are not so important to most people. Dropping the names of wealthy or famous people the family knows is done in the United States, but it is not viewed positively. More important is a person's own individual "track record" of personal achievement.

Thus, many cultural differences exist in family structures and values. In some cultures, the family is the center of life and the main frame of reference for decisions. In other cultures, the individuals, not the family, is primary. In some cultures, the family's reputation and honor depend on each person's actions: in other cultures, individuals can act without permanently affecting the family life. Some cultures value old people, while other cultures look down on them.

### Questions

1. What cultural values can be found behind the family structures?
2. Is there anything in common in the values behind Asian family relationships?
3. Do you think there are some changes in the Chinese family structure? How do you account for them, if there are any?

## 【Activity 3】

*Read the passage below concerning world family structure, which may help you have a better understanding of family change and child well-being outcomes. Then think about the questions that follow.*

Although two-parent families are becoming less common in many regions, they still constitute a majority of families around the globe. Children are particularly likely to live in two-parent families in Asia and the Middle East. They are more likely to live with one or no parent in the Americas, Europe, Oceania, and sub-Saharan Africa than in other regions.

Extended families, which include parent(s) and kin from outside the nuclear family, are common in Asia, the Middle East, Central/South America, and sub-Saharan Africa, but not in other regions of the world.

Marriage rates are declining in many regions. Adults are most likely to be married in Asia and the Middle East, and are least likely to be married in Central/South America, with Africa, Europe, North America, and Oceania falling in between. Cohabitation (living together without marriage) is more prevalent among couples in Europe, North America, Oceania, and, to an especially high degree, Central/South America.

Childbearing rates are declining worldwide. Sub-Saharan Africa has the highest fertility rates of any region; for instance, in Nigeria, a woman gives birth to an average of 6.0 children over her lifetime. Moderate rates of fertility are found in the Middle East, while the Americas and Oceania have levels of fertility that are sufficient to replace, but not expand, a country's population in the next generation (about 2.1 births per female). Below-replacement-level fertility is widespread in East Asia and Europe.

Amid the decline in marriage rates, childbearing outside of marriage—or nonmarital childbearing—is increasing in many regions. Central/South America and Western Europe have the world's highest rates of nonmarital childbearing, with moderate rates found in North America, Oceania, and Eastern Europe. Countries in sub-Saharan Africa display varying rates of nonmarital childbearing, and the lowest rates are found in Asia and the Middle East. (*source*: *An International Report from Child Trends and Social Trends Institute*)

## Questions

1. With the change of family structure, what family structures still constitute the main majority of families?
2. To your knowledge, is there any change to the extended families in Asia?
3. In your opinion, what are the possible reasons and cultural values for the decline of marriage rates and the prevalence of cohabitation?
4. What do you think of reasons for the decline of childbearing rates worldwide?

## Discussion

The nature, function, and everyday experience of marriage vary tremendously around the world. Marriage looks and feels different in Sweden than it does in Saudi Arabia; in China, compared with Canada; and in Argentina, compared with Australia. Nevertheless, across time and space, in most societies, marriage has been an important institution for structuring adults' intimate relationships and connecting parents to one another and to any children that they have together. In particular, in many countries, marriage has played an important role in providing a stable context for bearing children, rearing them, and integrating fathers into their lives.

However, today, the hold of the institution of marriage over the adult life course and the connection between marriage and parenthood differ significantly from one country to another. Dramatic increases in the prevalence of cohabitation, divorce, and nonmarital childbearing in the Americas, Europe, and Oceania over the last four decades suggest that the institution of marriage is becoming less relevant in these regions  than in other regions. At the same time, the meaning of marriage appears to be shifting in much of the world. Marriage is becoming more of an option for adults, rather than a necessity for their and their children's survival. Cohabitation has emerged as a common precursor or alternative to marriage in many countries for any number of reasons. Adults may look for more flexibility or freedom in their relationships than that marriage seems to offer, or they may feel that they do not have sufficient financial or emotional resources to marry, or they may perceive marriage as a risky undertaking, or simply unnecessary once they are cohabiting.

Children's lives are influenced by the resources and care provided by parents, siblings, and other adults that they live with, as well as by whether their parents are married.

# 【Activity 4】

*When you say "my family," what members do you usually include? What do you think the answers of an American and a Korean will be respectively to this question? Work in pairs.*

## Discussion

Family is important to all peoples in the world. But they may have different ideas as to what people compose their family members. Szalay and Fisher conducted a survey on the concepts of family members and relatives in different cultures. The subjects were Americans and Koreans. Adopting the Association Group Analysis, they asked the subjects to give the words associated with family and relatives respectively.

The result showed the difference: Koreans tend to include grandparents as family members, while Americans take them as relatives.

As a result, married American adults very often name their husband or wife and their children, if they have any, as their "immediate family." If they mention their father, mother, sisters, or brothers, they will define them as separate units, usually living in separate households. Aunts, uncles, cousins, and grandparents are considered "extended family."

From our experiences, we know that in this respect we Chinese are more like the Koreans. In some other cultures family often extends to include not only grandparents, but also cousins, second cousins, third cousins, aunts, uncles, great aunts, great uncles, and even godparents.

The differences lie within different cultures. It is the distinctive cultures that create different families, and socialize different attitudes toward individuals and families.

# 【Activity 5】

*Read the case story concerning different attitudes toward family members and relatives, and answer the questions below. Compare your answers with your neighbor.*

Rosa (Mexican-American) and Annie (American) shared a small dormitory room at a university. They liked each other very much and got along well until a problem came up.

One day, Rosa told Annie, "My second cousin wants to come and see the university. She might want to go to school here next year. Do you mind if she stays with us while she visits?"

"Gee, it's pretty crowded with just the two of us. Where's she going to sleep?"

"Oh, that's no problem. She can sleep in my bed, with me."

"Well, okay," said Annie. "It's up to you."

"Great!" answered Rosa. "She's coming tomorrow."

Two weeks later, the cousin was still with them. Since she did not bring enough money, Rosa paid for all her meals. Rosa missed many of her classes so that she could help her cousin find her way around.

Rosa never complained about any of this to Annie, but Annie decided to speak to her friend.

"Rosa," she said. "I know it's none of my business. But I don't like to see you being treated this way. It's not fair of your cousin to take advantage of you, using your time and your money like this. And how do you ever get any sleep, anyway? I think you should tell her you have your own life to live. After all, she's only your second cousin."

Rosa was surprised. She answered, "Oh, the bed doesn't bother me! It reminds me of sleeping with my sister as a child. You're right, though, about my schoolwork. I know I'm missing too many classes. But family comes first. I just couldn't leave my cousin here by herself."

Even after their conversation, Annie still could not understand her friend. Before her cousin arrived, Rosa had always seemed like such an independent, responsible person, who never missed a class. Annie just could not understand why she had changed.

## Questions

1. Why was Annie confused?
2. Why did Rosa continue to help her (second) cousin?
3. Do you think Rosa's and Annie's ideas are typical of their cultures?
4. Would you do the same for your second cousin as Rosa did? Why or why not?

## Discussion

One of the reasons that Annie could not understand Rosa is this: in American culture, the nuclear family is much more important to the individual than the extended family. Most Americans feel little responsibility toward their second cousins, and may never even have met them. Therefore, Annie was confused because Rosa put so much effort into helping "just" a second cousin. But in Rosa's culture there is not such a big difference between nuclear and extended family responsibilities. For many Hispanics, Asians, Africans, and Arabs, the extended family is very important in child rearing, in social life, and in caring for older people. In these societies, the extended family is the main financial and emotional support for people in times of crisis. This is not so for most Americans, who rely more on friends, institutions, and professionals.

Another reason why Annie and Rosa could not understand each other is their possession of different cultural values. Rosa felt that "family comes first," which means that her own needs come second. Annie had a hard time understanding that point of view because in her culture the individual usually comes first. In the United States the person who can "make it on his own" without help from family is respected, although of course many people do get help from their families. For Americans, it is very important for the individual to be independent of others. For example, U.S. history books are filled with stories of "self-made men," "rugged individualists" who "pulled themselves up by their own bootstraps," "left their pasts behind," and went from "rags to riches" to attain the American dream, "proving" that "God helps those who help themselves." In Hispanic and Asian cultures, however, family members depend on each other more, and families are built around the value of interdependence.

Because of these differences, it is sometimes difficult for people to understand and accept the way family members in other cultures seem to treat each other. It is important, however, to remember that families show their love in different ways. These differences sometimes make it hard to see the reality of family love in every culture in the world.

# 【Activity 6】

*Compare the following two cases about family relations and try to find out differences between them.*

A. An Iranian student who had earned a doctorate in the United States returned home to teach in an Iranian university. He was offered positions at three universities, and had to decide which one to accept. An American friend who was visiting him in Iran noticed that the man's older brother had accompanied him to all the interviews at the universities, and she asked him about it. The man, who was nearly 40, explained that he would follow the advice of his brother in choosing the position. "But why?" asked the American in amazement. "Oh," replied the Iranian, "because he is the head of the family now, and I must do whatever he thinks will be best for the family."

B. John and Jane have two daughters. John works for a large corporation and his wife is an independent contractor.

They own a big house and lead a comfortable upper middle class life. By the time their elder daughter turned 21, John and Jane found an apartment and moved her out. This daughter now goes to college and works part-time as a waitress at a local restaurant. John told me that he didn't like his daughter's job but she assured him that it is temporary. She promised that once she finishes her undergraduate courses, she will find a better job and support herself through graduate programs.

Although she still depends on John and Jane for her college education, she says staying in her parents' house is impossible. She wants to be on her own. Having her own space and with an income from her own work makes her feel independent. John and Jane are proud of what they did. They believe that all parents should let their children go out on their own once they are ready. As their second daughter is approaching her 17th birthday, John and his wife are preparing themselves to face it when the day comes for her to leave home.

When we talked about the empty nest, Jane said, "It is sometimes hard for me to think about the change and our future, but that's the way it is. They are both grown-ups now and they should be on their own."

"They probably also have had enough from our no-this-no-that kind of talks too, and can't wait to get out of the house," John added.

Then I asked whether they would some day move in with their daughters as they grow older, they both said no. Before they were too old or too sick to take care of themselves, they said, they also wanted to be independent from their children! And if, unfortunately, they needed special care, they would move into senior homes rather than living with their daughters and grandchildren. "There would be too much interference in our own way of life," they said.

## Discussion

In Case A, the American was surprised because in a similar situation an American would expect to decide what job would be best for oneself as an individual. Young Americans are encouraged by their families to make such independent career decisions. What would be best for the family is not considered to be as important as what would be best for the individual. For more information about individuality, refer to Chapter Two. But for the Iranian, the primary responsibility of a person is to advance the family as a group, either socially or economically, to bring honor to the family name. What do you think is the Chinese concept in this respect?

In Case B, both parents and children value individual freedom more than dependence on each other. This also reflects their distinct value systems.

We know from Chapter 2 that there are, generally speaking, two types of culture: collectivistic and individualistic. The former is typical of the Iranian culture as can be seen in Case A, and many Asian cultures as well. The latter is often used to describe Western cultures, and the American culture in particular. These two cultures view kinship relationships in different ways. That's why the American in Case A failed to understand what the Iranian man did. In collectivistic cultures kinship relationships emphasize that people are connected to each other by having descended from common ancestors. In doing so, kinship relationships emphasize, first of all, that ascending generations are before, prior to, and even superior to descending generations.

This hierarchy of relationship manifests in the relationships between fathers and sons, mothers and daughters, and even elder brothers and sisters and younger brothers and sisters. This hierarchy extends beyond the family boundary in a collectivistic society, where hierarchy is also established on the basis of age, experience, education, gender, geographical region, political affiliation, and many other dimensions of social organization.

Another aspect of collectivistic culture is the value of loyalty to the family, typical of families in Mexico, Latin America, Africa, parts of Europe, the Middle East, and Asia. In such families, a son's primary motivation for action is thought to be to bring credit to his parents (in the case of the Iranian man, to his extended family) and to provide security for his own and his extended family's descendants. He is not thought of as acting on his own behalf or for his own purpose. In China this loyalty takes the form of filial piety, an important cultural value. Traditionally Chinese children felt a lifelong obligation to their parents, ideally exemplified by an unreserved devotion to please them in every possible way. In China today conflicts often arise between the traditional view of children completely obeying their parents and the modern view of children choosing their own way of life. This is often the subject of many Chinese novels and movies: parents force their son or daughter to marry a person they may not love, but very often the child obeys out of filial piety.

But it doesn't follow that parents do little in return. Instead, parents assume the responsibility of taking care of their children's welfare, including education, job hunting, marriage and so on. In short, parents and children have mutual duties and obligations. It is clear that there is a lot of interdependence in the family.

In contrast, the individualistic culture lays emphasis on egalitarianism, where even in the family, independence is highly valued. That's why in Case B the daughters move out of their parents' house when they are over a certain age, and the parents don't want to stay with their adult children when they are old. When it comes to achievement, an American might say, "I will achieve mainly because of my ability and initiative," while a Mexican whose culture emphasizes family attachment might say, "I will achieve mainly because of my family, and for my family, rather than for myself."

The egalitarian relationship can be seen from the simple fact that children can address their elders by first name, which is impossible in such cultures as Chinese, Korean, Mexican, and the like. The United States is typical of this kind of culture where people assert an extreme of independence from kinship or other hierarchical relationships.

Although many Americans attempt to care for their aging parents in their own homes, many others place parents in nursing homes when permanent health care is required. This need arises, in part, from the fact that in a lot of American homes, both husband and wife work outside the house, leaving no one in the family to care for aging parents and grandparents. Elder people do not like to be burdens of others, even their own children.

# 【Activity 7】

*From the previous activities we have known something about different family structures. This activity is about the way children are reared in different families.*

*Before you read the passage on the way of child-rearing in China and Australia, think about the questions below:*

1. What do you think is the central relationship in a family: that between husband and wife or that between parents and children?
2. Should college students pay their own tuition or should their parents pay?
3. If you had a son of college age, would you pay for his tuition or would you lend him money and then he would repay you when he began to work?
4. Should college students work whole summer to make money and gain experience?
5. What values are reflected from the distinctive ways of child-rearing in China and Australia?

In Australian families the central relationship is usually that between husband and wife, with children being thought of as independent individuals from an early age. The central relationship around which Chinese families revolve is quite different... Couples with children view the roles of mother and father as coming before those of husband and wife.

It is the parents, usually the father, who make all important decisions for the children... This is in marked contrast to Australian families where children play an increasingly important role in deciding such matters as they grow older. This independence is also shown in the Australian custom of children leaving home to live independently of their parents long before marriage...

Australian children are more expected to work while they are studying than their Chinese counterparts. This can also apply to household chores, with Chinese parents expecting their offspring to devote their time to their studies. Children may be excused from such duties right up to marriage, so that married life can sometimes come as a rude awakening to the need to cook and clean.

Whereas in Australia students may work during the holidays or part-time during terms, such activity is rare in China. The situation has changed somewhat since the end of the 1980s, with some students taking work as tutors or providing various services such as dressmaking, but the initial public reaction was one of shock.

It is, then, still viewed as primarily the parents' responsibility to support their children while they are pursuing their education. Money spent in this way is under no circumstances regarded as a loan, to be repaid when the children finish their education and have secured a job. University students in Australia also receive financial assistance from their parents and there is in some families an understanding that this will be repaid once they are financially independent. To many Chinese this may smack of lack of love and family feeling.

The Australian emphasis on fostering independence in children from an early age runs counter to the Chinese view. Chinese children are not expected to be autonomous of their families to the same extent, with dependence on parents up to the time they are married. The protection and care of their children is the duty of parents. Chinese parents would look upon the failure to fulfill this duty as violating the most basic of parental responsibility. Dependence is the inevitable corollary and not something to be shed as soon as possible but the expression of strong family bonds of affection.

## Discussion

The answers to the first two questions are explicitly stated in the passage. Questions 3 and 4 are open. For the answer to question 5, you may go back to the previous activity. Here we would like to say something about overgeneralization. You may find that some of the statements in the passage may not be true in your situation. One reason may be that some facts have been over-generalized. This defect is very difficult to be completely not guilty of, as culture is extremely complex and so exceptions are often found. You should notice that the author of the above passage tries to prevent his statements from being too sweeping by using words like "usually," "more likely," "may" and so on. The statements may show the general trend in Chinese and Australian families, but they may not apply to every family in the two countries.

## 【Activity 8】

From the previous activity, we know that the relationship between parents and children take precedence over that between husband and wife in China. Now we shift to another two pairs of relationships: that between husband and wife and that between parents and married sons in a traditional Chinese family. It is true that things have changed considerably today. The influence of Chinese tradition, however, is still felt to a large degree.

*What is the most important relationship in the traditional Chinese family? According to the tradition, with whom should a man side in the event of any quarrel between his wife and his mother? What would an American man do in the same situation? How many do you know of those traditional ideals for a Chinese family life? Discuss in small groups.*

## Discussion

Traditionally, Chinese parents have enjoyed the freedom to decide their children's future. The most important difference in the relationship between parents and children in Chinese and American families is that the Chinese ask what children should do for their parents, and Americans ask what parents should do for their children. The children are said to "have ears but no mouth." An interruption in the adult's conversation usually brings severe punishment upon the children.

关爱 老 人

养子不孝害如比

The children are fully expected to fulfill their parents' wishes of whether they seem reasonable or not, as illustrated in the tales from Chinese literature called *The Twenty-four Examples of Filial Piety*. The sentiment of Chinese children toward their parents is called filial piety (xiao), which requires unconditional sacrifice to parents in any situation. Thus, "Filial piety is the chief of the hundred virtues." The statement "Parents are always right" reflects the absolute respect children pay to their parents.

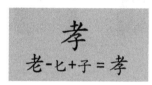

The most important relationship in a traditional Chinese family is believed to be that between parents and married sons. From this point of view a man's relationship with his parents takes precedence over that with his wife. Thus in the event of any quarrel between his wife and his mother, a man should side with his mother. At most he might hope to remain neutral, although this was not regarded as very honorable. To side with his wife would definitely be judged wrong. Contrast this with the situation in contemporary America where the relationship between husband and wife is paramount. The husband would be expected to side with his wife. He might even be counseled to move away from the vicinity of his parents' home to ease the conflict.

If the parent-son relationship is primary, then the arranged marriage is a logical correlate. In this system it is never enough for the wife to please only her husband. Her selection inevitably involves how well she will be able to serve her parents-in-law. This leads to the duty on the part of the sons to support their parents under the same roof. Providing parents with attentive daughters was part of that support.

Support itself, however, was not enough. Sons must respect and obey their parents' wishes. This extended to such matters as not traveling to faraway places during parent's lifetime and not doing anything to invite physical danger for this might deprive the parents of a son (never run any risks). Filial piety found further expression in the notion that children must not bring shame on their parents (even ancestors), and must do everything possible to make them proud of their offspring.

This relationship is a two-way street. Parents, in turn, are intimately tied to their children as are children to parents. Parents are responsible for their sons' education, marriage and support. In the case of daughters this responsibility was limited to education and marriage. Parents had no right to dispose of their property as they wished. It was to be shared equally among the sons.

This support and reverence toward parents continues even after death. Spirits must be placed in household shrines and graves should be tended regularly. Regular rites and sacrifices at shrines and cemeteries are expected to provide continued support and signs of respect for the spirits of the dead.

Today things in China have changed and are still changing. The relationship between husband and wife is assuming a more and more important position in modern families, in urban areas especially. The impact of tradition, however, is still easily found.

# IV Friends and Friendship

All people need friendship in their lives, which is established in different interactions with others, in offices, in schools, on social occasions, and so on. Generally speaking, among various cultures, there are both similarities and differences in how people make friends, how friendship is maintained, how long friendship usually lasts, how the circles of friends are formed, and what friends can talk about with one another.

## 【Activity 9】

*What are your ways of making friends? Do most or many of your friends know each other? Read the following case and express at least one way how Americans may make friends.*

Are you short? Tall? Do you like pumpkins but hate mayonnaise? Whatever your interests, there's a club, society, or group for you.

America is home to about 25,000 clubs, associations, federations, societies, fraternal organizations, and other groups that all sorts of people join. If you are very short, there are the "Short Stature Foundation" and the "Little People of America." If you're tall, there are dozens of clubs for tall people.

If you can't stand mayo, there's the "I Hate Mayonnaise" club; members get the No-Mayo newsletter, and a list of mayo-free restaurants.

Many people claim to have seen the rock star Elvis Presley, even after his death in 1977. Maybe that's because so many people dress up and act like Elvis. Some of them formed the "Elvis Presley Impersonators Association International".

If you like to sing along through a microphone as you listen to music, you might consider the "Karaoke International Sing-Along Association."

The "International Organization of Nerds" has more than 10,000 members. It is led by a man in Cincinnati, Ohio, who calls himself the Supreme Archnerd. He says membership may be for you if your eyeglasses are held together with tape, you keep at least 37 ball-point pens in a plastic pocket protector, and you wear slacks and shirts of clashing plaids.

Many clubs are devoted to food. The "International Banana Club" wants people everywhere to smile more in a world that is "going bananas" (变得野蛮或疯狂). The club has a library and museum of about 12,000 important banana artifacts. The "International Pumpkin Association" is devoted to growing giant pumpkins. "Slow Food Foundation" is a club that objects to fast-food places and promotes the joy of leisurely dining.

Because so many people love animals, there are many clubs to protect favored creatures. For instance, "Bat Conservation International" wants people to know about the many good points of bats. One example: Bats eat tons of insects, which would otherwise bug people.

## Questions

1. Why do you think there are so many clubs in the United States? Is this a way of making friends?
2. Are there so many clubs in China? Why or why not?
3. How do Chinese people make friends?

*Now study the two graphs on the right. One represents the type of friends of a Chinese, and the other, that of an American. Discuss in small groups which is which. What differences are there between the two types of friends? Try to explain why.*

A
B

## Discussion

People from both cultures make friends when they come into contact through diverse activities. Still there are differences in the way people make friends. In the U.S., one's friends tend not to share all aspects of one's life but rather to be linked to specific activities. A person may have work friends, leisure activity friends (like golfing, jogging, bridge, and so forth) and neighborhood friends. They exchange different things with different circles of friends as shown by graph A. Friends of one circle (linked by a particular interest activity such as the card game of bridge) may not know friends of another circle who pursue a different interest activity. For example, two friends who have known each other for years because

of their career and who often talked about work, politics, social problems, and so forth, may know little about each other's family.

In China, on the other hand, one may add friends by knowing friends' and relatives' friends, with their circle of friends becoming larger and larger, as Graph B indicates. One special aspect of friendship (or "connections" is a better word in this case) in China is that friendship may be strengthened by establishing a pseudo-kinship relationship. Thus we hear such terms as "dry father," "dry mother," and "sworn brothers." Sometimes "dry father" is rendered into "godfather" in English. But there is a difference. The bond of godfather-godson is confined to the son and to the older man alone, if the religious affiliation is put aside. This is not so with the Chinese. My "dry father's" wife is my "dry mother" and his children are my "dry siblings." Exactly the same thing holds true with reference to sworn brothers' parents, spouses, and children.

# 【Activity 10】

*How do you think friends should support each other? Look at the following situations and share your ideas in small group.*

Xiao Li is a Chinese student. One day her friend Linlin asked her to go shopping together. She was busy and really had no time to do that but she kept silent, put aside her work and went shopping with Linlin. Would you do the same as Xiao Li did? Do you think an American would do the same in similar situations? Why or why not? Sometimes when you arrive in the States and ring your friend up from the airport, he may tell you on the phone, "Take a 106 from the terminal," or "Get a taxi. Mind you get here in time for dinner." What would you think of your American friend? Would you think he was giving you a cold welcome?

## Discussion

In both cultures friendship is highly valued, but somewhat differently. In the United States you can certainly ask a friend to do something with you as Linlin did, but you would not expect a friend to recognize and respond to your wishes without stating them. Nor would you expect a friend to drop everything to respond to a non-urgent need such as going shopping. In fact an American friend would feel that they had imposed too much if the friend gave up a real need to study to go shopping. One's duties and obligations toward friends, even best friends are understood to have limits; one

does not expect friends to assume burdensome, long-term responsibilities toward oneself. A close friend in the U.S. is a person that one feels free to ask for help, recognizing, however, that the friend may say no, if they give you a reason. This general pattern is especially true of American men; American women tend to accept a greater degree of mutual dependence in their close friendships.

The reason behind this may be that, as with so many other things in the West, people prefer to be independent rather than dependent, so they do not feel comfortable in a relationship in which one person is giving more and the other person is dependent on what is being given. For Westerners friendship is mostly a matter of providing emotional support and spending time together.

On the other hand, the duties and obligations of Chinese friendships are virtually unlimited for all practical purposes. One has enormous responsibility to one's friends. Chinese friends give each other much more concrete help and assistance than Western friends do. For example, they give each other money and might help each other out financially over a long period of time. This is rarely part of Western friendships, because it creates dependence of one person on the other and it goes against the principles of equality and reciprocity. A friend in China is someone who, sensing that you are in need in some way, offers to assist you without waiting to be asked. You can feel free to tell your friend (usually a best friend) what he/she can or should do to help you or please you. This pattern of friendship tends to characterize both males and females in China. Hold onto good friends, they are few and far between.

In times of trouble, both American and Chinese friends give each other emotional support, but they do it differently. A Westerner will respond to a friend's trouble by asking, "What do you want to do?" The idea is to help the friend think out the problem and discover the solution he/she really prefers and then to support that solution. A Chinese friend is more likely to give specific advice to a friend. For instance, if in a friendship between two Chinese women, one woman is arguing with her husband, the friend might advise and she says so directly. An American friend in a similar situation may

want her friend to choose wise actions too, but she will be very cautious about giving direct advice. Instead she may raise questions to encourage her friend to consider carefully what may happen if she does one thing instead of another.

There is another interesting point regarding how friends communicate with each other in these two cultures. In Chapter 4 we noted that Chinese people often communicate indirectly while Westerners tend to be more direct. In close personal relationships such as friendship, the opposite is often the case. Talk between Chinese friends would probably sound too direct to Western ears. We have seen Chinese codes of etiquette require more formal and polite interactions with strangers or guests than what is typical in the West, but relationships with friends are much more informal than similar Western relationships.

Americans apologize to their friends for minor inconveniences such as telephoning late at night or asking for some specific help. Even in close friendships Americans use polite forms such as "could you…" and "would you mind…" They phrase their need in the form of a question that may be declined. Because Chinese do not use these polite forms in their close relationships, they probably do not use them when speaking English with Westerners they know well. As a result they may seem to be too direct or demanding to their Western friends. At the same time an American person who is a friend with a Chinese may continue to be formally polite after two have established their relationship.

## 【Activity 11】

*What is your friendship like? Do you try to keep your friendship lasting through all changes and stages in life? What do you think Americans would do in this respect? Discuss in small groups.*

### Discussion

Here is another difference concerning friendship. In the U.S., a person usually has numerous friends at any one time, but these friendships are usually tied to specific circumstances or activities and will gradually change over the years when circumstances and activities change. Even one's best friends (the few toward whom one feels the greatest emotional attachment and in whom one is most likely to confide) may change several times as the decades roll

by. Their friendship can be close and strong for a while, but then wanes or disappears as soon as the individuals move away from each other. But if these people should meet again, even years later, they would be delighted to continue the friendship.

One important reason for this kind of friendship may be people's high mobility there. Most Americans enjoy moving from place to place very often. In some states only one house in five has people living in it that have been there for more than five years. One may be born in one city, and go to school in another.

He may finish his middle school education in two or three cities and attend a college far across the country. And when he has entered business, he may possibly move from job to job. This job-hopping is a very common practice in the United States. People think that every chance to change a job offers the worker an opportunity to gain or use new experiences in order to move up to a higher position as well as get higher wages or salaries. And job-hopping also gives employers, the bosses, and other managers the chance to benefit from the new ideas and skills that different people bring to their firms or factories. Most Americans love traveling. People often drive their automobiles 100 kilometers or more just to have dinner with a friend or even fly to Europe and back just to watch a football match.

It is clear that the friendship of Americans, like so many other relationships in the United States including marriage, depends on frequent interaction with the other person. If the people involved do not see each other and interact regularly, the relationship is likely to wither and die.

In contrast, in China people seem to expect their friendships to stay the same over a long period of time, maybe for a lifetime. A true friendship is a relationship that endures through changes in the lives of the friends. This is especially true of close friends, whose number is quite limited. Close friends share most aspects of their life. Chinese people rarely allow such friendships to wither and die.

# 【Activity 12】

*From the above case studies, we know that Chinese and Americans enjoy different kinds of friendships. Do you think that friendship means the same to Frenchmen, Germans and Englishmen in the same way as it does to Americans, since they are categorized as Westerners who share quite a lot? Read the following passages. The first is written by E. S. Glenn, an American. The second is written by an American anthropologist, Margaret Mead (1901–1978). The readings will help you find some differences. After you have understood them, make a comparison of the Chinese friendship with those of the Frenchmen, Englishmen, Germans and Americans. The questions that follow may give you some clues for your task of comparison.*

A. The American rhythm is fast. It is characterized by a rapid acceptance of others. However, it is seldom that Americans engage themselves entirely in a friendship. Our friendships are warm, but they are casual—and they are specialized. By specialized I mean, for example, you have a neighbor who drops by in the morning for coffee. You see her frequently, but you never invite her for dinner—not because you don't think she could handle a fork and a knife, but because you have seen her that morning. Therefore, you reserve your more formal invitation to dinner for someone who lives in a more distant part of the city and whom you would not see unless you extended an invitation for a special occasion. Now, if the first friend moves away and the second friend moves nearby, you are likely to reverse this.

We are, in other words, guided very often by our own convenience. We make friends easily, and we don't feel it necessary to go to a great amount of trouble to see friends often when it becomes inconvenient to do so. There is a family whom my family and I like very much, but we haven't seen them for years. It has become inconvenient. Most of us have had that experience, and usually no one is hurt by it.

B. Few Americans stay put for a lifetime. We move from town to city to suburb, from high school to college in a different state, from a job in one region to a better job elsewhere, from the home where we raise our children to the home where we plan to live in retirement. With each move we are forever making new friends, who become part of our new life at that time … Surely in every country people value friendship?

They do. The difficulty when two strangers meet is not a lack of appreciation of friendship, but different expectations about what constitutes friendship and how it comes into being. In those European countries that Americans are most likely to visit, friendship is quite sharply distinguished from other, more casual relations, and is differently related to family life. For a Frenchman, a German or an Englishman friendship is usually more particularized and carries a heavier burden of commitment.

But as we use the word, "friend" can be applied to a wide range of relationships—to someone one has known for a few weeks in a new place, to a close business associate, to a childhood playmate, to a man or woman, to a trusted confidant...

In France, as in many European countries, friends generally are of the same sex, and friendship is seen as basically a relationship between men. Frenchwomen laugh at the idea that "women can't be friends," but they also admit sometimes that for women "it's a different thing." And many French people doubt the possibility of a friendship between a man and a woman...

For the French, friendship is a one-to-one relationship that demands a keen awareness of the other person's intellect, temperament and particular interests. A friend is someone who draws out your own best qualities, with whom you sparkle and become more of whatever the friendship draws upon. Your political philosophy assumes more depth, appreciation of a play becomes sharper, taste in food or wine is accentuated, enjoyment of a sport is intensified.

And French friendships are compartmentalized. A man may play chess with a friend for thirty years without knowing his political opinions, or he may talk politics with him for as long a time without knowing about his personal life. Different friends fill different niches in each person's life. These friendships are not made part of family life. A friend is not expected to spend evenings being nice to children or courteous to a deaf grandmother. These duties, also serious and enjoined, are primarily for relatives. Men who are friends may meet in a café. Intellectual friends may meet in larger groups for evenings of a conversation. Working people may meet at the little bistro (small restaurant or bar) where they drink and talk, far from the family. Marriage does not affect such friendships; wives do not have to be taken into account. ...

In Germany, in contrast with France, friendship is much more articulately a matter of feeling. Adolescents, boys and girls, form deeply sentimental attachments, walk and talk together—not so much to polish their wits as to share their hopes and fears and dreams, to form a common front against the world of school and family and to join in a kind of mutual discovery of each other's and their own inner life. Within the family, the closest relationship over a lifetime is between brothers and sisters. Outside the family, men and women find in their closet friends of the same sex the devotion of a sister, the loyalty of a brother. Appropriately, in Germany friends usually are brought into the family. Children call their father's and their mother's friends "uncle" and "aunt." Between French friends, who have chosen each other for the congeniality of their point of view, lively disagreement and sharpness of argument are the breath of life. But for Germans, whose friendships are based on mutuality of feeling, deep disagreement on any subject that matters to both is regarded as a tragedy. Like ties of kinship, ties of friendship are meant to be irrevocably binding. Young Germans who come to the United States have great difficulty in establishing such friendship with Americans. We view friendship more tentatively, subject to changes in intensity as people move, change their jobs, marry or discover new interests.

English friendships follow still a different pattern. Their basis is shared activity. Activities at different stages of life may be of very different kinds—discovering a common interest in school, serving together in the armed forces, taking part in a foreign mission, staying in the same country house during a crisis. In the midst of the activity, whatever it may be, people fall into steps—sometimes two men or two women, sometimes two couples, sometimes three people—and find that they walk or play a game or tell stories or serve on a tiresome and exacting committee with the same easy anticipation of what each will do day by day or in some critical situation. Americans who have made English friends comment that, even years later, "you can take up just where you left off." Meeting after a long interval, friends are like a couple who begin to dance again when the orchestra strikes up after a pause. English friendships are formed outside the family circle, but they are not, as in Germany, contrapuntal to (relating to) the family nor are they, as in France, separated from the family. And a break in English friendships comes not necessarily as a result of some irreconcilable difference of viewpoint or feeling but instead as a result of misjudgment, where one friend seriously misjudges how the other will think or feel or act. So that suddenly they are out of step.

## Questions

1. How do the Frenchmen, Englishmen, Germans and Americans form their friendships?
2. What do they expect to get from friendships?
3. What are the unique features of their friendships respectively?
4. How is the Chinese friendship similar to and different from theirs?
5. What are some possible reasons for the similarities and differences?

## Discussion

As cultures differ, it is natural to find differences underpinning the friendships of different peoples. In spite of that, friendships of the above mentioned peoples share a lot. Each is related to a whole way of life. There is the recognition that friendship, in contrast with kinship, invokes freedom of choice. A friend is someone who chooses and is chosen. Related to this is the sense each friend gives the other of being a special individual, on whatever grounds this recognition is based. Our friends, in a very real sense, reflect the choices we make in life. And between friends there is inevitably a kind of equality of give and take. It is these similarities that bridge societies.

## ■ Relationships Between Males and Females

## 【Activity 13】

*Read the following story and try to define some different cultural assumptions about men and women. A cultural assumption, shared by the people of a culture, is a belief about the way the world works, a way to understand reality. The questions that follow may give you some clues.*

Kevin was leaving work one Friday, when he stopped to talk to Blanca, a new worker. On Wednesday, they had talked at lunch. She had told him that she had just come from the Dominican Republic two months before. Kevin liked her.

"So, Blanca, what are your plans for the weekend?" asked Kevin.

"Oh, hi, Kevin," Blanca smiled. "I have to go shopping with my cousin for a winter coat."

"Tonight some of us from work are going out to a place called 'The Blue Hat' for beers and something to eat. Would you like to come? I could pick you up at eight if you tell me where you live."

"Okay, Kevin. That sounds nice. I hope it's O.K. if I bring my little sister along."

"As your chaperone (someone who goes out with two unmarried people so that they are not alone together)?" laughed Kevin, in a joking way.

"That's right," said Blanca. "I guess you know something about Dominican culture. It's the only way my parents will let me go."

"Are you serious?" Kevin stared at her. "Well, I'll be there at eight."

When Kevin, Blanca, and her sister arrived at "The Blue Hat", they sat down with Kevin's friends, who were already eating. A waiter came and asked, "What would you like to have? And shall I put this all on one check or will you all pay separately?" "Separate checks, please," answered Kevin. "I'll have a hamburger and French fries and a beer, please. Blanca?"

Blanca opened her purse under the table. Then she whispered something to her sister in Spanish. She looked at the waiter and said, "My sister and I aren't hungry. A coke and a beer, please."

## Questions

1. Why did Blanca bring along her little sister?
2. Why was Kevin surprised?
3. Why did Kevin say "Separate checks, please"?
4. Why did Blanca say she wasn't hungry?

## Discussion

Blanca thought that Kevin was going to pay for her because he had invited her to go out. Until recently, this was the American custom, as well. But things are changing. One reason is that many more American women work today. So, many men and women think it is unfair for men to always pay for everything when they go out. Another reason is that some women say that if a man pays for them, they feel like they owe him something. And some American women prefer to pay because they like to feel like an equal partner on a date. They don't feel equal if they are taken places and paid for.

But lots of American men still do pay for women on dates. They feel it is the man's role to do so. Many American women agree. With women's and men's roles changing so fast in the United States, it is often confusing to know what to do, even for Americans. Blanca's understanding that Kevin was going to pay for her is an example of a cultural assumption. Our cultural assumptions are so much a part of us that many times we cannot believe that the whole world does not see things as we do. Trying to understand cultural assumptions that other people make can help to explain their way of thinking and acting.

For example, Kevin was surprised, maybe even shocked, that Blanca's parents sent a chaperone with her on a date, because to the American way of thinking, Blanca's parents were treating her like a child. American parents assume young people will never learn to act responsibly unless they are given some responsibility and independence. Because of this, American parents allow their unmarried children to go out alone on dates after they reach a certain age. So we see that in different cultures parents care about their children in different ways.

Most Hispanic parents assume the worst will happen if they let their daughters go out alone with a man. "Men will always try to make love to a woman whenever they have the chance" is a Latin American cultural assumption about men. And the Hispanic assumption about women is that they will not be able to stop a man. As a result, most Hispanic parents feel that it is their responsibility to make sure that their daughters are not left alone on a date.

What do you think are the Chinese cultural assumptions about men and women? Are there any changes in the assumptions today?

## ■ Computer-mediated Communication with Other Cultures

## 【Activity 14】

Bruce: Greetings from Sydney. Wanna chat? I work for an Australian university.

Yoko: Greetings from Honolulu. Yes, I work at the University of Hawaii as a graduate tutor. I am in my final year of my doctoral dissertation.

Bruce: great :-), what area of research?

Yoko: I am studying oceanography.

Bruce: I would like to ask you a question..

Yoko: Yes?

Bruce: I am doing some research , can you tell me the Japanese word for "start" on a computer? (PAUSE)

Yoko: You are very rude. I think you are taking advantage of me. If you want to know the answer to this question, then you should consult a dictionary!

Bruce: I am sorry I offended you, good-bye.

### Questions

1. Why did Yoko say " you are very rude. I think you are taking advantage of me"?

2. Why Yoko felt being offended?

3. What has terminated the conversation?

4. What are the underlying causes of the conflict?

### Discussion

This is a fictitious re-enactment of a real chat discussion, which occurred on the Internet chat system called ICQ (short for I Seek You). Thousands of such discussions occur daily on dozens of global chat systems, such as MSN Messenger, AOL groups, IRC, yahoo chat, and CU-SeeMe. What is remarkable about the excerpt is the unresolved misunderstanding, which terminates the conversation. The underlying causes of the conflict are perplexing. A possible cause might be the cultural differences between the two participants. Another explanation could be a mismatch between the perceived social context of ICQ and the unexpected work-related question. A third explanation is that Japanese ex-patriots are often isolated in foreign countries and much more sensitive than Japanese people on their own soil.

Most professionals would agree that the Internet has enabled us to communicate more effectively with our professional colleagues, both locally and overseas. The ease, the speed and the convenience of e-mail, bulletin boards, chat systems and instant messaging has revolutionized our professional practice. But there is one area of concern, which seems overlooked: how does online communication affect intercultural communication? Does our Western, informal and very direct use of computer-mediated communication (CMC) technologies conflict with the way other cultures use these technologies? Or has the whole world become a homogeneous community, each country indistinguishable in terms of their online communication behavior?

We do not think that 5,000 years of civilization can be changed by a mere decade of Internet usage. This means that our enthusiasm for online communication is naive and misplaced when it comes to communicating with members of other cultures. With vastly increased opportunities for communication to take place, we believe that there is an equivalent increase in the amount of miscommunication that is occurring between cultures. We cannot be certain of this however, because there is very little research, which has studied the intersection of communication technology and intercultural communication.

# REVISION TASKS

1. *Review this chapter with the help of the following questions.*

(1) How do you think interpersonal relationships affect communication? What are some positive factors contributing to a successful interpersonal relationships?

(2) Are there any changes in the Chinese family structure now? If yes, what are the changes? Since China has lift restrictions on the one-child policy, what might be the changes for the Chinese family structure?

(3) What do you think is the central relationship in present-day Chinese families: husband and wife or parents and children? Why? Will this kind of relationship affect the education of children, and the relationships between husband and wife?

(4) Why do you think the DINK family now appears in China as well as in some Western countries?

(5) What is emphasized in the Chinese family and the Australian family respectively? Can you explain the differences behind the different ways of child-rearing?

(6) How important is kinship relationship to you? And Why?

(7) How are friends important to you? And why?

(8) What are the differences in the concepts of friends between the Chinese and American cultures?

(9) What do the differences in friendships of various countries tell us about intercultural communication?

(10) Is there anything unique in the Chinese personal relationships?

## 2. Complete the tasks below.

(1) Read the poem① and then express the meaning in your own words.

> Your friend is your needs answered.
>
> He is your field which you sow with love and reap with thanksgiving.
>
> And he is your board and your fireside.
>
> For you come to him with your hunger, and you seek him for peace.

(2) E. S. Glenn says: "My father, when he lived, did not want to live with me. I would have been a pain in his neck." ("a pain in one's neck" means a person, thing or situation that is very annoying but difficult to avoid or get rid of.) Would you have your parents live with you when they are retired? Would your parents choose to live with you when you get married? Work out the reasons for your answer.

(3) Joe Barrett, an American High School Spanish teacher, describes a critical incident experienced by one of his American students during an exchange program in the Dominican Republic. Study the incident written by Mary about her homestay sister Luz. What troubled her and why? How would you respond if you were Mary?

> I brought a Sony Walkman and three of my favorite tapes with me to the Dominican Republic because I like to listen to music when I go on long trips. The other day, when Luz asked to borrow my Walkman to do her English listening homework, I said yes because I wasn't using it at the moment. Later that night, I saw her with the headset on, the Walkman in her hands, and she was dancing merengue. She returned the Walkman to me that night but every day since then, she takes the Walkman to listen to music. What bothers me is that she doesn't even bother to ask; she just takes it without my permission. I would loan it to her sometimes but the way it's going, the batteries will soon run out and I won't be able to listen to music on the trip this Sunday. What should I do?

(4) Read the passage about divorce and see whether you agree with the statement about divorce in China.

> In America, nearly half of all marriages end in divorce. Some states even allow "no-fault" divorce where a justification for divorce is unnecessary. In China, although divorce is becoming more common, marriage is still considered a permanent arrangement and divorce is disapproved of by many people.

(5) Read the following story and answer the questions below.

> Tom (Australian) and Lili (Chinese) are preparing to get married. Before being officially married, they sign a pre-nuptial agreement regarding their separate property. The assumption Tom holds is that as an individual each of them should protect their own rights and property in the event of a future divorce. Tom has had a bad experience from a legal perspective where his divorce made him quite poor when his ex-wife whom he loved for 20 years left him. What is different here is that he states this openly to his would-be wife. This kind of talk gives the Chinese woman the impression of preparing for a divorce instead of marriage, as they seem to be dividing property,

---

① Khalil Gibran, *The Prophet*. 纪伯伦诗集, 2006: 29.

making it very clear what is yours and what is mine.

In his talk about the agreement, Tom says that with the agreement when Lili dies, he could claim her property if she did not bestow it to others in the form of a will, and vice versa. He talks about death as naturally as about shopping. This is unacceptable in China. Such an agreement does focus attention on the motives and trust between the couple. It seems that Westerners are more materialistic, not bothering about any bad luck that might be brought about by mentioning something unwelcome.

## Questions

a. Have you ever thought of signing an agreement before marriage (pre-nuptial agreement on separate property)?

b. How would you feel if the person you loved made such a suggestion?

c. What values can be found behind this kind of agreement?

d. Should people marry for money and wealth first rather than for love?

# Chapter 7

# Social Interaction Customs

*All life is an experiment. The more experiments you made the better.* (Ralph Waldo Emerson)

*Human beings draw close to one another by their common nature, but habits and customs keep them apart.* (Wang Yinglin)[①]

*Two roads diverged in a wood, and I—I took the one less traveled, and that has made all the difference.* (Robert Frost)

---

① Wang Yinglin: 王应麟(1223—1296), Author of *The Three Character Classic*.

# I Warm-up: Read and Say

*Look at the following unhappy experiences of those people in foreign cultures and try to explain why they felt so.*

A. "When I traveled in China, I talked with many people. I knew they were friendly to me, but sometimes their questions made me feel a bit uncomfortable, such as questions about my age and salary."

B. "Once my British friend drove me to a museum. She said she was thirsty and wanted some soft drinks. She asked me if I'd like some, I said no. Then she stopped the car and bought herself a drink, coming back and drinking it alone. I felt very uncomfortable. In China when we go out, we share food and drink, even when the other says no."

C. "People here call me Lao Wai (old foreigner). At first I was quite upset, I looked at myself in the mirror, I wasn't old: I was only in my twenties."

# II Understanding Social Customs

Social customs are very important part of culture. No communication is done without involving some custom rules, explicit or implicit. Customs vary of course from culture to culture. The above incidents illustrate how differences in cultural conventions can lead to difficulties in the communication between people with different cultural backgrounds. Such differences can cause misunderstanding, unsatisfactory interaction and even unpleasant physical reactions.

A saying from *The Three Character Classic* goes "Human beings draw close to one another by their common nature, but habits and customs keep them apart." The first part of the quotation means that humans are social animals, and no one in normal circumstances can live without any contact with others. The second part tells us that there are differences in individuals and groups as well. These diverse habits and customs may cause problems in people's communication, especially when this communication takes place between people with distinct cultural backgrounds. Therefore, to improve our intercultural communication competence, we need to understand differences regarding social customs.

Social customs are closely related to the deep structure of a culture (the focus of Chapter 2) that determines how a person responds to events and other people. Even though what members of a particular culture value and how they perceive the universe explain a lot why people behave the way they do, we shouldn't try to connect every human behavior with a certain value.

**Forms of Address**

In all cultures, every time one person speaks to another, he/she has to choose what is considered the most appropriate option of address to the occasion. This is just one of those seemingly small things in which cultures differ greatly.

# 【Activity 1】

*Read the following cases and think about the questions after each one.*

A. The young lady Marilyn, a major character in *Family Album*, *USA*, addresses her mother-in-law by her first name, Ellen. How do you account for this? Could the same thing happen in China? Why?

B. In China we address a stranger with an advanced age "Grandpa" or "Grandma." Why do we do so since that stranger is not connected to us by blood? How does this sound to an English ear?

C. We Chinese routinely use many position-linked or occupation-linked titles to address people, such as 王经理,马局长,张主任,李医生,etc. Do English native speakers have similar customs? How do you usually address each other?

## Discussion

Nowadays, more and more English native speakers address others by using the first name—Tom, Michael, Linda, Jane, etc. This is especially common among Americans, even when people meet for the first time. This applies not only to people of roughly the same age, but also of different ages. It is not uncommon to hear a child calling a much older person— Joe, Ben, Harry, Helen, etc. This, however, is not accepted in China and other Asian countries. In the case of Marilyn, the use of first name shows that the two ( daughter-in-law and mother-in-law) are very close and on intimate terms.

The following paragraph written by an American may help us have a better idea of how family members address each other in America.

In most American families, children call their parents "mom" and "dad." In a very few families that are especially informal, children call their parents by their given names—a practice that people in other families may find troubling or shocking. On the other hand, calling a stepfather or stepmother by a given name is far more common, and there is a good deal of resistance on the part of teenaged children to calling their biological parent's new spouse "mom" or "dad." Some children feel that there is something objectionable in such use of parental title with newcomers. Sisters and brothers, whether elder or younger, always call each other by their given names, most often in the form of a nickname. A daughter-in-law calls her mother-in-law "mom," "Mrs.—" or by her personal name, depending on the formality or ease of their relations. Frequently a son-in-law will stick to Mr. and Mrs. plus surname in the early period of a marriage and gradually go over to something more intimate—their given names or "mom" and "dad"—at some later stage, often at a signal from his in-laws.

It seems that English native speakers, Americans especially, are quite informal when they communicate with each other. Young employees are free to call older, even much older, co-workers by their given names. University students address their instructors as "professor" or "Professor Smith" or "Mr. Smith" or John, if the instructor prefers to be on a first-name basis with students. University instructors usually don't regard being addressed by the given name as a sign of disrespect, but rather, as an indication that the professor is considered affable and has a sense of equality. If an instructor has a PhD degree, however, he may prefer to be called "Dr.—."

This doesn't mean that there is no sense of hierarchy at all in their culture. A professor from a North American University told a story concerning the point in question. On the day he was granted the doctor's degree, he was about to thank his professor who immediately asked to be addressed on the first name basis instead of the usual Dr. So-and-so, because they were now equals.

But we cannot conclude that mutual use of first names implies friendship and intimacy in every situation. In many offices the use of first names among colleagues is customary, even for colleagues who dislike one another. Use of title plus last name in such a circumstance is still avoided. It would be taken as being too frosty, an open declaration of dislike which would chill relationships still further.

Chinese custom in this aspect certainly seems counter to what is practiced in the English speaking countries. In China seniority is paid respect to. Juniors are supposed to address seniors in a proper way. The use of given names is limited to husband and wife, very close friends, juniors by elders or superiors. What underlies this is probably hierarchy that is prevalent in the society.

Now we turn to case B. In China kin terms are not only used within one's own family but also to other people not related by blood or marriage. These terms are used to show politeness, respectfulness, and friendliness. For example, a child may call a policeman 警察叔叔 (police uncle); a young street peddler may address a middle-aged female customer as 大姐 (elderly sister). Literary translation of these terms would sound odd to an English ear. The English equivalents of the above kinship terms are not so used. In English speaking countries, even with relatives they tend to use just the first name and leave out the term of relationship. We may find Brother Joseph or Sister Mary in English, but these terms would commonly be understood as referring to persons belonging to a Catholic group or some religious or professional society.

Case C mentions another difference in addressing. From the viewpoint of sociolinguistics, forms of addressing can serve as an indication of the relationship of power and solidarity in the society. In calling their superiors or elders, the Chinese are accustomed to the nonreciprocal or asymmetrical addressing, in other words. They use "title +surname" or occupation-linked titles to address their superior or elders rather than call them surnames, while the superior or elders call the addressers their names. The Chinese tend to abide by the polite principle of depreciating oneself and respecting others to show appropriate respects towards the persons being addressed, otherwise, the addresser may be considered as ill mannered, ill educated or rude. So we have Li Ju ("Li Bureau" or "Bureau Li"), Wang Zhuren ("Wang Director" or "Director Wang"), to name just a few. But in English speaking countries, people have a tendency to follow the reciprocal or symmetrical addressing. Although they are different in age and status, they can call the other directly, namely, their names, even first names. Bosses are not addressed by their title and surname, much less by their surname plus their position. There are only a very limited number of such titles to be used with surnames—Doctor, Professor, Judge, President, Senator, Governor, Mayor, General, Colonel, Captain, Father, etc. not arousing offence between them, but demonstrating the sense of intimacy and the conception of "Everyone is created equal." The difference may lie in how people view titles. Chinese seem to recognize who they are, while people from the English world seem to emphasize what one does.

Chinese people feel unnatural addressing a westerner by his given name, feeling that it indicates too close a relationship, and westerners, on the other hand, may feel that if a Chinese insists on using his surname, it indicates an unwillingness to be friendly and maintains a gap between them. So the use of forms like "Miss Mary" or "Mr. Smith" may be a Chinese forms of compromise. With Miss Mary, the use of the given name indicates friendliness, but the addition of the title indicates the respect they feel they ought to show. And with Smith, the lack of a title indicates friendliness, but the use of the surname prevents if sounding too intimate. However, both addressing used by the Chinese sound very strange and uncomfortable to the westerner.

It may be interesting to mention two more Chinese words 老 and 小 that go before the surname. These "prefixes" do not carry disrespect, offense or any negative implications; instead they embody friendliness, equality, and informality. But 老 can also be used as a "suffix" adding to the surname to address a certain elderly person who is highly respected in society, like 郭老. But the number of people who can enjoy this treatment is very small. Again there is nothing comparable in English, where "old" and "young" are used only to describe, never as a title.

## 【Activity 2】

We all know that names have meanings. For example, Chinese names can give all sorts of information about a person. They may give clues about where and when the person was born. Or they may tell us something about family relationships, ethnic group, parents' expectation for the children, sex (though nowadays it is more difficult to tell a girl's name from a boy's), values or even personal characteristics. However, naming is different in other cultures, and so it takes effort to understand the implication of foreign names and the rules governing their use.

*A common practice among students in China who learn a foreign language is to have a name in the target language. When we do so, we need to be careful about the meanings of foreign names. The following passage by Ann Aungles① may help bear out this point.*

When my mother was a young girl, her father was killed in a work accident on the London Docks. Her mother, unable to care for five children, sent three of them, my mother and a younger brother and sister to be looked after in an orphanage in 1910. At that time orphanages in England had two functions: to care for the children and to fill the constant demand for trained domestic servants. In 1916, my mother, 14, became a housemaid in a castle in Scotland. The lady of the house instructed the housekeeper that this new maid was to be known as "Florrie" instead of her own name "Florence".

It was the standard of the day. The upper classes regularly renamed their servants to fit their "servant class" which were lesser beings in the household.

Renaming, of course, was also a feature of slavery and servitude in Australia and the USA. Today Afro-American and indigenous Australian historians record this enforced cultural dispossession of their grand parents and great grandparents as a significant aspect of the gross racism of that era.

So it is a shock to some visiting lecturers in Beijing that students are willing to adopt English names. Names are loaded with symbolism, sometimes positive, sometimes negative. Yet the connotations attached to any one name may not be clear unless one has lived in that country from which it has been derived. But how are students to know the subtleties of naming without fully participating in the life and culture that create these complex layers of meaning.

The results can be disturbing. There is an unease in speaking with a sophisticated, wise, mature young person whose name would be used only by children in England or America. In addition, Western societies are notorious for their consumerism. They are societies of instant disposability. In some ways names are like clothes. Out-of-date names can be an awful embarrassment to young adults.

I am glad that I do not have to take on a name whose cultural underpinnings are a mystery to me. However, it would be good to know what students feel about their English names. Is renaming a pleasure or an inconvenience? Does it instill a sense of alienation and cultural dispossession or of cultural advantage? Or is taking on an English name simply an insignificant aspect of being an English learner in China?

---

① Dr. Ann Aungles, a lecturer at the University of South Australia and at the University of Wollongong in NSW, has been visiting Beijing Foreign Studies University since 2000. This passage is taken from her article "The Political Economy of English Names" (*English Language Learning*, Aug., 2004, p.1.).

## B Greetings and Farewell

### ■ Greetings

Anthropologist J. R. Firth (1972) holds that greeting is the confirmation that communication is possible and thus helps to establish and carry on personal relationships. It may embody politeness, status, position and/or the equality of both parties.

## 【Activity 3】

*Work in pairs. List some common forms of greeting used by the English native speakers and Chinese people. Then try to spot some differences, if there are any.*

### Discussion

The most common forms of greeting among the English-speaking people are *Good morning*, *Good afternoon*, *Good evening*, *How are you*? *How do you do*? *Hello*! *Hi*! *How's everything going*? etc.

In today's China more and more people, especially those in urban areas, tend to use "你/您好!" which is close to *How are you*? or *Hello*! or *Hi*! But some traditional ways of greeting in China differ a lot from English greetings.

One of the most conventional ways to greet a Chinese is simply to say his/her name, perhaps adding a term of respect: Li Xiansheng, Mr. Li, Teacher Li, etc. This type of greeting may give an American an impression that the Chinese person is preparing to ask a question or make a comment. For example, on hearing "Prof. Smith," the American's response is likely to be "Yes?" Of course no question or comment is forthcoming because this is only a greeting.

Another typical Chinese greeting is literally "where are you going?" or "What are you going to do?" or "Have you eaten?" In fact, it is not a genuine question for Chinese, but only a form of greeting. Still another functional greeting in Chinese is to make casual comments about whatever another person is doing to show acknowledgment. For example, a Chinese may say, "Oh, you're working at the computer" to a person who is actually doing so. For native English speakers, this may be saying or asking about the obvious.

Another Chinese term 辛苦啦 might be interesting. It is a good warm expression showing concern with many functions. It may be used in recognition of the fact that a person has put in considerable effort or gone through some hardship to achieve something. It is also used as a greeting to a person who has just completed a long trip, and as a greeting complement to a person who has just done something. For example, a Chinese administrator was heard to warmly greet a foreign teacher by saying "你好,辛苦了!"

The English expressions used to commend people who have finished a difficult task or are still working on it could be *Well done*, *That was/You've got a hard job*. An interpreter translated "您一路上辛苦啦!" as "I am afraid you must have had a tiring journey." It sounds unnatural to an English ear, though it's grammatically correct. The proper expression should be: Did you have a good trip? /Did you enjoy your trip? /How was the trip? etc.

On the other hand, some English greetings have no equivalents in Chinese. For example, when most English speakers meet for the first time, they often have some set expressions such as "I'm pleased to meet you." "Nice to see you." etc.

When two people in Europe meet each other, they may bow, shake hands, or kiss. English people, when they meet for the first time, shake hands and say "How do you do?" A man wearing a hat raises it when he meets a lady, but if he is a soldier, sailor or airman in uniform he salutes, as he does when he meets an officer.

Germany people shake hands also, but before doing so a man clicks his heels together and very stiffly. When he is introduced to a stranger for the first time, he repeats his own name in case the other person did not hear it clearly during the introduction. In some parts of Africa, the correct greeting is to press the thumb ainst that of the other person, while in India a person places his hands together with the fingers pointing up and touches his forehead.

In France, men as well as women often kiss each other on both cheeks. To kiss a lady's hand was once considered very polite all over Europe, and though it is no longer an everyday custom it is still done sometimes on special occasions. In some parts of the world people do not kiss each other at all. The people of the Andaman Islands in the Bay of Bengal and the Australian Aboriginals hug each other violently on meeting, but without kissing. Lapps, Eskimoes and the natives of Polynesia rub noses instead of kissing.

In Europe a man greets a person who is superior to him in position by taking off his hat and standing up, but a Chinese in the same circumstances covers his head. A Polynesian sits down quickly, so that the man of higher rank may look down on him. In the Congo district of Africa a man will politely turn his back whenever an important person speaks to him.

When greeting someone, an American's first instinct is to stick out his or her hand, look directly at the other person, and smile. In some situations, this habit can mean making three mistakes at once. And the moment of greeting is when crucial first impressions are made. Methods and styles of greeting vary greatly around the world, and you need to know which practices apply in different circumstances.

In many eastern countries it is a sign of respect to uncover the feet. Therefore, instead of taking off his hat on entering a house, as a European does, a Burmese or a Hindu will remove his shoes before he crosses the threshold, leaving them outside until he returns.

When greeting Asians for the first time, do not initiate the handshake. You may be forcing a physical contact that the other person finds uncomfortable. Many Asians, particularly Japanese, have learned to accept the handshake when dealing with Westerners. Because the bow is the customary greeting in Japan, a slight bow of the head when responding to a proffered handshake is appropriate. Westerners generally are not expected to be familiar with the complex Japanese bowing protocols.

Most Latinos are more accustomed to physical contact. Even people who know each other only slightly may embrace when greeting.

Middle Easterners, particularly Muslims, avoid body contact with the opposite sex, but persons of the same sex commonly hug when greeting each other. When shaking hands, men should be careful not to pull their hand away too quickly. Orthodox Jews also avoid all physical contact with those of the opposite sex who are not family members.

People from France, Spain, Italy, and Portugal greet friends by kissing on both cheeks.

The smile is the near-universal gesture of friendliness, and in America its meaning is usually clear.

The person smiling is happy, amused, and/or sending out a friendly signal. In other cultures the smile may be sending other signals. In some Latin cultures, for example, the smile may be used to say "Excuse me" or "Please."

If a person from another culture does not return your greeting smile, it doesn't indicate hostility or bad manners. In some Asian cultures, smiling is a gesture to be reserved for informal occasions, and smiling while being formally introduced would be considered disrespectful.

In many cultures, avoiding eye contact is a sign of respect, but such behavior can lead to misunderstandings. For example, some Korean shopkeepers have been accused of disrespecting their non-Korean customers because the shopkeepers avoided making eye contact. The same sort of misunderstanding has occurred between American teachers and Asian students who do not look at the teacher while he or she is speaking.

From the above discussion, we may say that Chinese tend to show more concern for the matters in personal life of others, which are usually taken as privacy by Americans and other Westerners. What you have learned in the previous chapters may help understand the differences here.

## ■ Farewell

Ordinary, daily farewells among both Chinese and Americans occur in two phases. In the first phase, the idea is explicitly introduced that one or more of the parties should depart. In the second phase, one or more of the parties actually does depart from the home, office, or other location.

## 【Activity 4】

Western people believe that to be willing to visit and converse with someone is to have respect for him. To terminate the visiting is not of one's own free will, but because of some other arrangements, therefore they always try to make their leaving sound reluctant by finding some reasons and apologize for it to make the leaving acceptable for both parties.

Among the Americans, phase one tends to be played out as follows. One of the individuals initiates this phase by noting that he/she should depart soon, but no immediate move to depart is actually made. Both continue their conversation or other shared activity for a while longer; this delay may last from a few minutes to as much as an hour. An exception occurs when someone suddenly discovers that a virtually important event will be missed if he/she does not depart at once; in this case, abrupt moves to depart will occur but with apologies.

An American who intends to depart usually explains that a factor in his/her own personal situation compels the departure. They often signal several times before leaving. "Well, it's been nice to see you again. I do enjoy our talk and the lovely dinner, but I must be going soon." "I've got to study for that test tomorrow, so I'd better be going." "Thank you very much for asking me over. I hope we'll be able to get together again before long…" Consolidation in a wider range of common acquaintances also occurs, in expressions such as "Say hello to Jack for me" or "Remember me to John." Sometimes they excuse themselves because of some factor in the life of their interlocutor—"I know you need to get back to work, so I'm going to go now."—but this type of justification is not often thought necessary in a culture where each individual is expected to look out for his/her own welfare.

When phase two arrives, an American visitor goes to the door (thus ending phase one). His/Her exit from the scene (phase two) occurs quite efficiently. The host accompanies the leaver to the door and may briefly exit a short distance beyond it, offering a farewell wave as the leaver disappears.

Now discuss in small groups. What happens among the Chinese during the two phases? Is what the Chinese do similar to or different from what the Americans do?

Parting may be divided into two steps. Before the final prating, there is usual a leave-taking. Western and Chinese cultures have diverse ways to deal with leave-takings. Firstly, in English society, during the closing phase of an encounter, from "I" perspective, reasons for terminating the encounter are presented in mitigatory comments. Typical comments are associated with expressions of apology, such as "I'm afraid I must be off, I have to relieve the baby-sitter" etc.

In Chinese society, during the closing phase of and encounter, usually, from a "you" perspective, reasons for ending the encounter are set forth in mitigatory expressions. Such expressions include "You are busy now, I'm not trouble you anytime." "You must tired, have a rest early, I gone." etc. With these words, they may stand up from their seats. Chinese leave-taking is very short and quick. Western people think it so abrupt that they have not prepare for it. While moving to the door, Chinese employ expressions of apology like "sorry, excuse me." "Sorry, can I have you a while?" It should be noted that these expressions employed by Chinese guests to show concern for their hosts can only be appropriate for business visits in the English environment.

## Discussion

Among the Chinese, phase one tends to occur in a very short period of time. A Chinese also offers a reason for leaving, but it is unlikely to be related to the leaver's own personal situation. The explanation is more often related to the other person's presumed needs.

For example, in a meeting between people in superior and subordinate roles, the subordinate is likely to relate his/her imminent departure to a disinclination to "take up any more of your time." The reason behind this may be that China is a collectivistic culture where a person is not expected to emphasize personal needs as a reason for acting.

Among the Chinese, phase two is typically played out over an extended time, and over an extended space. The two people exit from the door together and continue walking some distance while continuing to converse. The distance that the host accompanies a guest is an indication of the esteem in which he/she is held. It is not uncommon for a host to accompany the guest down several flights of stairs and out of the building before saying the final good-bye.

The final words of the hosts are usually 慢走, 走好, 慢点儿骑, 不远送了, 有空再来, etc. often accompanied with a smile and a gesture of farewell. The English expressions when parting are "See you" "So long" "Good-bye" "Have a nice day." "Take care." etc. with also a smile and a gesture of farewell.

## © Compliments and Responses

Compliments and praises, part of verbal communication, are of important social functions. They help establish good relationship which contributes to the smooth process of communication.

## 【Activity 5】

*Read the following cases and answer the questions after each one.*

A. A young Chinese woman who was new in the U.S. was complimented for the lovely dress she was wearing. "It's exquisite. The colors are so beautiful!" How do you think she responded? What would an American woman respond?

B. A Canadian woman acquaintance of a Chinese art teacher asked him to look over an article that she had written about Chinese painting. He agreed, but added something politely. What do you think he would like to add?

C. A famous Chinese actress married a German. One day when she was acting, her husband was there watching, saying again and again that she was the best actress. The actress' colleagues present asked her afterwards to tell her husband not to praise his own wife like that in public. On learning this, the German wondered what he did wrong.

When the actress and her husband were talking with their Chinese friends at a party, the husband politely praised a Chinese lady on her beauty. The lady's husband said that his wife was moderately good looking when young, but now she was old and no longer so. The lady nodded in agreement with a smile. The actress' husband was surprised. Explain why the German was confused in the first situation and surprised in the second.

## Discussion

In almost all cultures people compliment on others' intelligence, talents, performance, manners, clothes, houses, furniture, cars, and good personal qualities. Appropriate compliments can serve as effective supplementary means in inter-personal communication. But cultural differences exist.

Western and Chinese culture are at polar opposites about compliment. An western hostess, if she is complimented for her cooking skill, is likely to say, "Oh, I am so glad that you liked it. I cook it especially for you." Not so is a Chinese hostess, who will instead apologize for giving you "Nothing." They will say "It's up to you, not very delicious." If translate this into English "I just made some dishes casually and they are not very tasty." Perhaps the foreigner will think why you invite me to you family and have the untasty food. You aren't respect me. The English-speaking people are more active to praise others and to be praised than Chinese people. For example, the Americans are "straight forwardness," the Chinese take pride in "modesty." That modesty has left many a Chinese hungry at an Americans table, for Chinese politeness calls for three refusals before one accepts an offer and the Americans hosts take "no" to mean "no," whether it is the first, second or third time. Still bigger differences exist in people's attitude toward compliments, i.e., in the response to compliments. Chinese are tend to efface themselves in words or refuse it, although they do feel comfortable about the compliments. So many westerners simply feel puzzled or even upset when their Chinese friends refused their compliments. The Chinese people are not intending to be modest with the sacrifice of friendship in so doing, but it is rather due to the traditional Chinese philosophy, that of modesty. The Chinese people regard modesty as a most valuable virtue, so they seldom agree to the compliment on their own.

In case A, the Chinese woman was pleased but somewhat embarrassed. In the typical Chinese fashion, she replied, "Oh, it's just an ordinary dress that I bought in China." But to an American, the reply could imply that the taste of the person who gave the praise in clothing was questionable.

In case B, the art teacher added that "I really know so little about the subject." This would, to a Western ear, be suspicious of "fishing for a compliment," even though the intention might have been quite sincere. Then the Canadian had to say, "Oh, come on, I know you're an expert on Chinese art."

In the case of the actress, her husband was confused in the first situation because in the Western culture it would be natural for family members to praise each other. And the one who is praised usually feels pleased. For example, it would not be unusual to hear an American woman talking about how hard her husband works and how well he has done his job, and about the promotions and honors that he has received. She might do the same about her children, how bright they are, what good marks they earn in school, how active they are in their stamp-collecting groups, etc. But Chinese simply do not praise members of one's own family in front of others.

In the second situation, her husband was surprised because of the same reason mentioned above, and also because in the Western culture, generally, saying that someone is old is impolite, even among family members, both privately and in public. By the way, complimenting a man on his wife's looks or giving remarks as "You have a lovely wife" would be considered perfectly natural and even highly appreciated. But the same compliment would be regarded as almost indecent by many Chinese, especially when concerning those beyond their youth. When it comes to responses to compliments Westerners tend to accept compliment with thanks, while Chinese generally murmur some reply about not being worthy of the praise.

## D Gratitude and Thanks

Expressing thanks is universally held as being civilized. When people have helped you, you usually give thanks to them, indicating your appreciation of the favor. This is true of both the Chinese and Western cultures. Yet differences are easily found between them in how people express their gratitude and thanks, and how they respond to the expressions of gratitude and thanks from others.

## 【Activity 6】

A. If a teacher answered a question you asked, would you say "Thank you"? If your mother bought you a book that you needed, would you say "Thank you" to her? Explain why you would do so or not.

B. Some American tourists said "Thank you" to the interpreter who helped them during the tour. The interpreter replied, "It's my duty to do so." This is appropriate in the Chinese context. But is it appropriate in the English context?

## Discussion

In case A, a Chinese student would always thank the teacher for the latter's help, but would seldom do so to their parents because Chinese people don't usually say "Thank you" to those who are very close. Sometimes they might say something like "累了吧?" "辛苦了" "快歇歇吧" etc. to show their gratitude and concern. One traditional Chinese concept holds that it is the duty of the young and the junior to do something for the elderly and the senior, and so the latter don't have to say thanks.

"Thank you" not only shows politeness but also carries a person's grateful feeling for those who offer help. Without using expressions of gratitude, misunderstandings may arise because the help seems to be taken for granted and is mot appreciated, For westerners, each person is an equal individual, whether he is a family member of not.

Saying "Thank you" is very common in Western cultures, even between parents and children, husband and wife and for very small and most ordinary things. So they thank people all day long. For instance, you will thank the saleswoman after she has attended to you. You will say "Thank you" to the waitress when she brings you a cup of coffee. You will say "Thank you" to the cashier when you have paid for your food and got your change. A teacher will say "Thank you" to a student who has just answered the question. At home, the husband will thank the wife when she brings him a glass of water. The wife will thank the husband if he helps her with her chair.

In contrast, In Chinese, "Thank you" is not frequently used between intimate friends and family members because it may imply a certain distance between the addresser and the addressee. Traditional Chinese customs don't require people to express thanks for the small favors that others have done them. On the other hand, however, native Chinese speakers tend to repeat the terms of thanks many times to show their courtesy and heartfelt thanks especially to those whom they are not familiar with and for what they think are important favors. But this practice which is not done in the West may give Westerners the sense of empty thanks and insincerity, and make them uncomfortable. For example, if an American advisor has spent half an hour helping you edit some letters, you will, of course, want to say, "Thank you, gratefully appreciate your time." That's enough. More statements of thanks would be embarrassing to them.

All cultures require their members to respond to thanks, but they have different expressions. For example, some English expressions such as "It doesn't matter" or "Never mind" can be confusing to Chinese. They are responses to apologies in English, not to thanks as in Chinese. Similarly, some Chinese set expressions like "This is what I should do" or "It's my duty to do so" are confusing to English native speakers. They are responses to thanks in Chinese, but not so in English. Therefore, in the second situation, native English speakers would find it inappropriate to respond with "It's my duty to do so" which means that "you don't have to thank me. I had no choice but to do it because it is my duty, otherwise I would not have done so." This is, of course, far from the message the Chinese interpreter intended to convey.

## 【Activity 7】

*Read the following passage about how Americans and Greeks accept or deflect compliments. Figure out the cultural differences and then talk about how the behavior of Chinese people in similar occasions will be different.*

A personal experience in Greece made me aware of the cultural convention involved in exchanging compliments, which I, in my naive pre-linguist state, had assumed to be evidence of personality. I was invited to a dinner party at the home of a man who was an excellent cook. He had prepared an elaborate dinner, including many small individually-prepared delicacies. During dinner, I complimented the food:

"These are delicious." My host agreed: "Yes they are delicious." I praised: "It must have taken hours to prepare". "Oh, yes," he agreed. "These take many hours to prepare." Taking for granted that a host should not compliment his or her own cooking and should minimize his or her effort, I decided that this host was egotistical.

When leaving the dinner party, I said, "Thank you for the wonderful meal." And the host retorted, "What, those little nothings?" with a dismissing wave of his hand in the direction of the table and a self-deprecation grimace on his face. I was surprised again, and even felt hurt, as if he were implying I had been making too big a deal about the effort involved in preparing the meal. I expected him to accept the compliment this time, saying something like, "The pleasure was mine; come again."

So I say that we differed not about whether compliments should be accepted or deflected, but rather which compliments should be accepted and which deflected—and how. What I had interpreted as a personality characteristic was a cultural convention. This interpretation was repeatedly confirmed when I heard other Greek speakers accepting and turning aside compliments in similar ways.

## E Invitation

There are formal and informal invitations. The ways of inviting may vary in different cultures. Take the Chinese and American practices. For formal invitations there isn't much difference between them. The invitation is usually in the written form and sent out quite some time in advance. In the culture of British and America, it is very important to consult a time before you invite somebody to attend a banquet or take part in social activities. Esp. in America, invite somebody means you are borrow times of others. So they respect time very much. But in informal invitation, there can be confusion, especially when the invitation is done verbally. While in China, people are prefer to an uninvited guest. And otherwise, you will be thought unfriendly if you cannot receive an uninvited guest very well.

## 【Activity 8】

*Now study the following statements and think how you would respond to each of them. Discuss in small groups.*

1. Let's get together soon.
2. I haven't seen you for a long time. You must come round for dinner sometime.
3. It's good seeing you. I'll invite you to tea later.
4. I'm going to give a party this weekend. Come if you like.
5. How about joining us for dinner this Friday night?
6. If an American friend of yours suggests you have lunch with him, you might simply say something

like this, "I'm afraid it'll have to be some place inexpensive, as I have very little money." Your friend may say, "O.K., I'll meet you at McDonald's." Who do you think would pay for the meal?

## Discussion

In 1, 2, and 3, the speaker doesn't give specific time and place for the get together, and doesn't inquire whether the other party would like to accept it. So those statements are just expressions of goodwill rather than genuine invitations. They just indicate that the speaker feels positive toward the other party. The proper response would simply be "Thank you. I'd love to very much." No questions about "when" and "where" should be asked. If ever such questions were raised, the speaker would be embarrassed because he/she doesn't really mean to do any invitation. However, we Chinese rarely do this. We usually take these statements at their face value. So in a joking way this is like "We Chinese mean what we say."

Numbers 4 and 5 are invitations as they give specific time. But they may sound uncertain to an Asian ear because of the tone of the verbal invitation. If a Chinese were to invite a friend to dinner or some other occasions, he/she would most likely say something like: Do come. Please do come...

The likely explanation for the difference is that the Americans who value individual freedom a lot hate to impose anything on others, which they don't like themselves. We Chinese who are accustomed to collectivism tend to show our concern for the others, and we sound a little too eager because we know our culture requires people not to accept invitation immediately.

The sixth statement by your American friend means it is agreed that you two will go Dutch, that is, each person pays for himself/herself. If one says, "Oh, no. I want to take you to lunch at Johnson's." or "I want you to try the steak there. It's great." , this means that he/she intends to pay the bill for both of you. If you feel friendly toward this person, there's no reason why you shouldn't accept the invitation. You may simply say, "Thank you. That would be very nice."

There is one more point about invitation. In both cultures, if anything happens that prevents you from going after you have accepted the invitation, you'd better let the host know either by writing or by phone call.

## F Appointment and Visiting

In many cultures today official meetings are by appointment and the visitors' arrival is expected to be punctual. Still there are differences. In the non-official context, more differences are found.

## 【Activity 9】

*If you were to visit a friend of yours, would you just go or would you make an appointment beforehand? Ask your parents or other elders over forty whether they made an appointment before visiting someone about twenty years ago. How are things changed? What is the practice of people in countries like Germany, France, and Italy in this respect?*

# Discussion

Years ago unannounced visiting of friends was the common practice in China, probably because at that time few Chinese were accessible to telephones. Today, however, with the popularity of telephone and other communication means, more and more Chinese are making appointments before visiting others. Yet there are still unannounced visits. Hosts are usually not very upset when such a visit occurs. Some people believe that the more guests the better, just as an old saying goes: "The frequent visit of guests indicates the hospitality of the hosts."

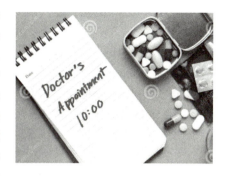

In America any visit, whether it is to see a doctor, a professor, a friend and even a relative, is usually arranged by appointment. This is the courtesy to be observed. When an American is making an appointment, he/she tries to be polite, and leaves room for the other party to refuse if not convenient. Examples are: "I haven't seen you for a long time. I was wondering whether I could come round to visit you sometime." "I'd like to come and see you sometime. Would you be free one afternoon next week?"

Germany is similar to many other northern European countries, including Scandinavian countries and England. In these countries, people living next to each other are not necessarily expected to interact unless they have already met socially. "Dropping in" is simply not an option; you are considered very rude if you do not call in advance to arrange a visit in countries like England, Belgium, Luxembourg, Finland, Norway, and Denmark. Even in Austria, where there is a customary visiting hour at 3:00 p.m., you still must call in advance. Only in certain countries (Sweden is an example) can you drop in unannounced—and this can occur just in the countryside or at summer homes, never in the city.

In France never drop in unannounced to a home, no matter how well you think you know the hosts. French people—like Germans—can live next to neighbors for years and still have no relationship with them at all. Living near people is no reason to strike up a friendship.

In Italy, the next-door neighbor of France, things are different. You can drop in anytime without calling first, except for the resting hours of 2:00 to 4:00 p.m. Many Italian families are much more comfortable with drop-in guests than French families are. Privacy and formality are not as important to Italians as to the French. Italians are legendary for their warmth and friendliness.

Spanish people are not as carefree about visitors as Italians. Spaniards prefer that you call ahead to make sure it is convenient to visit. Normal visiting hours are 4:00 to 6:00 p.m. It is not good to visit immediately after lunch, when many people are resting. An invitation to a Spanish home is very special. Spanish people rarely invite foreigners to their homes until they know them well. They think carefully before inviting people and are very formal when they offer the invitation.

People in most Latin American countries feel comfortable if guests drop in without warning. In fact, the more guests the better, some people feel! Guests are greeted warmly, often with hugs and kisses. Do not be surprised if you are asked to stay for a full meal even if you have just come by for a chat.

# 【Activity 10】

*When one of your colleagues or classmates is sick in hospital, will you go and visit him/her? If you do, will you give notice before you go? You are to read a story concerning hospital visiting. After reading it, try to explain why the visitors were upset and the patient and his wife were unhappy.*

Jim had to have an emergency operation during his one-year teaching post in China. Starting from the next day after the operation, his Chinese colleagues went to the hospital to see him during visiting hours. To the discomfort of Jim and his wife, none of them gave any notice before their visit, and some came at inconvenient times. For the first three days, Jim had a hard time recovering from the operation, and his wife would stop the visitors at the door, and briefed them about how Jim was doing. But the visitors were very upset about not seeing Jim.

## Discussion

In China it is a common practice to visit patients in hospital. It is believed that a patient needs to know that others care about him/her. In fact, a patient would be upset if no one from his/her work unit makes any hospital visits, and might take it a sign of his/her own unpopularity. People also tend to think that the patient is bored in the ward and would always be happy to see a visitor. It is usually not considered necessary to inform the patient of an intended visit because the patient is doing nothing other than lying in bed. What is behind this practice may be that Chinese who are generally group-oriented lay much stress on mutual care within their inner-groups, believing that harmony and unity will be thus achieved.

In North America, however, visitor access to hospital patients is tightly controlled by hospitals. The number of visitors and time of visits is regulated to ensure that the patient can rest and recuperate. This is especially true immediately following surgery. At such times, normally only immediate family are allowed to visit. This may be because Americans who believe in individualism tend to be private about their personal lives. Having a large number of acquaintances drop by unexpectedly at a time when Jim is very fragile proves stressful for his wife, and possibly to him if he is alert enough to know he has visitors.

It is important for us to know that all people care for others, but they have different ways to show their concern for others due to their cultural backgrounds.

## G Hospitality

Hospitality, which refers to the friendly and generous reception and entertainment of guests, visitors, or strangers, is universal, but what is hospitality varies from culture to culture. Trouble may result if you are ignorant of the conventional practices of hospitality in cultures other than your own.

# 【Activity 11】

*From the following story Different Lunch Boxes you will find that the well-intentioned practice on the Chinese side was ill-interpreted. Discuss with your partner why there was such misunderstanding. Try to offer at least two possible reasons for each side.*

Peter was one of the American technicians who came to China to help set up a coffee plant. He was in China for six months. Before leaving for home, one of his Chinese colleagues took him out to dinner. Peter decided to ask him a question that had puzzled him for as long as he worked in the plant.

"Why is it that the Chinese workers have stainless boxes for their lunch, while we foreigners have lunch put in the disposable plastic boxes?"

The colleague smiled, "It is because the plastic boxes are more convenient—they are disposable. With the stainless boxes, you have to wash them after every meal."

But Peter was not convinced. "I don't think so. Stainless boxes are much better than plastic boxes. They look more professional, they are more durable, and they protect your lunch better."

## Discussion

From the Chinese perspective, hospitality is always behind the way Chinese treat their guests. It is a deep and honored Chinese tradition. Though stainless boxes are nice to have, having to wash them after every meal is not as convenient as a plastic box that can be thrown away.

But the North Americans look at the same issue differently. They think that plastic is less expensive than stainless. The worth of many objects (other than those given as a gift) is usually proportional to cost. By being given a less-costly lunch box, Peter felt that he and his team were being discriminated against. From a North American perspective, Peter's interpretation of being given plastic rather than stainless boxes as second-class treatment was predictable. He did not recognize that he and his team were given the same lunch as their Chinese colleagues in a form that eliminated the need for them to do the dishes.

The lesson we can draw here is that it is risky to assume that the other side understands the motivations behind actions or traditions when cross-cultural understanding is involved.

# 【Activity 12】

*If you and some of your friends go for a meal at a restaurant, who is going to pay the bill? Read the following passage and then discuss in small groups why we Chinese behave differently from Westerners when it comes to paying the bill.*

In America and England it is quite common for friends to share the cost of the meal equally between them, to go Dutch, as we say. Hence in China you can come across the sight of Westerners at the end of a meal busily pooling their money in order to put together the right amount to pay the bill. All this before bemused Chinese who would typically rather fight over who is to pick up the tab, thinking it seems mean to only pay for oneself. In fact to Western eyes going Dutch, splitting the bill, implies equality between friends. Invited out by one's boss one would not expect to pay, but to grab the bill when with friends and refuse to let them contribute may seem to some to suggest that they are too poor to pay their own way. On other occasions, however, Westerners will treat a friend to a meal and then, as in China, there is usually the expectation that the guest will return the favor by inviting the host to a meal later. The same thing applies, of course, if they invite one another to their homes. When meeting at a pub for drinks, a popular pastime in England, each person in the group will take it in turns to buy his round, asking everyone what they would like and then going to the bar to get the drinks. Those who don't buy a round when it is their turn are frowned upon. While no one is likely to complain to their face they may well earn a reputation as scroungers and be gossiped about behind their backs if they do it habitually.

## 【Activity 13】

*Study the following cases and then answer the questions after each one. Better discuss with your partner.*

A. At the opening ceremony of a training program, a Chinese employee (director of the Training Dept.) at an overseas company introduced an American instructor: "Now, let's welcome Mr. Smith to give us an excellent and enlightening speech." Is this remark appropriate in the Chinese context? And in the American one? If the speaker were a distinguished person, how would the Chinese welcome him/her to an organization?

B. The following is what an American wrote of a Chinese banquet. Can you see some characteristics of the Chinese way of entertaining guests to dinner from the account?

The first six or seven dishes seemed to fill the table to overflowing, with plates precariously wedged one on top of another. With my American-bred expectations, I assumed this vast first wave of food was surely the total number of dishes to be served, and I dug in greedily, dazzled by the variety and sheer quantity. The Chinese guests around me, however, had a different reaction. They seemed merely to  take a bite or two of each dish and then put their chopsticks down, continuing to chat. "They must not be very hungry," I thought with a shrug, and continued my feast. To my surprise, more dishes soon were piled on top of the already mountainous stack. Plus two or three soups, side dishes, desserts, and delicacies of various kinds, all seemingly enough to feed the entire People's Liberation Army. No wonder my fellow guests had merely sampled a few bites of each dish; they knew very well that these first few items were just the tip of a titanic culinary iceberg. I, however, was so stuffed after the first fifteen minutes that I could only watch in a bloated stupor as the remainder of the banquet took its course.

### Discussion

In case A, to the surprise of all the Chinese present, the American instructor appeared quite unhappy on hearing the remark. The reason is that to an American ear this remark implies that the Chinese host seemed to be encouraging him to try his best because the host had little confidence in him in doing the training job.

Similarly, there is difference in what a host says when the guest speaker finishes his/her speech. He Ziran gave an example in Pragmatics and English Learning: "Dr. Smith, you've made a wonderful lecture!" It is all right in Chinese, but sounds a little too much to an English ear, for in the West, the academic report should be factual, and thus can't be "wonderful." The appropriate response might be something like: "I really appreciate your lecture, Dr. Smith."

Moreover, in China if a distinguished visitor is coming to a certain institution, there will always be banners, large boards or posters with expressions like: "热烈欢迎尊贵的、著名的……光临我院(所、厂等)考察/来做学术报告/来进行学术交流", etc. The English way, however, is much simpler, just "Welcome to...".

One interpretation for case B is that when entertaining guests Chinese people usually prepare a lot of food, quite more than enough, even though it may mean that they have to tighten their budge on food for a few days. They would feel embarrassed if the food tends to be not enough or even just enough. The Chinese host usually goes to trouble to make sure there is something left after the meal. Such is the traditional Chinese custom.

The "wastefulness" of this practice has been criticized in China recently, and some advocate ordering more sensible quantities if at a restaurant, or at least taking the leftovers home in a lunch box. But there remains a deeply-ingrained tendency on the part of a host to provide much more than the guests could possibly eat.

The dinner Westerners give is usually, compared with ours, much simpler. The president of the college where one author of this book once worked jokingly summed up the western banquet this way: first, running water, then some thick liquid (soup), followed by raw vegetables (salad) and a piece of meat, finally some fruit or ice-cream. One such example is as follows:

Guangdong TV's 1998 Chinese New Year's Festival Show was filmed in Los Angeles, with many performers and technicians from mainland China flown over to the U.S. to collaborate with the American TV people on the broadcast. The Chinese performers stayed at a Holiday Inn (a popular and reputable motel chain in the U.S.).

The first lunch the motel provided was a rather perfunctory but quite typical American meal in such situations: a smorgasbord(瑞典式自助餐) arrangement, with sandwiches, cold cuts, fresh fruit, salad, and soup. No hot dishes, no rice. The performers were disappointed and confused. Some asked, "Is this some kind of preliminary snack, or what?"

We know why the performers felt that way, because the Chinese way of entertaining guests is quite different from the American one.

In addition, traditional Chinese custom requires that during the course of entertaining, the host has to always pour more wine or tea to the guest's glass or cup, and always adds more food to the guest's plate or bowl without asking whether it's wanted or even facing a refusal. Why? The Chinese guests know how to respond to this hospitality. They simply leave the wine or tea or food in the container and stop having any more. But this may be confusing to people with different cultural backgrounds.

In the West, it is impolite for the host to keep offering something again and again or press something on the guest. Without any knowledge of such differences, a Chinese guest in a Western situation would suffer from hunger or thirst, because in our culture it is good manners for the guest to refuse the offer of food or drink even though he/she needs it badly.

# 【Activity 14】

*Suppose a respectable elderly gentleman is having dinner with a young lady in a restaurant. Who do you think would be first served in China? And who would a Western waiter first serve? Answer these questions and try to explain why.*

## Discussion

In China it is normally the elderly man who gets the first service, because in China where hierarchy is prevalent, it is the elderly or the superior who is supposed to get special respect. But in the West, it is likely the young lady who is first served because of their "ladies first" tradition.

This tradition is manifested in many other ways in the West. At a formal party, when a lady guest goes into the sitting room, most men in the room are likely to stand up. The ladies there may not rise whether the new comer is a man or a woman. Men usually open doors for women and women generally walk ahead of men into a room or a restaurant, unless the men have to be ahead of the ladies to choose the tables, to open the door of a car or render other services. On the street, men almost always walk or cross the street on the side which is close to the traffic. But if a man walks with two ladies, he should walk in-between them.

The courtesy "ladies first" can trace back to different sources. One of them may be Christianity, where Maria is respected as embodying noble and lofty emotions. Knighthood that originated in the Middle Ages Europe might be a direct source. The knightly code embodies courage, piety, honor, loyalty and respect for women. This practice requires men to take care of women in many occasions. But since the 1960s some women have protested against being taken special care of. This is partly because they are quite independent, and partly because they believe "ladies first" implies that women are inferior to men.

## 【Activity 15】

*Suppose you work at a school and you are married. One day the school invites you to a banquet. Do you think the invitation should include your spouse who doesn't work in the same school? The following is a letter an American teacher wrote to his friend James. Read the letter and give him a reply, explain the practice in China.*

Dear James,

Teaching in China is a real pleasure, but people here can sometimes be a little mean with their hospitality. Yesterday I was invited to an official banquet in the evening by the university. As you know, I enjoy Chinese food and would have loved to have gone, but for some reason Janet was not included in the invitation. Naturally I couldn't accept and leave the dear old wife at home so I had to make an excuse to get out of it. Can't think why they should want to snub her in that way, but it has made both of us feel that we are not really welcome...

## Discussion

To us Chinese the American teacher's accusation of meanness is unfair—his hosts were not being ungenerous. However, his complaint is understandable given his lack of knowledge of Chinese culture. Expectations about when spouses should be included in invitations differ between China and the West. Generally speaking, in the West for invitations to any meal taking place in the evening, ranging from those given at someone's home through to dining out together or attending formal banquets, both husband and wife will be included. This is not expected in the case of mid-day meals, probably because couples often work in different places and some jobs involve taking a "working lunch" with clients or colleagues. Here in China, however, it is quite common for only the husband or wife to be invited to a meal, either in work unites or between friends, and neither husband or wife will feel offended if one of them is not invited.

# REVISION TASKS

1. *Review this chapter with the help of the following questions.*

(1) Do you have an English name? If yes, why? How did you choose it? Do you know some popular English names for girls and boys? If yes, do know the meaning of these English names?

(2) List some of the differences in addressing people in Chinese and Western cultures.

(3) Why do you think kinship terms in China are not only used within one's own family but also extended to other people not related by blood or marriage?

(4) What are the traditional Chinese ways of exchanging compliments? How many of them are still used?

(5) Why do you think there is hospitality? What is its importance in communication?

(6) Why does hospitality differ in different cultures?

(7) List some differences in showing hospitality in Chinese and Western cultures.

(8) We know that there remains a deeply-ingrained tendency in China that the host should provide much more food than the guests could possibly eat. If you treated some foreigners in this way, and they told you that they "eat to live, not live to eat," how would you feel and what would you say to them?

(9) What do you think of going Dutch? In what social situations, do you practice "going Dutch?"

(10) What do you think of the "Ladies first" principle? Does it connote sex discrimination?

2. *Complete the tasks below.*

(1) Suppose one of your classmates is in hospital, you go to visit him/her. What will you say to him/her? Would a Westerner make similar remarks in the similar situation?

(2) Why is there gift-giving/receiving in society? What are the rules in China for doing this? Should people give expensive gifts? Why? If you were a manager, one of your employees one day gave you an expensive suitcase as a gift, how would you take it? Why?

(3) Read the passage about an American's experience of the French conversational style. Discuss in small groups how the Chinese conversational style is similar to or different from it.

One of the most challenging cultural practices I have had to learn is the conversational style of the French (and other francophone), specifically, how they participate in casual conversations or discussions. Their style, broadly speaking, stands almost in direct opposition to the mainstream

American conversational participation I grew up with. The first time I encountered this style was at a faculty party in Bondoukou, Côte d' Ivoire. A collection of teachers had gathered at a teacher's home for the aperitif. The group included a combination of French nationals, Ivorians, a Ghanaian, and me, the sole American. We sat around the courtyard, drinks in hand, nibbling on hors d'oeuvres, and, of course, talking. The conversation was full of force, and it was like nothing I'd ever experienced before.

I could not follow what was being talked about. Topics seemed to jump from one theme to another, arising from everywhere around me. I didn't know where to put my attention. Everyone was talking at once, except for me and perhaps Kofi, the Ghanaian. As soon as I turned my head to follow what I thought was the thread of the conversation, talk erupted behind me, or to one side or another. People there seemed to be able to listen and talk at the same time, sometimes actually speaking to more than one person at once. I saw absolutely no way to enter the conversation. I heard no hesitations, no moments of silence. The direct questions I waited to bring me into the conversation were never asked. Nursing my drink, I sat silently, nodding, showing attentiveness and interest, feeling intensely uncomfortable.

(4) Look at the following generalizations about the U.S. culture and decide whether they are true or false.

a. Most young people in the U.S. start dating around the age of twelve.

b. The bill in most restaurants in the U.S. includes a service charge.

c. In the U.S., shopping for groceries is usually done by going to a supermarket once a week.

d. Most Americans do their own housework.

e. In American cities, people who walk their dogs in public are required to clean up after them.

f. It is polite to ask Americans questions about their salary.

g. When invited to a birthday party in the U.S., you are expected to give a gift of money.

h. In the U.S., saying "Thank you" is a common way of reacting to a compliment.

i. The cost of university tuition is so expensive in the U.S. that only the very rich can afford it.

j. In families, it is often the mother who does most of the food shopping.

(keys[1])

(5) Imagine that the situations below take place in an English-speaking country. What would you do in each situation? In some cases, more than one answer is possible.

1) You've been having digestive problems for a week, and have just started to feel better. You meet a British friend at a party. You friend says, "How are you?" What would you do?

a. Start talking in detail about your problem.

---

[1]  a, b, f, g, and i are false.

b. Say "Fine, thanks. How are you?"

c. Say "Not bad, thanks. How are you?"

d. Nothing.

2) You're visiting an American friend in her new apartment. You like the apartment and you want your friend to know. What would you do?

a. Say "Your apartment is nice. How much is the rent?"

b. Say "Gee, this place is really nice."

c. Say "I really like your apartment."

d. Say nothing, but show that you are interested by walking around, looking at everything in the apartment, and picking up everything that is movable.

3) You've been invited to dinner at a friend's home. You're about to sit down to eat, but you want to use the toilet first. What would you do?

a. Say "Excuse me. Where's the toilet?"

b. Say "Could I wash my hands before dinner?"

c. Say "Do you mind if I use the bathroom?"

d. Say nothing and start looking around the house for the toilet.

4) You're a guest in a British or American friend's home. Your friend asks if you would like something to drink. You really would like a drink. What would you do?

a. Say "Yes, please."

b. Say "Yes, that would be lovely."

c. Say "No, thank you" and wait for your friend to ask you again.

d. Say "That's OK. I can get it myself."

5) You've just been introduced to a British or American friend's parents. What would you do?

a. Say "Hello," and bow.

b. Say nothing and shake hands.

c. Say "Nice to meet you," and shake hands.

d. Say "Hi!"

(keys①)

---

① 1) b and c are right. You should respond by saying something like "Fine. How are you?" or "Very well, thanks. And you?" You should not start to talk about your medical problems. 2) b and c are right. It's polite to praise the apartment, but it is impolite to ask how much the rent is. 3) b and c are right. You should not mention the toilet directly. 4) a and b are right. Your friend will probably not ask you again. 5) c is right.

# Chapter 8

# Improving Intercultural Competence

*Tolerance for each other's differences is the only way we can survive.* (Whoopi Goldberg)

*The highest virtue here may be the least in another world.* (Khalil Gibran)

*As the traveler who has once been away from home is wiser than one who has never left his own doorstep, so a knowledge of one other culture should sharpen our ability to scrutinize more steadily, to appreciate more lovingly, our own.*" (Margaret Mead)

# I Warm-up: Look and Say

*Study the two pictures. First, look at the picture "Sheep on Boat."*
*Where are the sheep? What are they doing? Does it remind you of a certain*
*idiom in the English language?*

Now look at the picture "Two Men." How does each of them look alike? What are they holding in their hands? What are they doing? Do they understand each other? Why or why not? Does this picture give you some clues about the study of intercultural communication?

The English idiom related to the picture above reminds us of "all in the same boat." It means that people who are in the same boat must work as a team because they face the same challenges together, so they need to cooperate in order to succeed. In today's world all of us live on the same planet, so we have to work together to ensure a better environment where peace and development bring us a better life. To that end, we have to try to understand each other, which is the basis of working together. This chapter deals with some points that we should be aware of and some endeavors that we should commit to if we are to understand each other.

It is certain that a lack of knowledge of others leads to misunderstanding, but knowledge of others may also lead to misunderstanding, especially if the knowledge is false or only partly true. This is what the picture of men with books tells us.

Misunderstanding impedes communication. This kind of problem may come up between people within the same culture who share a lot, let alone between people with different cultural backgrounds. In the field of intercultural communication there are other problems that we have to study so as to become effective when we interact with people from other cultures.

# II Intercultural Communication Competence

Greek philosopher Heraclitus said, "You can never step into the same river twice." "Everything flows, nothing stays still." What he meant was that change is the most important fact about the world. In fact, it has been happening all the time and at all places, and is especially characteristic of our modern world. The obvious feature is the figurative shrinking of the earth, the emergence of the "global village" where people of different countries are brought into closer and more frequent contacts with each other. As a result, intercultural communication has become increasingly important.

As we know, commu-nication, language and culture cannot be separated. Successful intercultural communication demands cultural fluency as well as linguistic fluency. If we are to communicate effectively in English, we need more than just competence in English grammar and vocabulary. To be culturally fluent, we should be aware of and sensitive to the culturally determined patterns of verbal and nonverbal communication which speakers of the target culture follow, how they treat time and space, and why they think and behave the way they do (their values, beliefs, attitudes and assumptions in diverse aspects of life).

There can be four levels of awareness. When we first get in touch with another culture, we are aware of some superficial or very visible cultural traits, and we feel it is unbelievable, exotic or bizarre and possibly entertaining. When we get to know more about that culture, we will be aware of some meaningful cultural traits, quite different from our own, and we may feel that things are unbelievable but in a somewhat frustrating way. Then with more and deeper understanding, we begin to be aware of more significant and subtle cultural traits, and we feel believable but only at thinking level. Finally, if we get into that culture and live in it, we will be aware of how a culture feels to someone who is a member of it, and we may feel it is believable at an emotional level as it is a lived experience.

Cultural competence requires some adaptation to the cultures by both parties participating in the communication. It means that either party has to make a certain compromise, or to make some changes in behavior that are different from one's own culture. For example, Chinese don't usually accept a present without several refusals. But when some Chinese people get a present from an American, they accept it at once and open it immediately in front of the guest while giving complimentary remarks. On the other hand, the Americans who know that in China handshaking is often practiced take the initiative to shake hands while visiting China. The purpose of such adaptation is to achieve smooth communication. But it doesn't mean that we should "go native," to do exactly as the people of the other culture do. It is both impossible and unnecessary. To sum up, intercultural communication competence means being able to communicate efficiently and effectively with people from other cultures, to achieve mutual understanding and to gain better cooperation. In other words, with adequate competence, we will be able to know when, where, how, to whom to say/do what, understand why and in what ways people are similar and different, to facilitate further understanding and communication worldwide so as to promote friendship that contributes to a better world.

## 【Activity 1】

*Read the case story concerning the communication across cultures and discuss in small groups what problems may arise in this kind of communication and why. The questions that follow may give you some clues.*

John, an American, was happy when his Saudi Arabian neighbor invited him to a party at his apartment, just down the hall in the same apartment building. After work, John made a special trip to the neighborhood liquor store to buy a bottle of his favorite white wine for the party.

When John got to the party, his host, Mazen, greeted him at the door in a friendly way. He put his arm around John's shoulders and said, "Oh, John. I'm so glad you could come."

John answered, "How're you doing, Mazen? Looks like a great party. Here, I brought you some of my favorite wine."

Mazen took the wine but said nothing about it. Then he said, "I'd like you to meet my sister who came from Riad, my city, just two days ago."

John reached out to shake Mazen's sister's hand, but she just stood there, and stopped smiling. John decided that she was probably shy. So he tried to be especially friendly to her. They had a nice conversation until Mazen ended it.

John was saying to Mazen's sister, "So, it looks like your brother is going to show you the town." Because John was feeling very friendly to his host and his host's sister, he put one arm around each of them. Mazen suddenly looked very serious.

He stood up and took John by the arm and said, "Come over here and try some of our food."

John enjoyed himself very much at the party that night. He couldn't believe how much food Mazen had prepared. As he was leaving, he realized that he had not seen his bottle of wine. He decided that in all the confusion, Mazen had probably forgotten to open it.

## Questions

1. Why did John buy the wine?
2. Why didn't Mazen say anything to John about the wine?
3. Why didn't Mazen's sister shake hands with John?
4. Why did John put his arm around Mazen and his sister?
5. Why did Mazen suddenly end John's conversation with his sister?
6. What does this story tell us about communication across cultures?

## Discussion

In many aspects there are cultural differences. For example, what is polite in one culture is sometimes impolite in another culture. In this case, John tried hard to be a polite guest according to the rules of his culture. In the United States, people often bring wine or beer to a party. In fact, the invitations to many American parties have the letters "B.Y.O.B.," which means "Bring your own booze" ("booze" is a slang expression for alcohol). However, most Muslims, like Mazen, do not drink alcohol. Their religion forbids it. So John's wine was not welcome at the party, although his host was too polite to say so. (Even in the United States it is not always a good idea to bring alcohol: most states do not allow anyone under the age of 18 or 21 to buy alcohol, and some religious groups forbid it.)

John also showed little understanding of Arab culture when he tried to shake hands with Mazen's sister. By American customs, he was just trying to be polite. But in Muslim cultures, the most impolite thing a man can do is to touch a woman who is not his wife. John put his arm around Mazen and his sister to show his friendship. But to an Arab, that gesture would show the opposite: that John did not respect his sister. For that reason it was an insult to Mazen as well.

People all over the world want respect from others, but cultures show respect in different ways, as John's experiences at Mazen's party indicate. Some of these differences are explained by the values that each culture thinks are important. For example, the American custom of "B.Y.O.B." can be explained by the fact that most Americans think it is important to be informal and direct. And Mazen did not serve wine at his party because one of the most important Saudi values is living by the laws of the Muslim religion.

As cultures vary, misunderstandings and difficulties in intercultural communication arise when there is little or no awareness of divergent cultural values, beliefs, behaviors and so on. How can we overcome as many of those difficulties as possible so as to ensure smooth communication with people from different backgrounds? Cultural awareness plays an important role. If John and Mazen had been aware of the differences between each other's culture, Mazen and his sister wouldn't have been offended.

There are three assumptions in the field of intercultural communication that account for the importance of cultural awareness. First, culture, however defined, is overtly manifest in language, foods, music etc., but the greater part of culture is hidden. More important by far is the covert culture, which is concealed from one's conscious awareness. Second, most of the harm that may appear in intercultural relations is due to ignorance rather than malice. In short, we can assume that we mean well but that in acting "naturally" we cause others and ourselves much irritation or worse. Third, only when we become aware of what guides our behavior can we alter our ways and attitudes and thus improve our intercultural behavior. It is important to achieve "cultural literacy" (awareness and knowledge of other cultures as well as our own), for it would better enable us to "read" the meaning of the behavior of others and of ourselves, thus successfully communicating with different individuals in our "global village."

From this story we should know that it is inevitable that we will meet problems in communication across cultures, because we grow with our culture and everything we say and do is culturally defined. But with adequate cultural awareness and competence, we will be able to anticipate potential problems and to deal with them when they arise.

## III Potential Problems in Intercultural Communication

As indicated by the previous story, problems may arise in contacting people with different cultural backgrounds, if neither side understands the other's cultural rules. It is not surprising that such problems come up because everyone lives in a certain culture and is thus conditioned by his/her culture to behave in accordance with the rules of that culture. Problems in intercultural

communication may, theoretically, be potential because every intercultural encounter contains the elements for both success and failure. If we know some possible causes of problems, we could anticipate them and thus be prepared to better deal with them. In this section we will examine four of them.

##  Cognitive Barriers

## 【Activity 2】

*Study the following cases and suggest an answer to the question below each one. Think about what kind of problems they may be.*

A. Soon after Li Ying arrived in the States, an American friend invited him to a party. He got to the party on time, only to find that many people were late and dressed in a very casual way. There were only a few kinds of beverages and some simple foods. Few people there knew him, and he at last found Mark, his friend, and began to talk with him. They only talked about ten minutes before Mark said that he had to talk with another friend and left, to Li's great disappointment. The host introduced him to a couple of people and then he left too. Two hours later, Li found an excuse and returned home. He had to cook some noodles, as he was still hungry. He thought he would never participate in this kind of party again. Why was he so disappointed?

B. One Japanese student in America said: "On my way to school, a girl whom I don't know smiled at me several times. I was a little surprised." Why was he surprised?

C. A South Korean student in America wrote: We went to visit an American friend. When we saw him, he opened the window and said to us: "I'm sorry, I don't have time. I have to work on my studies." Then he closed his window. This student was confused. Why?

### Discussion

The communication participants in all the cases met some problems because of ignorance of the culture of the people they met. They tended to assume, though often unconsciously, that the other party of the communication had the same values, beliefs, behaviors, and customs as they themselves. When what happens is different from their expectations, they are likely to feel disappointed, depressed or even angry. These kinds of problems can be classified as cognitive barriers.

In the case of the Japanese student, it is because in his culture girls don't smile at strangers, let alone at strange men. For an American, however, this smile often means nothing special but is a way of showing goodwill.

The Korean student was confused because in his country, when a visitor comes, the host should, whether he likes it or not, or whether he is busy or not, welcome the guest. He should never speak to the guest without even opening the door. But in the USA, as mentioned in the previous chapters, people feel free not to receive a visitor.

## B Stereotyping

## 【Activity 3】

*Read the short story and answer the questions that follow.*

Mr. Bias is the director of a small private company. He is interviewing candidates for the position of assistant manager. He selects a bright and ambitious applicant. Later, he discovers that this applicant is from the country of Levadel (a fictitious nation). Since he thinks all Levadelians are stupid and lazy, he decides to select someone else for the position. What do you think of Mr. Bias' decision? What mistake did he commit?

## Discussion

STEREOTYPES ARE THE VIEWS OF
THE SMALL-MINDED.

The story is fictitious. Mr. Bias made his decision based on a stereotype of that applicant's nation. As the name Bias suggests, stereotyping may lead to prejudice.

Stereotypes, found in nearly every intercultural situation, are a means of organizing our images into fixed and simple categories that we use to represent an entire collection of people. The reason for the pervasive nature of stereotypes is that human beings have a psychological need to categorize and classify. The world we confront is too big, too complex, and too transitory for us to know it in all its details. Hence, we want to classify and pigeonhole. Stereotypes, because they tend to be convenient, help us with our classifications.

There are a number of reasons that stereotypes, as a form of classification, hamper intercultural communication. First, stereotypes fail to specify individual characteristics. They assume that all members of a group have exactly the same traits. In other words, they don't recognize internal differences within a group, and do not recognize exceptions to its general rules or principles. Second, stereotypes also keep us from being successful as communicators because they are over-simplified, over-generalized, and/or exaggerated. They are based on half-truths, distortions, and often untrue premises. Therefore, they create inaccurate pictures of the people with whom we are interacting. Such an attitude based on erroneous beliefs or preconceptions is called prejudice. Stereotypes and prejudice often occur together. In fact, prejudice is a learned tendency by which we respond to a given group of people or even in a consistent, usually negative way. Just as the case indicates, if you meet one person from *Levadel* who is lazy, it is oversimplifying or stereotyping to attribute that particularly bad quality of that person to all members of that culture. Third, stereotypes tend to impede intercultural communication in that they repeat and reinforce beliefs until they often become taken for "truth." For years, women were stereotyped as a rather one dimensional group. The stereotype of women as "homemakers" often keeps women from advancing in the workplace.

Where do we acquire stereotypes? Stereotypes and prejudice do not appear when we are born. We gradually develop our stereotypes and prejudice through the process of learning and socialization. First, people learn stereotypes from their parents, relatives, and friends. Second, stereotypes develop through limited personal contact. If we meet a person from Brazil who is very wealthy, and from this meeting we conclude that all people from Brazil are wealthy, we are acquiring a stereotype from limited data. Finally, many stereotypes are provided by the mass media. TV has been guilty of providing distorted images of many ethnic groups.

Now the problem is how we can learn about another culture without falling into stereotyping. As was mentioned before, any culture is extremely complicated and varied in itself. Without some generalizations, it is hard to form a picture of a particular culture. The paradox is that any generalization is theoretically stereotyping to some extent. So here the dilemma we have to face is that, on the one hand we have to make generalizations so as to get some knowledge about another culture, and this knowledge is essential in communicating with its people; while on the other hand generalizations tend to cause stereotypes which hamper communication between people from diverse cultures.

Therefore we have to be aware that no two groups are either polar opposites or exactly alike. We carefully make generalizations, but we constantly remind ourselves that people are different even within one culture in spite of the many things they share, and that these generalizations may apply to some people to a certain extent at certain times, but certainly not to everyone at all times. In other words, we should always be aware of the limits of generalizations about any culture.

# 【Activity 4】

*Study the two statements: "All Americans are rich." "There are some very wealthy people in the United States." Are they stereotypes? Explain.*

## Discussion

The former is a stereotype because it doesn't allow for individuality, and often encourages critical or negative judgment, and may lead to misunderstanding which hampers cross-culture communication. The latter is a generalization because it is non-judgmental and allows for individuality.

What we have to remember is that cultures vary internally and are changeable. The following principles may help us avoid stereotyping in our interaction with people from other cultures.

- Generalizations are inevitable in the study of cultures, but exceptions are also inevitable. Overgeneralizations are dangerous because they lead to stereotyping and prejudice.
- Stereotyping due to generalizing may be inevitable among those who lack frequent contact with another culture.
- All cultures have internal variations.
- Personal observations of others about another culture should be regarded with skepticism.
- Many cultures often exist within a single race, language group, religion or nationality, differentiated by age, gender, socioeconomic status, education, and exposure to other cultures.

## C Ethnocentrism

## 【Activity 5】

*A. Rosamine and Merita are from two different cultures. They are talking about one aspect of family life. They seem to have different points of view. Who do you agree with? Why? Discuss these questions in small groups.*

Rosamine: I think it's terrible that in your country children leave their parents when they are so young. Something that shocks me even more is that many parents want their children to leave home. I can't understand why children and parents don't like each other in your country.

Merita: In your country parents don't allow their children to become independent. Parents keep their children protected until the children get married. How are young people in your country supposed to learn about life that way?

*B. Read the short passage about two terms that refer to the same people. Explain why there is difference in their names.*

We call a group of primitives in North America Eskimos; this name, originated by certain Indians to the south of the Eskimos, means "Eaters of Raw Flesh." However, the Eskimos' own name for themselves is not Eskimos but Inupik, meaning "Real People." By their name they provide a contrast between themselves and other groups; the latter might be "people" but are never "real."

## Discussion

The two cases are examples of ethnocentrism ("Ethno" means "race" or "people"). Ethnocentrism refers to the tendency to think of one's own culture as being the center of the world, or the belief that one's own culture is primary to all explanations of reality.

We learn ethnocentrism very early in life, and primarily on the unconscious level. It might be the major barrier to intercultural communication. The negative impact of ethnocentrism on intercultural communication is clearly highlighted by the following passage:

First, ethnocentric beliefs about one's own culture shape a social sense of identity which is narrow and defensive. Second, ethnocentrism normally involves the perception of members of other cultures in terms of stereotypes. Third, the dynamic of ethnocentrism is such that comparative judgments are made between one's own culture and other cultures under the assumption that one's own is normal and natural. As a consequence, ethnocentric judgments usually involve invidious comparisons that ennoble one's culture while degrading those of others.

In today's world few people would openly claim that their own culture is superior to other cultures. But people unconsciously tend to make judgments based on their own value systems. Some scholars maintain that no one can be completely immune from ethnocentrism as we grow up with our own culture, the software of our mind. For example, the map published by a particular country places that country in the center. Thus, when we face a map from another country, we often feel strange. Another case in point is that the history book of a particular country usually bears out their own contributions to the world's civilization process. These are  evidences that no country is without any degree of ethnocentrism. Ethnocentrism is to a certain extent a universal phenomenon.

We know that ethnocentric attitudes should be avoided. In many things between cultures there is no right or wrong, better or worse. For example, Chinese people use chopsticks while Western people use knives and forks when eating. Chinese celebrate the Mid-Autumn Day, whereas Americans celebrate Thanksgiving Day. Jews cover their heads when they pray, but Protestants do not. Is one more correct than the other?

## 【Activity 6】

*The following passage by Ken Barger (2003) may help you to have a better understanding of ethnocentrism. Then you will know why we should be aware of its harms and how we should try to reduce its negative impact when interacting across cultures.*

A snowmobile race was sponsored by the Inuit (Eskimo) community council in a village on the Hudson's Bay in the Canadian Arctic, Christmas 1969. Inuit friends urged me to join in a snowshoe race across the river ice, but, knowing I was inexperienced at this, I was reluctant to participate. They persisted, however, and, recognizing that they wanted me to be involved, I agreed. Of course, I was the last one to return, way behind everyone else in the race. I was very embarrassed, but to my surprise, people came up to me and congratulated me, saying, "You really tried!" A month later, when I was on a caribou hunting trip with three Inuit men in a remote area, we got trapped by a winter storm and had to go several days without food. This was when I learned that trying was much more important than winning. While the Inuit like to win, their greater value on trying has a distinct adaptive function. One way anthropologists learn about other cultures is "participant observation," being involved in their daily life, watching what they do, and doing what they do. We seek to learn the meanings and (more important) the functions of their ways. We are also involved in "cross-cultural comparison," comparing their life experiences with other groups (mostly our own). In the case of the snowshoe race, I learned about Inuit values on trying, but I also learned about American values on competition and winning.

"Ethnocentrism" is a commonly used word in circles where ethnicity, inter-ethnic relations, and similar social issues are of concern. The usual definition of the term is "thinking one's own group's ways are superior to others" or "judging other groups as inferior to one's own." But this definition only reflects part of the attitude involved in ethnocentrism, and, more important, does not address the underlying issue of why people do this. Most people, thinking of the shallow definition, believe that they are not ethnocentric, but are rather "open minded" and "tolerant." However, as explained below, everyone is ethnocentric, and there is no way not to be ethnocentric... it cannot be avoided, nor can it be willed away by a positive or well-meaning attitude.

To address the deeper issues involved in ethnocentrism calls for a more explicit definition. In this sense, ethnocentrism can be defined as: making false assumptions about others' ways based on our own limited experience. The key word is assumptions, because we are not even aware that we are being ethnocentric... we don't understand that we don't understand.

One example of ethnocentrism is seen in the above comments on the Inuit snowshoe race. I assumed that I had "lost" the race, but it turns out the Inuit saw the same situation very differently than I did. Westerners have a binary conflict view of life (right or wrong, liberal versus conservative, etc.), and I had imposed my "win or lose" perspective of life on the situation. As a result, I did not understand how they experience life, that trying is a basic element of life. This did not necessarily involve thinking that my ways were superior, but rather that I assumed my experience was operational in another group's circumstances.

......

The assumptions we make about others' experience can involve false negative judgments, reflected in the common definition of ethnocentrism. For example, Anglos may observe Cree Indians sitting around a camp not doing obvious work that is needed and see Crees as "lazy." Westerners generally value "being busy" (industriousness), and so may not appreciate the Cree capacity to relax and not be compelled to pursue some activities of a temporary nature... nor realize how much effort is put into other activities like hunting.

Assumptions can also reflect false positive attitudes about others' ways. For example, we in the urban industrial society frequently think of Cree Indians as being "free of the stresses of modern society," but this view fails to recognize that there are many stresses in their way of life, including the threat of starvation if injured while checking a trap line a hundred miles from base camp or when game cycles hit low ebbs. False positive assumptions are just as misleading as false negative assumptions.

......

Everybody is ethnocentric, as all of us around the world assume things about other people's ways. The question is why are we ethnocentric?

The definition given above emphasizes that we make false assumptions based on our own limited experience. If our own experience is the only "reality" we have, then it is normal to assume it is the "natural" basis of reality... because our own ways work for us. Our perceptions of colors, our time frames, our values on industriousness, our social roles, our beliefs about Life and the Universe, and all our other ways help us organize life experience and provide important meanings and functions as we move through daily life span activities. It is normal to assume these provide a meaningful and functional basis for life in general. How can we not be ethnocentric?

......

So what is the problem with ethnocentrism?

Ethnocentrism leads to misunderstanding others. We falsely distort what is meaningful and functional to other peoples through our own tinted glasses. We see their ways in terms of our life experience, not their context. We do not understand that their ways have their own meanings and functions in life, just as our ways have for us.

At the heart of this is that we do not understand that we do not understand! So we aren't aware that we can develop more valid understandings about how they experience life.

......

So what can we do about ethnocentrism?

Addressing ethnocentrism is not a matter of trying not to be ethnocentric. This is an impossible task, since we will never experience every life situation of everyone around the world. We will always have our assumptions about life based on our existing limited experience. So a much more productive approach is to catch ourselves when we are being ethnocentric and to control for this bias as we seek to develop better understandings.

In science, grounded understandings are not developed from the absence of biases, but rather the recognition and control of biases. The scientific process helps us have a clearer view of what we do understand in the context of what we do not understand. Ethnocentrism is a bias that keeps us from such understandings of other people's life experience, but it is possible to recognize this bias and control it... so that we can go on to develop more valid and balanced understandings. This calls for us to develop our learning skills.

......

When we go beyond ethnocentrism, there are whole new areas of understanding the possibilities in how all humans can experience life.

# Ⓓ Culture Shock

# 【Activity 7】

*Read the following story and discuss with your neighbor what culture shock is and how much you know about it from the story.*

Nguyen Chau Van Loc went to the United States in 1979 from Vietnam. His first impression of the U.S. was very positive. He felt that this new environment offered him many exciting opportunities.

However, Loc quickly found himself unprepared to take advantage of these opportunities. He knew almost no English. Even when he knew what to say on a bus or in a store, no one understood him, and he had to repeat and repeat.

In Vietnam, Loc was a technician, but in the U.S., he didn't have enough experience compared with other people. He had trouble finding a job. He felt that he did not have an important role or position in the city and missed the security and friendliness of his town in Vietnam. He felt that he would never learn English or feel happy in the U.S.. He began to feel very depressed and homesick.

With the help of a counselor in his English program, he understood that his feelings were normal and that they were only a stage in his adjustment to the new culture. He learned that many other Vietnamese felt the same way he did. Some, in fact, were more disoriented than he was and were afraid to go out into the city.

Eventually, Loc began to feel better about his life in the U.S. He developed a position in the Vietnamese American community and adjusted to his new role in American society. He is accustomed to his life in the new country but will always miss Vietnam.

## Discussion

"Culture shock" occurs as a result of total immersion in a new culture, as Loc's story manifests.

From Loc's experience we see that there are, generally speaking, three stages of culture shock. In the first stage, the newcomers like their environment. Then, when the newness wears off and problems arise, they begin to dislike or feel disappointed with things in the new culture. In the final stage, the newcomers begin to adjust to their surroundings and, as a result begin to enjoy their life more.

The main cause of culture shock is thought to be displacement from one's home culture. This lack of common experiences and familiar surroundings creates varying degrees of consequences. For the person who is constantly encountering other cultures, the anxiety period might be brief and include only a bit of "homesickness." However, for many people, culture shock can mean depression, serious physical reactions (such as headaches or body pains), anger, aggression toward the new culture, and even total withdrawal. All of these reactions would obviously hamper intercultural communication. In addition, there is a kind of reverse culture shock that takes place when people return "home" after a rather long period of time in another culture.

Study the following statements and you'll see why it is not inexplicable to experience culture shock to some degree in another culture.

- Feelings of apprehension, loneliness or lack of confidence are common when visiting and experiencing another culture.
- Differences between cultures are often experienced as threatening.
- What is logical and important in a particular culture may seem irrational and unimportant to an outsider.

## IV Efforts We Should Make

As we have known from the previous section that there are potential problems in intercultural communication, can we do something to deal with them if they ever occur? The answer is definitely in the affirmative. The following is what we can do to prevent them from happening, or to help us deal with them in real encounters.

**Knowing Ourselves**

# 【Activity 8】

To be able to conduct effective intercultural communication, we need to know about other cultures. We also need to know about our own culture of which we often are unconscious because we are too familiar with it.

*Look at the dialogue in Activity 5 again. If those two women had been aware of their own respective values regarding parent-child relationships and child education, and known that people's values were different, would they have said what they did? Discuss the answer to this question in small groups and try to give reasons why we should develop self-awareness.*

## Discussion

If the two women had been aware of the different values concerning children-parents relations of each other's cultures, they wouldn't have been so ethnocentric and wouldn't have had any prejudice against the other person's culture. Knowing ourselves is the first step for us to reduce ethnocentrism and guard against prejudice.

Knowing ourselves is necessary for developing cultural awareness required for effective intercultural communication, because what we bring to the communication event greatly influences the success or failure of that event. First, we have to identify our attitudes, prejudices, and opinions that we all carry and that bias the way the world appears to us. If we hold a certain attitude toward gay men, and when a man who is a gay talks to us, our pre-communication attitude will color our response to what he says. Knowing our likes, dislikes, and degrees of personal ethnocentrism enables us to place them out in the open so that we can detect the ways in which these attitudes influence communication.

The following questions may help us know our culture and our own specific beliefs, values, and behaviors. How has our own background influenced the way we express ourselves, verbally and non-verbally? How has it influenced the way we think about and relate to others? How has it influenced the way we choose our friends and keep our friendships? How has it influenced the way we choose our careers? Knowing ourselves involves discovering the kind of image we portray to the rest of the world. If we perceive ourselves in one way, and the people with whom we interact perceive us in another way, serious problems can arise. For instance, if we see ourselves as patient and calm, but we appear rushed and anxious to the person with whom we are talking, we will have a hard time understanding why people respond to us as they do. We should learn to recognize our communication style—the manner in which we present ourselves to others. The following questions help us in this area.

- Do I seem at ease or tense?
- Do I often change the subject without taking the other person into consideration?
- Do I deprecate (反对) the statements of others?
- Do often I smile? Do I interrupt repeatedly?

- Do I show sympathy when someone has a problem?
- Do my actions tend to lower the other person's self-esteem?
- Do I employ a pleasant tone of voice when I talk to people?
- Do I tend to pick the topics for discussion or do I share topic selection?
- What does my tone of voice suggest?
- How do I react to being touched?

## B Appreciating Similarities and Respecting Differences

## 【Activity 9】

Intercultural respect begins with the awareness that your culture is no more valuable or "correct" than any other. Being part of the majority culture in a given country does not change this; in fact, it only makes that awareness more important, since it may be even easier to see your culture as normal and dismiss or mock others for being strange. To show respect for any cultural differences you encounter, keep in mind that you see the world through a cultural "filter" that not everyone shares.

It is true that cultures are different due to a host of various factors, but it doesn't mean that there are no similarities or commonalities. On the contrary, we share a series of crucial characteristics that link the people of the world together. For example, we share the same planet for a rather short period of time. We all desire to be free from external restraint: the craving for freedom is basic, though the freedom can be of different degrees and with various implications.

*We have to remember that in describing another culture, people tend to stress the differences and overlook the similarities. Work in small groups and find out as much as you can about what people share in the world.*

### Discussion

There are many things people in the world share, otherwise intercultural communication would be impossible. Here are some more examples. There is a universal link between children and family: we all share the same thrill and excitement at a new birth. Mating and wanting good friends tie us together. All of us face old age and the potential suffering that often goes with it; and of course, we are joined in knowing that death, like birth, is a part of life's process. All cultures love music and art, play sports, tell jokes, believe in being civil to one anther, and search for ways to be happy. All people seek to avoid physiological and psychological pain while searching for some degree of tranquility in life. There are also philosophical values that bind us together. One of the most important of the common values is "be kind to others," which can be found in the teachings of different religions. The words may be different, but the wisdom contained is universal. The following are examples.

"Hurt not others in ways that you yourself would find hurtful." (Buddhism)

"All things whatsoever ye would that men should do to you, do ye even so to them." (Christianity)

"Do not do unto others what you would not have them do unto you." (Confucianism)

"This is the sum of duty: do naught unto others which would cause you pain if done to you."
(Hinduism)

"No one of you is a believer until he desires for his brother that which he desires for himself."
(Islam)

"Respect for all life is the foundation." (Native American)

# 【Activity 10】

From Activity 9 we see that we are alike in many ways. We are also different. Let's compare Beijing and Chicago. Outwardly there is little to distinguish what one sees on the streets of the two cities— hurrying people, trolleys and buses, huge department stores, blatant billboards, skyscraper hotels, public monuments—beneath the surface there remains great distinctiveness.

*What differences can you think of? How should we look at cultural differences?*

## Discussion

Beneath the surface there is a different organization of industry, a different approach to education, a different role for labor unions, a contrasting pattern of family life, unique law enforcement and penal practices, contrasting forms of political activity, and different sex and age roles. Indeed, most of what is thought of as culture shows as many differences as similarities.

If we are to succeed in intercultural communication, we should pay enough attention to the enormous differences (some of which have been discussed in the previous chapters) between our culture and the one we come into contact with.

If we can appreciate similarities and respect differences existing in cultures, we are able to better assess the potential consequences of our acts and be more tolerant of those of others. There are generally two attitudes toward differences. One is to take differences as polar opposites; the other is to see them as being different in degrees. In intercultural communication, we think the latter attitude is reasonable. We have noted that people, as human beings in the world, have a lot in common; they also vary greatly as they are conditioned by their own cultures.

Take the two women in Activity 5 as an example. Both of them love their children, but their love is shown in different ways. Moreover, both women's children are to leave their parents' home, but at different ages. So a continuum may help us see differences in proper perspectives. Differences are particular points on the continuum, not the two ends.

The remarks of Yu Qiuyu, the Chinese scholar and essayist, on cultural commonalities and differences sum up the attitude we should hold. At the 2006 Cross-Culture Communication Forum in Beijing, he stated in his presentation that at the highest spiritual level, culture is a shared spiritual value of all humanity. For example, the ultimate meaning of Chinese culture is not unique within all of humanity. Principles such as "What you do not

want for yourself, do not do to others" and "live in harmony with nature" arise in all human civilizations and are thus universals. Concepts like "peace," "science," "harmony," "balance," and "keeping pace with the times" share the support of the wise throughout all humanity. Similarly, values like democracy and human rights are not confined to the West, but are universally pursued. In other words, we share so much when we coexist on the same earth. However, the ways to realize those values may vary from culture to culture. Differences follow and should never be neglected. Our attitude toward them should be that of respect. We should know that cultural differences will not necessarily create conflict. Instead, they enrich our world, just as when the Euclid, Hegel, and Kant of our minds meet the Confucius, Su Dongpo, and Wang Yangming of our minds, in mutual appreciation and support rather than conflict and cancellation. In fact, beauty is in the coexistence of different cultures. In this sense, the saying of South African Archbishop Tutu that "We celebrate our diversities" should be supported.

##  Developing Empathy

### 【Activity 11】

To improve intercultural communication we need to develop empathy— be able to see things from the point of view of others or to see oneself in the other fellow's situation. It has been recognized as important to general communication competence and as a central characteristic of competent and effective intercultural communication.

*Since empathy is important in any communication, you must have experienced some empathy. Draw from your own experiences to indicate how we can improve empathy.*

#### Discussion

To improve empathy, first, we have to remind ourselves to pay attention to the spontaneous emotional expressions of others and the situation where the interaction takes place. Second, since empathy is a reciprocal act, both parties have to be expressive so as to achieve understanding. Third, empathy can be enhanced through awareness of specific behaviors that members of a particular culture or co-culture might find impertinent or insulting. Finally, we have to remember that empathy can be increased if you resist the tendency to interpret the other's verbal and nonverbal actions from your own culture's orientation.

##  Keeping an Open Mind

A standard scientific principle is that diversity is adaptive. The more different resources a group has, the more potentials it has for adapting to life challenges. We have come to realize this in ecodiversity, but perhaps we still have to realize this in terms of ethnic diversity. The more different ways of experiencing life available to a society, the more resources it has for meeting adaptive challenges. It is believed that one of the United State's greatest strengths is its ethnic diversity, for they have adaptive resources from peoples all over the world.

When we encounter people from other ethnic backgrounds, we have an opportunity to learn new ways of seeing and experiencing life which we never knew existed. In a larger framework, we can learn the tremendous potentials humans have for being human. Through intercultural encounters, we can develop more valid and balanced understandings of other cultural ways. We can also better understand ourselves, by contrasting our own ways with other life experiences and asking about our own meanings and functions.

Facing this opportunity, we should keep an open mind, not only being tolerant of others but also learning from others. A multicultural perspective helps.

Multiculturalism requires us to take different cultures as equals. It teaches us to accept as inevitable the contradictions implicit in everything we learn. Multiculturalism is a style of self awareness which involves frequent questioning about the expandable and arbitrary nature of one's own culture. If we are frequently conscious that cultural context influences our thoughts and behaviors and that these, while important to us, are neither static nor absolute entities, we will be more open to accept the fact that others can enrich our experience. Thus to be multicultural is to be aware and able to incorporate and synthesize different systems of cultural knowledge into one's own.

Multicultural people are those who are intellectually and emotionally committed to the fundamental unity of all human beings while at the same time they recognize, legitimize, accept, and appreciate the fundamental differences that lie between people from different cultures. This new kind of people cannot be defined by the languages they speak, the countries they have visited, or the number of international contacts they have made. Nor are they defined by their profession, their place of residence, or their cognitive sophistication. Instead, multicultural people are recognized by the configuration of their outlooks and worldviews, by the way they remain open to the outlooks and worldviews, and by the way they remain open to the imminence of experience.

## REVISION TASKS

1. *Review this chapter with the help of the following questions.*
(1) How do you understand intercultural communication competence? What does it include?
(2) What is the difference between the meanings of communication competence and intercultural

communication competence?

(3) Can you think of cases where stereotypes have turned into prejudice or hatred? Where do you think stereotyping comes from? How should we guard against it?

(4) How can we overcome cognitive barriers?

(5) What is the difference between having pride in one's identity and being ethnocentric?

(6) Do you agree that everyone is more or less ethnocentric? What harm does ethno-centrism usually bring to communication across countries?

(7) What behaviors would be expected of a person who has an inferiority complex about his/her own culture?

(8) How do you think culture shock can be reduced to the minimum?

(9) How should we look at different cultures?

(10) How do you account for the fact that people in this world are both similar and different?

(11) Why is empathy important in communication? How can we develop empathy?

## 2. *Complete the tasks below.*

(1) Read the passage below. Note how the African comments on individualism. Do you agree with him? Why or why not? How do his remarks reflect on cultural diversity in the world?

We often assume that our values are the right values simply because for us they are the obvious values. An African friend of mine, an ambassador in Washington, recently said, "One of the things which have caused misunderstandings between your people and mine is that you Americans always speak of individualism as being good. We do not consider individualism good. You always oppose government to individualism. What we oppose to individualism is not the government, but the family, the clan, the small community of natural primary relations. We feel that an individualist is a lonely man."

(2) Read the account of an African American's experience. Identify the problem he mentions. Try to explain why it arises and offer a possible solution.

When I walk through the streets of San Francisco's business districts, or any residential area except black ones, white people stare at me as if I were a circus clown.

Their staring eyes don't see that I get mostly A's in school, or that I am a captain of the football team, or that I belong to positive youth organizations. They can't see my future career in sports or journalism. All they see is that I'm 6-foot-4, young, black, and male—potential danger to them.

White men look at me as if I'm up to no good, or as if they are superior to me. White women just look at me with fear. Sometimes they cross the street when they see my friends and me coming, or walk in the street and only get back on the sidewalk after we pass by.

(3) Read the passage below. Then discuss in small groups the questions: Why does the school textbook say the dried fish, a delicacy of American Indian people, "tastes like an old shoe, or is like chewing on dried feather?" What was the response of the writer, an American Indian lady? Why?

Ever since I was a small girl in school, I've been aware of what the school textbooks say about

Indians. I am an Indian and, naturally, am interested in what the schools teach about natives of this land.

One day in the grammar school I attended, I read that a delicacy of American Indian people was dried fish, which, according to the textbook, tasted "like an old shoe, or was like chewing on dried leather." To this day I can remember my utter dismay at reading these words. We called this wind-dried fish "sleet-shus," and to us, it was our favorite delicacy and, indeed, did not taste like shoe leather. It took many hours of long and hard work to prepare the fish in just this particular fashion. Early fur traders and other non-Indians must have agreed, for they often used this food for subsistence as they traveled around isolated areas.

(4) Read the following passage and sum up the differences between Swedes and Americans. Think about what other clues this passage suggests that help us understand intercultural communication.

Swedes tend to think that Americans are superficial and openly proud of themselves because they talk a lot. Swedes generally don't mind silence. If you pause for a while before answering a question or saying something about the topic being discussed, to a Swede that means you find the question or topic important and you're thinking before you talk. It also tells a Swede that you're intelligent.

Also, Swedes don't like it when people talk about how good they are at something. You may be good at something, but you're supposed to deny it and say you need to learn more or something like that. And don't interrupt!

If someone offers you a gift, it would be suitable to seem a bit embarrassed or moved, and always offer to pay for your meal if you go out together.

Americans are always surprised when I say I think American women are not very liberated. In Sweden, men on the average do 40% of the house work. Younger men do more, and older men do less. In the U.S. men can't stay home with their babies. In the U.S. you find more women in top executive positions but it seems they had to give up a lot to get there.

(5) Read the following story, and discuss the reasons for the cultural conflicts between people of two different cultures.

John, a Korean American, and his American girlfriend, Rachel, decide to marry. When John tells his Korean mother, who is divorced, that he and his future bride will be getting their own place, his mother gets very upset. She is mad and blames Rachel for influencing his decision. Rachel is confused about John's mother's reaction. Why is John's mother upset over the news that John's and Rachel will be getting their own place? ( *Source*: *Heather Heater*, *University of Rhode Island*)

(6) Read the passage below, identify the problem and try to explain: What's happening to Huang? What are the possible reasons for Huang's problem?

Huang was the firstborn son of a well-to-do family in Hong Kong China. He had done well in his undergraduate studies at a prestigious American university. He made his initial adjustment fairly well, finding housing and joining a support group made up of other students from Hong Kong who lived near his university. After a time, however, he began to be disappointed in his work and was unhappy with life in America. He had become attracted to an American woman, but the relationship broke up because of personality differences. While not failing any of his classes, he was by no means among the best students in his department, as shown by both test scores and participation in class seminars. Not wanting his friends from Hong Kong to learn about his problems, Huang went to the student health center with complaints about upset stomach, severe headaches, and lower back pain. The doctor at the health center prescribed acetaminophen with codeine. Huang began to take the pills, but the problems did not go away. (*Source*: From R.Brislin, K.Cushner, C. Cherrie, & M. Yong, *Intercultural Interaction: A Practical Guide*, 1986, Sage Publications.)

(7) Read the story below, discuss in the group and try to find out: Why Mr. Tanaka so bewildered by M. Legrand's decision? Why did M. Legrand discuss the job opportunity with his wife before making the final decision? Compare the possible responses from the perception of Japanese and from the perception of French.

M. Legrand is a French engineer who works for a Japanese company in France. One day the general manager, Mr. Tanaka, calls him into his office to discuss a new project in the Middle East. He tells M. Legrand that the company is very pleased by his dedicated work and would like him to act as chief engineer for the project. It would mean two to three years away from home, but his family would be able to accompany him and there would be considerable personal financial benefits to the position—and, of course, he would be perform a valuable service to the company. M. Legrand thanks Mr. Tanaka for the confidence he has in him but says he will have to discuss it with his wife before deciding. Two days later he returns and tells Mr. Tanaka that both he and his wife do not like the thought of leaving France and so he does not want to accept the position. Mr. Tanaka says nothing but is dumbfounded by his decision. (*Source*: From R. Brislin, K. Cushner, C. Cherrie, & M. Yong, *Intercultural Interaction: A Practical Guide*, 1986, Sage Publications.)

(8) Please read the story below, discuss in groups and try to explain: What were the feelings of Mrs. Simpson when she encountered this incident? What were the problems of the Indian student in this incident from your perception? How would you help this Indian student in this incident?

Mrs. Jane Simpson enjoyed her job as department secretary in a large, well-respected university in the United States. She enjoyed trying to be helpful to students as they worked their way through departmental and university regulations on their way toward their bachelor's, master's and doctoral degree. One day, a student from India entered the departmental office and began demanding attention to his various problems with his visa, low course grades, and his thesis adviser. He never used words such as "please" and "thank you," talked in a tone of voice reminiscent of a superior talking to subordinates, and gave orders to Mrs. Simpson. Mrs. Simpson counted slowly to 10, but her anger did not subside. She went to see the department chairperson to see if someone else could work with this student in the future. (*Source*: From R.Brislin, K.Cushner, C. Cherrie, & M. Yong, *Intercultural Interaction: A Practical Guide*, 1986, Sage Publications.)

(9) Each of the following sentences contains some ethnocentric attitudes. First, identify them and then change some of the statements so that they are no longer ethnocentric.

Example:

Mentonia (a fictitious country) has produced the world's greatest literature. → Mentonia has many writers who have produced well-known works of literature./Mentonia has produced the finest works of art in the world.

    a. Mentonia is a superior country because it has produced the greatest technology in the world.

    b. Non-Mentonians do everything the wrong way round.

    c. The Mentonian language is the best language for poetry.

    d. The Mentonian people have been very generous in teaching people in other countries how to do things the right way.

    e. If everyone did things the Mentonian way, the world would be a better place.

(10) The following are common stereotypes of Americans, discuss in groups and decide whether they are true or false according to your knowledge.

    a. Americans are always in a hurry.

    b. Americans drive big cars.

    c. Americans talk a lot but say little.

    d. Americans have superficial relationships

    e. Americans do not care about old people.

    f. Americans are outgoing and friendly.

    g. Americans lack discipline.

    h. Americans are disrespectful of age and status.

    i. Americans are ignorant of other countries.

    j. Americans are extravagant and wasteful.

    k. Americans are loud, rude, boastful, and immature.

# Appendix Book List for Students

[1] Blanton, L. L. and Linda Lee. 1999. *The Multicultural Workshop*. Beijing: China Machine Press.

[2] Dai, Fan & Stephen L. J. Smith. 2003. *Cultures in Contrast: Mis-communication and Misunderstandings Between Chinese and North Americans*. Shanghai: Shanghai Foreign Education Press.

[3] Davis, Linell. 2001. *Doing Culture*. Beijing: Foreign Language Teaching and Research Press.

[4] Greene, Albert. 2005. *Christianity and Western Culture*. Beijing: Beijng University Press.

[5] Hall, E. T. 1959. *The Silent Language*. Garden City NY: Doubleday & Company, Inc.

[6] Hu, Wenzhong & Cornelius L. Grove. 1991. *Encountering the Chinese*. Yarmouth: Intercultural Press, Inc.

[7] R. Brislin, K. Cushner, C. Cherrie & M. Yong. 1986. *Intercultural Interaction: A Practical Guide*. Sage Publications.

[8] Samovar, Larry A., Richard E. Porter & Lisa A. Stefani. 1998. *Communication Between Cultures*. Belmont: Wadsworth Publishing Company.

[9] Snow, Don. 2004. *Encounters with Westerners: Improving Skills in English and Intercultural Communication*. Shanghai: Shanghai Foreign Language Education Press.

[10] 毕继万. 1999. 跨文化非语言交际. 北京: 外语教学与研究出版社.

[11] 邓炎昌, 刘润清. 1989. *Language and Culture*. 北京: 外语教学与研究出版社.

[12] 杜学增. 1999. 中英文化习俗比较. 北京: 外语教学与研究出版社.

[13] 贾玉新. 1997. 跨文化交际学. 上海: 上海外语教育出版社.

[14] 胡文仲. 1999. 跨文化交际学概论. 北京: 外语教学与研究出版社.

[15] 胡文仲. 2004. 超越文化的屏障. 北京: 外语教学与研究出版社.

[16] 乐黛云. 2002. 跨文化之桥. 北京: 北京大学出版社.

[17] 林语堂. 2000. *My Country and My People*. 北京: 外语教学与研究出版社.

[18] 朱永涛. 2000. 美国价值观——一个中国学者的探讨. 北京: 外语教学与研究出版社.

# References

Amant, Kirk St. 1999. *When Culture and Rhetoric Contrast*: *Examining English as the International Language of Technical Communication*. IEEE Transactions on Professional Communication, 12 (4): 42.

Blanton, L. L. & Linda Lee. 1999. *The Multicultural Workshop*. Beijing: China Machine Press.

Chen, Shen. 1999. *The Teaching of Cultures in Foreign Language Education*. 北京：北京语言文化大学出版社.

Colombo, Gary, Robert Cullen & Bonnie Lisle. 1992. *Reading America Cultural Contexts for Critical Thinking and Writing*. Boston: Bedford Books of St. Marin's Press.

Dai, Fan & Stephen L. J. Smith. 2003. *Cultures in Contrast*: *Miscommunication and Misunderstandings Between Chinese and North Americans*. Shanghai: Shanghai Foreign Education Press.

Davis, Linell. 2001. *Doing Culture*. Beijing: Foreign Language Teaching and Research Press.

Gillespie, S. & R. Singleton. 1996. *Across Cultures*. Allyn and Bacon Needham Heights: Mass. A Simon & Schuster Company.

Greene, Albert. 2005. *Christianity and Western Culture*. Beijing: Beijng University Press.

Gu, Yueguo. 2000. *Cross-cultural Communication*. Beijing: Foreign Language Teaching and Research Press.

Guo-Ming Chen, William J. Starosta. 2007. *Foundations of Intercultural Communication*. Shanghai: Shanghai Foreign Language Education Press.

Hall, E. T. 1959. *The Silent Language*. Garden City NY: Doubleday & Company, Inc.

Hall, E. T. 1976. *Beyond Culture*. Garden City NY: Doubleday Anchor Books.

Hanvey, Robert G. 1990. *Cross-Cultural Awareness*∥Hu Wenzhong. *Selected Readings in Intercultural Communication*. Changsha: Hunan Education Press.

Hofstede, G. H. 1997. *Cultures and Organizations*: *Software of the Mind*. USA: McGraw Hill.

Hofstede, G. H. 2001. *Culture's Consequences*: *Comparing Values*, *Behaviors*, *Institution*, *and*

*Organization Across Nations*. Thousand Oaks, California: Sage Publications, Inc.

Hu, Wenzhong & Cornelius L. Grove. 1991. *Encountering the Chinese*. Yarmouth: Intercultural Press, Inc.

Klippel, Friederike. 1991. *Keep Talking*. Cambridge: Cambridge University Press.

Kluckhohn, F. R. & F. L. Strodtbeck. 1961. *Variations in Value Orientations*. Evanston, Illinois: Row, Peterson and Company.

Levire, Deena R. & Mara B. Adelman. 1982. *Beyond Language*. Englewood: Prentice Hall, Inc.

Moran, Patrick R. 2004. *Teaching Culture: Perspectives in Practice*. Beijing: Foreign Language Teaching and Research Press.

Moser, David. 2000. *A Foreigner Encounters Chinese Food Culture*. English Language Learning, 4: 38.

Myon W. Lustig & Jolene Koester. *Intercultural Competence: Interpersonal Communication Across Cultures* (5 th Edition). Shanghai: Shanghai Foreign Language Education Press.

Orem, Richard A., Shouyuan Wang & Byoung chul Min. 1997. *Ugly Chinese, Ugly Americans*. BCM Publishers, Inc.

Oshima, Alice & Ann Hogue. 1983. *Writing Academic English*. Reading: Addison Wesley Publishing Company.

R.Brislin, K. Cushner, C. Cherrie & M. Yong. 1986. *Intercultural Interaction: A Practical Guide*. Sage Publications.

Samovar, Larry A., Richard E. Porter & Lisa A. Stefani. 1998. *Communication Between Cultures*. Belmont: Wadsworth Publishing Company.

Scollon, Ron. & Suzanne Wong Scollon. 2000. *Intercultural Communication: A Discourse Approach*. Beijing: Foreign Language Teaching and Research Press & Blackwell Publishers Ltd.

Seligman, Scott D. 1999. *Chinese Business Etiquette*. NY: Time Warner Book Group.

Smith, P. B. & M. H. Bond. 1999. *Social Psychology Across Cultures*. Boston: Allyn and Bacon.

Snow, Don. 2004. *Encounters with Westerners: Improving Skills in English and Intercultural Communication*. Shanghai: Shanghai Foreign Language Education Press.

Stella Ting-Toomey. 2006. *Communication Across Cultures*. Shanghai: Shanghai Foreign Language Education Press.

Tomalin, Barry & Susan Stempleski. 1998. *Cultural Awareness*. Shanghai: East China Normal University Press & Oxford University Press.

Trompenaars, Fons. 1998. *Riding the Waves of Culture: Understanding Diversity in Global Business*. 2nd ed. USA: McGraw Hill.

Xu Lisheng. 2004. *Intercultural Communication in English*. Shanghai: Shanghai Foreign Language Education Press.

Zanger & Virginia V. 1985. *Face to Face—The Cross-cultural Workbook*. Newbury House Publishers.

Zuo Biao. 2001. *Lines and Circles*, *West and East. English Today* 67，17（3）：4.

毕继万. 1999. *Cultural Characteristics of Indirectness.*∥胡文仲. 跨文化交际面面观. 北京：外语教学与研究出版社.

毕继万. 1999. 跨文化非语言交际. 北京：外语教学与研究出版社.

陈治安，李力，刘承宇. 2005. *Intercultural Communication from Theory to Practice*. 重庆：重庆大学出版社.

陈申. 2001. 语言文化教学策略研究. 北京：北京语言文化大学出版社.

邓炎昌. 1988. *American Society and Culture I*. 北京：高等教育出版社.

邓炎昌. 1988. *American Society and Culture II*. 北京：高等教育出版社.

邓炎昌，刘润清. 1989. *Language and Culture*. 北京：外语教学与研究出版社.

窦卫霖. 2005. 跨文化商务交际. 北京：高等教育出版社.

杜学增. 1999. 中英文化习俗比较. 北京：外语教学与研究出版社.

段连城. 1993. 美国人与中国人. 北京：新世界出版社.

高旭东. 2004. 中西文学与哲学宗教. 北京：北京大学出版社.

关世杰. 1995. 跨文化交流学. 北京：北京人民大学出版社.

何自然. 1988. 语用学概论. 长沙：湖南教育出版社.

胡曙中. 1993. 英汉修辞比较研究. 上海：上海外语教育出版社.

胡文仲. 1994. 语言与文化. 北京：外语教学与研究出版社.

胡文仲，高一虹. 1997. 外语教学与文化. 长沙：湖南教育出版社.

胡文仲. 1999. 跨文化交际学概论. 北京：外语教学与研究出版社.

胡文仲. 1999. 跨文化交际面面观. 北京：外语教学与研究出版社.

胡文仲. 2004. 超越文化的屏障. 北京：外语教学与研究出版社.

纪伯伦. 2006. 纪伯伦诗集. 北京：北京出版社.

贾玉新. 1997. 跨文化交际学. 上海：上海外语教育出版社.

乐黛云. 2002. 跨文化之桥. 北京：北京大学出版社.

李力，陈治安. 1997. *Language*，*Culture & TEFL*. 重庆：西南师范大学出版社.

李瑞华. 1996. 语言文化对比研究. 上海：上海外语教育出版社.

林语堂. 2000. *My Country and My People*. 北京：外语教学与研究出版社.

王墨希，李津. 1996. 中国学生英语语篇思维模式调查.∥李瑞华. 英汉语言文化对比研究. 上海：上海外语教育出版社.

王宗炎. 1996. 自我认识与跨文化交际.∥李瑞华.英汉语言文化对比研究. 上海：上海外语教育出版社.

徐行言. 2004. 中西文化比较. 北京：北京大学出版社.

衣俊卿. 2004. 文化哲学十五讲. 北京：北京大学出版社.

应惠兰. 1999. *New College English*. 北京：外语教学与研究出版社.

张爱学. 1999. *Foreigners with Something to Say*. 北京：兵器工业出版社.

赵毅，钱为钢. 2000. 言语交际. 上海：上海文艺出版社.

郑立信，顾嘉祖. 1993. 美国英语与美国文化. 长沙：湖南教育出版社.

朱万忠. 2001. *Spoken English Test*. 重庆：重庆大学出版社.

朱永涛. 2000. 美国价值观——一个中国学者的探讨. 北京：外语教学与研究出版社.

*Family Album USA*. 1993. 北京：外语教学与研究出版社 & 阶梯股份有限公司 & 麦克米伦出版公司[美国新闻总署参与策划].